REBELLION OR REVOLUTION?

Books by Harold Cruse:

The Crisis of the Negro Intellectual
Rebellion or Revolution?

REBELLION
OR
REVOLUTION?

Harold Cruse

Foreword by Cedric Johnson

University of Minnesota Press
Minneapolis • London

Acknowledgment is gratefully made for permission to reprint material in this book. "Rebellion or Revolution?" (including essays originally titled "The Roots of Black Nationalism"), "Marxism and the Negro," and "The Economics of Black Nationalism" were originally published in *Liberator;* copyright 1963, 1964 by Afro-American Research Institute, Inc. "The Blacks and the Idea of Revolt" was first published in French as "Les Noirs et l'idée de révolte" in *Les Temps Moderne,* no. 247 (December 1966); it is published for the first time in English in this collection. "Negro Nationalism's New Wave" was originally published in *The New Leader;* copyright 1962 by The American Labor Conference on International Affairs, Inc. "An Afro-American's Cultural Views" was first published in *Présence Africaine,* Paris, no. 17 (December 1957/January 1958). "Revolutionary Nationalism and the Afro-American" originally appeared in *Studies on the Left* 2, no. 3 (1962); copyright 1962 by Studies on the Left, Inc. The film and theater reviews "King Solomon's Mines," "Call Me Mister," "Josephine Baker," and "Green Pastures" originally appeared in issues of *The Daily Worker* in 1950 and 1951.

Originally published in 1968 by William Morrow and Company, Inc.

First University of Minnesota Press edition, 2009

Published by the University of Minnesota Press
111 Third Avenue South, Suite 290
Minneapolis, MN 55401-2520
http://www.upress.umn.edu

Library of Congress Cataloging-in-Publication Data

Cruse, Harold.
  Rebellion or revolution? / by Harold Cruse ; foreword by Cedric Johnson. — 1st University of Minnesota Press ed.
    p.   cm.
  Originally published: New York : Morrow, 1968.
  Includes index.
  ISBN 978-0-8166-5901-2 (pbk.)
  1. African Americans. 2. African Americans—Politics and government—20th century. 3. Black nationalism—United States—History—20th century. I. Title.
  E185.C93   2009
  323.1196'073—dc22   2009003104

Printed in the United States of America on acid-free paper

The University of Minnesota is an equal-opportunity educator and employer.

18 17 16 15 14 13 12 11 10 09   10 9 8 7 6 5 4 3 2 1

Contents

Foreword

Cedric Johnson

I fell in love with the work of Harold Cruse during the 1990s. Like so many other black youth coming of age amid the crack cocaine epidemic, rising street violence, and the neoconservative reaction of the Reagan–Bush years, I was captivated by the pointed critique of ruling class hypocrisy and strident calls for self-determination offered by the Black Panther Party and Malcolm X and popularized through the music of Boogie Down Productions and Public Enemy. For many living through this period such identification with black radical politics was short-lived and faddish, but for others this initial infatuation grew into deeper political commitments and more extensive intellectual exploration. My growing scholarly interest in Black Power and gnawing dissatisfaction with black liberal and black nationalist thinking spurred me toward a more careful consideration of Cruse's work.

As a graduate student during the mid-1990s, I carried a tattered paperback copy of *The Crisis of the Negro Intellectual* along with me on my routine trips from the Maryland suburbs into Washington, D.C., where I was working as an adjunct lecturer. The forty-minute train commute passed quickly as I plunged headlong into the bevy of literary and political personalities, ideas, and events that populated Cruse's world. A few times these sessions were so engrossing that I missed my station stop. Even as I quarreled with his claims, I relished the clarifying effect they necessitated in my thinking. I was often overcome by a sense of déjà vu reading Cruse during an age of Afrocentrism and cultural studies. I was amazed at how commonsensical his arguments had become. His critique of mainstream cultural appropriations of black working-class idioms, his pluralist reading of American society, and his calls for black economic and cultural independence were all too familiar themes of postsegregation black public discourse. Some of Cruse's observations about identity and American society had become orthodox but his critical approach to class and political matters had not. Since his passing in 2005, many have begun to give his work a well-deserved second look.

In many respects, *Rebellion or Revolution?* is Harold Cruse's finest work. This essay collection first appeared some forty years ago during one of the most tempestuous periods of the 1960s. The year 1968 was defined by planetary struggles against patriarchy, racism, war, and imperialism and equally by political assassinations and brutal repression of these popular social forces. The Cold War was made hot. Although many of the essays included here were written twenty years before the book's first publication, *Rebellion or Revolution?* spoke directly to the ongoing political rebellions enveloping the United States and the globe during the late sixties. Together, these thirteen essays stand as a prescient but imperfect critique of Cold War left orthodoxy and as an enduring challenge to the American Left to develop a politics capable of summoning deep, systemic changes in U.S. society. Unfortunately, the publication of *Rebellion or Revolution?* was overshadowed by the controversy surrounding Cruse's first book.

Published in 1967, *The Crisis of the Negro Intellectual* was a bestseller that elevated Cruse out of obscurity and into a prominent role in black public debate during the late sixties. *The Crisis of the Negro Intellectual* drew heated reviews from Ernest Kaiser, Robert Chrisman, Julian Mayfield, and others who objected to Cruse's criticisms of Jewish–Black political alliances, his nativist dismissal of the West Indian contribution to African American cultural and political development, and his highly personal attacks on renowned black artists such as Paul Robeson and Lorraine Hansberry. Ironically, his fierce critique of liberal integrationism helped to expedite Cruse's integration into academe. Within a few years of the publication of *The Crisis of the Negro Intellectual*, Cruse was appointed chair of the University of Michigan's AfroAmerican Studies program (which evolved into the Center for AfroAmerican and African Studies), and he became a highly sought speaker on the collegiate lecture circuit. When the editors at William Morrow contracted *The Crisis of the Negro Intellectual* in 1965, they also agreed to publish a collection of Cruse's earlier essays one year after this first book was released. For decades, *Rebellion or Revolution?* has stood like a reticent child in the shadows of her more gregarious older sibling, waiting to be acknowledged and heard.

The Crisis of the Negro Intellectual brought Cruse widespread recognition, celebrity within black activist circles, and infamy in some corners of the American Left, yet *Rebellion or Revolution?* is a much more remarkable and enduring intellectual contribution. This collection is comprised of essays Cruse penned during the fifties and sixties for various movement organs such as the *Daily Worker, Studies on the Left, Présence Africaine*, and *Liberator* magazine. In this collection, we find a slightly less acerbic, more disciplined, and lucid Cruse. *Rebellion or Revolution?* retraces his evolving critique of the postwar American Left and in particular the failings of the Communist Party and liberal civil rights leaders. At various turns, Cruse rehearses lines of criticism that would become common among Black Power radicals during the late sixties.

This book maps Cruse's intellectual and personal journey in writing *The Crisis of the Negro Intellectual.* In his self-effacing Introduction, Cruse offers glimpses of his "personal memorabilia," his experiences as a soldier and struggles as a writer in New York intellectual circles. In the book's autobiographical passages we get a sense of his personal failures, triumphs, and motivations as a writer and social critic. Cruse never obtained a college degree; instead, his intellectual abilities were forged by his life experiences and the grand historical events of the twentieth century. Jim Crow segregation, the Great Depression, World War II, and the Communist Party were his classrooms.

Born in Petersburg, Virginia, on March 8, 1916, Cruse described himself as the product of "the broken family syndrome" who spent much of his childhood shuttling back and forth between New York City and his southern birthplace. At age twenty-five, Cruse joined the army and served during World War II in the British Isles, Northern Africa, and Italy. After the war, Cruse joined the Communist Party and would remain an active member until 1952. During these years, he worked as a librarian and reviewer for the cultural department of the *Daily Worker.* After leaving the Communist Party, Cruse lived for a time in Greenwich Village, where he began working on a novel and tried his hand at playwriting. He completed three plays but was unsuccessful in having his works staged. Finding the doors to New York's theater scene slammed shut, Cruse turned to nonfiction writing and found his calling. During the late fifties, he hit his stride as a political essayist and became increasingly active in anticolonial politics. In July 1960, Cruse joined LeRoi Jones, Robert F. Williams, Julian Mayfield, and other black artists and activists for a historic expedition to revolutionary Cuba organized by Richard Gibson and the Fair Play for Cuba Committee. Subsequently, Cruse became involved in such black radical organizations as On Guard for Freedom, AMSAC (American Society of African Culture), and the Freedom Now Party.

Cruse's intellectual project evolved within the context of Cold War attempts to rethink class struggle and the strategies and organizational forms that might support a viable transformative left politics. Like C. Wright Mills, Grace Lee Boggs, James Boggs, Herbert Marcuse, and many other American leftist contemporaries, Cruse's writings during the late 1950s and 1960s attempted to reinvent American radicalism in light of the taming of radical trade unionism through the labor-management accord, McCarthyism, and the growing significance of the southern civil rights movement and anticolonial struggles.

Despite his anticommunist reputation, Cruse should not be included among those ex-communists (such as the contributors to the 1949 book *The God That Failed*). whose repentant words were used to shore up Western capitalist hegemony. Cruse never completely rejected the possibility of anticapitalist revolution in American society, but through his engagement with the organized left he concluded that the Communist Party, the Trotskyites, and other left factions had failed at this task. His turbulent relationship with the Communist Party pushed him toward a more critical posture regarding left orthodoxy and his original rethinking of Marxist ideas. His problems with the party stemmed from his assertive position on cultural affairs and what he saw as the failure of party bureaucrats to deal effectively with the American racial question.

In his theater and film reviews for the *Daily Worker*, Cruse offers a perceptive analysis of mass media that illuminates their increasingly powerful role in maintaining racist ideology in the United States and throughout the colonial world. Although his characterizations of black culture often retreated to notions of racial authenticity that read the complexity out of black and American cultural development, Cruse thought that the storied contributions of blacks to American culture placed black creative intellectuals in a uniquely privileged position. He argued that "the Afro-American cultural ingredient in music, dance, and theatrical forms . . . has been the basis for whatever culturally new and unique that has come out of America." What was needed, according to Cruse, was the seizure of those media that might allow blacks to gain greater economic autonomy and to promote more humanistic portraits of African American life and history.

Cruse's critical perspective of the American racial problematic finds its most concise, powerful statement in his 1962 essay "Revolutionary Nationalism and the Afro-American." A cornerstone of this collection, this essay captures the spirit of the New Nationalist militancy that became a critical alternative to liberal integrationism in the wake of the Supreme Court's historic 1954 decision in *Brown v. Board of Education–Topeka, Kansas*. Originally published in *Studies on the Left*, this essay became required reading among young activists in such proto–Black Power organizations as the San Francisco Bay Area's Afro-American Association and the Revolutionary Action Movement. Along with Malcolm X, Robert F. Williams, and *Liberator* magazine, Cruse's essay would lay the groundwork for the racial militancy that flourished during the Black Power movement of the late sixties.

Cruse was among the first to employ the colonial analogy to describe African American social reality. Against the grain of liberal interpretations that viewed black oppression as an exception to liberal democracy, Cruse declared that the "Negro is the American problem of underdevelopment." For Cruse, the economic and political conditions endured by blacks under slavery and Jim Crow segregation in the United States were comparable to those of colonized people, with the main difference being their residence within the mother country. For the Negro, Cruse contends, "his national boundaries are the color of his skin." This distinctive social position of African Americans as a domestic colony placed them at the vanguard of the U.S. struggle. Since black radical activists had failed to fully appreciate this social reality, in Cruse's estimation they could not generate a native revolutionary theory that transcended the limitations of left officialdom.

In his influential 1962 essay and others included here, we also find an interpretative conundrum that would mark all of Cruse's subsequent writings. He acknowledges the presence of distinctive class interests among the black population, but embraces a political strategy that negates those differences. He chastises Marxist historians such as Herbert Aptheker for their reliance on such tropes as "the Negro People" and the "Negro liberation struggle" (an antecedent of "the Black freedom movement" favored by latter-day historians) because such sweeping categories undermined serious class analysis of the black population. Cruse contends that with the exception of civil rights there is "no unity of interests between the Negro middle class and the Negro working class." And yet he does not carry this analysis to its most progressive political conclusions. Often in his writings, this critical historical interpretation is shelved in favor of an elite pragmatism. Cruse revisits Booker T. Washington and W. E. B. Du Bois's turn of the twentieth century debate over the pursuit of full citizenship rights and defends Washington's gospel of industrial education and economic self-help as a matter of historical practicality. In the end, Cruse does not encourage a politics grounded in the experiences and interests of the black working class, but instead he rehabilitates the racial uplift politics of the Jim Crow era where black elites serve as the role models and legitimate voice of the masses.

These interpretative problems should not steer readers away from Cruse. Rather, these very contradictions make his work all the more intriguing and rewarding. Much of American society has changed since these essays were first published. Unfortunately, many of the social realities and ethical problems that troubled Cruse remain with us in newer, more daunting forms. The ascendancy of black political elites, the dismantling of the welfare state, and the shifting societal demographics have all made U.S. racial politics more complex. Inequalities of material wealth, rights, and resources have grown sharper under corporate globalization. Mass media technologies have proliferated in radically democratic ways even as media ownership has become more oligarchical. Cruse's gift to black political culture and the American Left was his willingness to disturb conventional wisdom and pose difficult questions. These writings embody the kinds of critical perspective and intellectual courage that are sorely missing in contemporary American public life.

Rochester, New York
June 2008

Introduction

Very often a writer's first published work does not represent his first fledgling efforts, but a matured reflection of those efforts. So it was with my first revealed book, *The Crisis of the Negro Intellectual*. I chose this title after much deliberation. Many of the young "black militants" would have much preferred "Black Intellectual" because they have succeeded in casting the term "Negro" out of *their* vocabulary as a semantic symbol of the "Afro-American's" slave status wherein we suffered the ignominy of having a pejorative name imposed on us. (*German-Americans come from Germany, Italian-Americans come from Italy, Jewish-Americans come from ——?; but whence comes the American Negro? Not from Negro-Land, since there is no such place.*)

However, I stuck to the word Negro because my intended audience embraced more than the numerical body of the black militants; I was also addressing "Negroes." I can say that the response has been surprisingly positive and I wish it were practical to quote sentiments from some of those responses, one of which came from a certain black magazine editor who asked: "Where have you been all these years? Why haven't we heard from you long before now?" This was a good question, since I don't properly belong to the current generation of young black militants, but am a carry-over from the World War II generation that came to maturity in the 1940's. Because of this

7

it is *easy* to see that I am cast in a challenging, if not dubious, role; the young wave distrusts anyone over thirty years of age. Hence, the publication of this collection of articles and essays, aside from revealing the line of critical progression which led to the publication of my first book, will also answer the editor's question—Where was I?—and, in addition, will explain some of the activities in which I was involved.

Certain unfriendly critics of my book have complained that I was overly "modest" in not talking very much about myself and my own political exploits during the forties and fifties. But that would have necessitated another kind of a book—a political autobiography, a genre I was not interested in. Life, circumstances, my creative psychology, plus the vagaries of the publishing field, have made of me a social critic almost against my will. Over the last eighteen years or so, I have written many things, both little and ambitious, in different literary forms. For a variety of reasons—subjective, objective, and external—none of my output, except some articles, was ever published. One of the external reasons was that the politically repressive and intellectually vapid decade of the fifties was not a receptive atmosphere for genuinely critical and creative "black literature." This was true whether the atmosphere was of the Left, Center, or Right. In the early fifties I broke with the Communist Left for a variety of reasons, one of which was that I could not function in the Left as a creative writer and critic with my own convictions concerning the "black experience." As the reader will learn from this collection, my very first efforts at critical writing were published in a Communist journal. It was the Communists' response to these articles that quickly convinced me of the gulf between their views and mine on critical and creative approaches to the black experience. On the other hand, the non-Communist Liberal Establishment of the fifties was no less predisposed than the political Left against any real critical reevaluation of the black impact on America. Although the Supreme Court Decision of 1954 shook up a lot of racial complacency, the real fruits of black resurgency on the social fronts had to wait for the sixties, and critical literature had a longer wait. This partially answers the query, "Where was I?" I was thinking and writing alone, unnoticed in my Chelsea, Manhattan, garrett. Added to these literarily extenuating circumstances was the fact that I am my own harshest critic. Once having written something, I lose interest in it because of an egotistical need to excel it.

The sum total of the black experience in the Western world is so historically complex that a single essay on any aspect—political, economic, cultural—must be extremely limited in scope, for in its brevity it must oversimplify. More than that, the contemporary pace of the black and white confrontation towards new levels is so rapid that written responses in most forms become dated. For this reason most of what I have written over the last eighteen years is so dated that there is very little reason to publish it. This raises, of course, the question of what among his early efforts a writer-critic should attempt to rewrite in order to update. That is always a challenging problem, but for me it is, I think, too late for rewriting. The literary and critical demands of today are too great, as each cumulative event, each burgeoning development heaps new responsibilities and thrusts new challenges on the writer-critic. Like the purely social idealist, the literary idealist the world over is hard-pressed to be relevant.

What I have said so far ought to explain why the reader will find articles in this collection dating back to 1950 and 1951 which are presented exactly as they first appeared. They are not very outstanding as critical achievements in themselves, but they do not embarrass me in 1968 as being dated or sophomoric. They do, in fact, convey the essential evolution of a cultural concept groping towards definition, in the form of critical reviews of films (mass media) and theater. Whatever the reader may think of the literary or other merits of these pieces, it is important to know that *in 1950–51 a black writer was not supposed to write and think along such lines.* This was true even in the Communist Left, a movement which had pre-

tensions of a literary radical tradition. My discovery of this
attitude was a serious and ironic blow to my literary ambitions.
If my views were not acceptable in a radical political movement, *where would they find acceptance?* In 1950–51 these
critical ideas were not even acceptable in the newspaper of
the leading black radical of the times, Paul Robeson's *Freedom*
newspaper. What was revealed to me were the depths of a
very profound fact about American life—a biracial cultural
impasse, involving the cultural ingredients and life-styles of
two races, that was so deep, that had so many ramifications,
that was so uniquely American, that its sociological importance
transcended the political, economic, and "social" attributes
assigned to the problem by the social scientists. These were
the cultural realities presented in the fifties that pushed inexorably towards the eventual appearance of a book as controversial as my *The Crisis of the Negro Intellectual*.

Many things, of course, go into a controversial book. In my
case there were also the ingredients of both personal and
epochal history. We subsume such personal memorabilia under
the heading of experience, a rather broad concept that conveniently describes the character of one's life not always com-
prehensible to all of one's readers. For example, for those born
during or after the World War II era, it is impossible to grasp
what it meant to have one's teens coincide with the Great Depression of the 1930's, only to be faced with the army at
twenty-one. Most of the men in the Vietnam disaster of today
enter the army out of an era of spiritual poverty rather than
the material poverty of the thirties. It is debatable which is
worse for the psyche, but I speak most persuasively out of the
war experiences of my own generation. Personally, I have
never known spiritual poverty even during the days of physical hunger. As bad as times were in the thirties, the American
people did not experience moral and spiritual deterioration
such as we know today. Rescued from hard times, I carried
with me into World War II a mixed bag of fear and chagrin,
a naive and youthful zest for adventure, an open mind rein-

forced with certain intellectual addenda gained from reading
Alain Locke, W. E. B. Du Bois, Richard Wright, Langston
Hughes, Eugene O'Neill, George Jean Nathan; Europeans
such as Marx, Schopenhauer, Marx, Shaw, and Ibsen (also
such plebeian classics as *The Shadow*, and other ten-cent pulp
fiction).

Yes, as with everybody else in this country, my intellectual
development began with certain American and European classics; and also, like most people, I read such classics with the
adopted belief that they represented the keys to "real" education. Little did I realize that I had already received a seminal
kind of education and exposure that would prove extremely
valuable for the kind of career I would naturally drift towards
—that of a cultural and social critic. As a boy I attended three
kinds of educational institutions—the completely integrated
schools of suburban Queens, the predominantly black Harlem
schools, and the segregated all-black schools of Virginia. As a
teen-ager in Harlem my relatives introduced me to the exciting
and impressionable black vaudeville world of the local theaters
—the Lafayette, the Lincoln, the Alhambra, the Harlem Opera
House, and the Apollo. The great personalities of this world
were Duke Ellington, Cab Calloway and his sister Blanche,
Earl Hines, Chick Webb, Count Basie, Fletcher Henderson,
Jimmie Lunceford, Lucky Millinder, Noble Sissle and Eubie
Blake, Ethel Waters, Gladys Bentley, Ivy Anderson, Earl
Tucker, the Cotton Club Revue, Bill Robinson, Ella Fitzger-
ald, and many others, all of whom left me with the indelible
impression that black theatrical art was not only unique but
inimitable. I can even remember myself as a small boy seeing
the legendary Florence Mills perform at the old Lincoln
Theatre, still standing today on Harlem's One Hundred and
Thirty-Five Street like a relic haunted with the ghosts of
Harlem's heyday. Florence Mills remains in my memory as a
stately female vision, faceless in time, a radiant form in a dark-
ened spirit house full of unseen worshippers murmuring in
cadence to rhythm and song. She died too young to be sainted

and enshrined even by her black and white devotees who called her the "Little Blackbird." [1]

There were many magic worlds within Harlem; the theater was one which was a reflection of many others. These magic worlds helped to shield the minds of youths from many of the grimmer realities of adult segregation. Even the desolation of Harlem's depression years could not blot out the will of most of the black youth to make dreams out of their own spiritual inheritance. This was true despite anger, revolt, crime, poverty and despair. This was the inheritance of my Harlem generation, the inheritance we had to cash in in the decade of the 1940's. Unavoidably for us, the forties became a decade of war, both hot and cold. It was a cruel sort of debut for the Class of Age 21, considering the backdrop. But we went into that brand new thing—the "citizen's army," as it was called at first, and I carried my Harlem inheritance through the Deep South of Louisiana, Mississippi, and Florida, the British Isles —Ireland, Scotland, England—North Africa and Italy up to the Po Valley. I added new "foreign" ingredients to my inheritance from North Africa and Italy. In England, however, the "foreign" elements of the culture remained relatively remote to me because the British, noting that it was *only the black regiments* whose rosters were completely made up of good old Anglo-Saxon names like Smith, Jones, Williams, Wright, Johnson, etc., tentatively welcomed us into their fraternity as Black Englishmen. After I returned home, however, my adult education was rounded out in a manner I could never have imagined in 1940.

World War II shattered a world irrevocably. But people who thought as I did were called upon in 1945 to treat the postwar era with intellectual and critical tools more applicable to the vanished world of the thirties—a world we had never had time to understand as we lived it. I spent the years from 1945 to about 1952 wrestling with this perplexity, and trying

[1] *See*: James Weldon Johnson, *Black Manhattan*, Alfred A. Knopf, New York, 1930, pp. 197–201.

to understand why I was such a glaring intellectual misfit—an incomprehensible gadfly to some, and a pretentious neophyte to others, those whose politics I criticized. When the newspaper sociologists talked about "postwar adjustment" after World War II, they meant economic, political and social adjustment more than psychological adjustment, since everyone's Americanism was taken for granted. It did occur to some that "foreign ideologies" extracted from Old World exposure or Oriental seduction could possibly undermine certain assumptions of the native faith. But no staunch American could ever believe that the seeds of cultural alienation were homegrown and planted in the home soil by so-called American history and so-called cultural historians of so-called American nationality.

Of course, the full implications of all of this were not that clear to me when I first began to write articles of cultural criticism. Very naively, I thought that what was obvious to me about the Negro in American culture would be obvious to everyone else. I was unaware of the long, tortuously difficult, intellectually booby-trapped road ahead of me. The path from my very first articles to *The Crisis of the Negro Intellectual* turned out to be a road eighteen years long, but I didn't know that then. In fact, I had no idea where I was headed. But as each year went by, I saw the road leading deeper into a peculiar kind of American cultural sickness, a pathological region of the American psyche defended by political and cultural antagonists of all kinds, an array of armed snipers and shock troops from the army of the intellectual defenders of a sick cultural faith. I came through it all badly mauled, scarred, traduced, defeated in a score of battles, but determined to win the war even if that required becoming a critical Kamikaze fighter on the cultural front.

This collection of articles (plus my commentary) will, I hope, convey to the reader the nature of the road I traveled. It is a selection which will show the progression of my critical perceptions leading, from certain tentative probings in the late

1940's of the black image in theater and film, to my more matured reflections on the anatomy of Black Power. Along this road I assumed certain critical approaches predicated on what I considered implied normative cultural values easily observed in the black and white exchange on all levels of cultural experience. I made certain critical postulates and, in qualifying them, referred them onto another conceptual level. The reader will encounter seeming contradictions in point of view from one piece to another, or even questionable logic in certain implied hypotheses. This represents for me a posing, and then a sorting out or modifying, of my ideas in the process of arriving at a more definitive critical construct.

The first four pieces are two film and two theater reviews —"King Solomon's Mines," "Call Me Mister," "Josephine Baker," and "Green Pastures." I must say again that whatever the reader might think concerning the literary quality or the importance of the insights of these pieces, the important thing about them is that *nowhere at the time in New York's publication world was anything like such views being expressed.* There was no craze in the air for knowledge and understanding of the "black thing" as in 1968. Although these reviews were contemporaneous with the first efforts of James Baldwin in 1948 and 1949, even he was generally unnoticed until 1954–55. The most outstanding black literary achievement of the 1950's was Ralph Ellison's *Invisible Man,* but there was little first-rate critical work out of the black experience to complement this excellent novel. Not only does this reveal the low cultural temper but explains something about Baldwin's rapid rise on the one hand and his critical flaws on the other. Negro writers lack a critical tradition to help sharpen the creative perception. Perhaps they also need more "involvement" with their own inner social trends, but I am not going to say how. My own first attempts at criticism were accomplished during my involvement in numerous community activities, a function I would not wish on any serious writer since writing *is* a full-time job.

"King Solomon's Mines" was not my first film review, but the first *and only* review on the "black experience" which the Communists liked and even reprinted. About a year or so before this review appeared my own political brashness had led me to open up a critical assault on the *Daily Worker's* foreign department for the editor's apparent lack of interest in African developments. This was also coupled with a blast at the paper's labor department for what I considered the editor's biased approaches towards A. Philip Randolph. At that time there were three other Negroes writing for the paper while I was being broken in as the librarian and part-time reviewer in the cultural department. Needless to point out, these three writers would not have dared to initiate such an attack themselves, but once the critical breach was made they had to fall in and back it up, whatever the embarrassment. It was a case of the young radical of those times challenging the complacency of the old-heads, and the effect was far-reaching. Those critics of my book who said I was suspect because I didn't mention my own party deeds should know that what they called my "modesty" had a most difficult time contending with my ego in these early issues of personal Communist involvement. I was never personally modest about my political views while in the Left, but the reader should note that my outspokenness at the time was not derived from what later came to be called "black nationalism." In the case of "King Solomon's Mines," I was simply responding to what W. E. B. Du Bois had taught me in his books on Africa. That such a film review was written about fifteen years before the present young black militant wave became Africa-conscious reveals that the awareness of Africa was never as scarce among black people as many present-day experts make out. It was always present in many Afro-Americans; it was simply not strident and had little to do with black nationalism. At any rate, the *Daily Worker's* foreign department beefed up its reportage on African affairs and everybody, black and white, liked my review and said so. *But they never forgave me*, the young black newcomer, for violating protocol and raising a fuss. I didn't learn until much later that my days were numbered.

Little was said for or against my review of "Call Me Mister," in which I attempted to call attention to the way Hollywood was trifling with the black image on the home cultural front while watering down the black soldier's experiences in World War II. I had an ulterior motive in writing this review, which was to initiate a running commentary on Hollywood's racial practices. As a matter of historical record, it should be noted that even while the Communist writers, who controlled Hollywood's Screen Writers Guild up to 1947, were prominent in Hollywood's affairs, the movie industry's racial policies remained the same. It was not until *after* the Hollywood Communist purge of 1947-48 that the first Hollywood cycle of Negro films appeared, which included such titles as "Lost Boundaries," "Home of the Brave," "Pinky," etc. Other Communist film critics immediately attacked these films as "distortions" as if to imply that they, the Communists, would have done better, which is extremely doubtful. At least they pushed no "Negro film cycle" when they were in power in the film capital. More than that, not one Negro screenwriter developed in Hollywood during the Communists' absolute control of the Screen Writers Guild, a fact which is highly significant. They would have said, of course, that they couldn't find any that were "qualified" in a field where expertise is achieved only by doing. The truth is, despite all the Communists' pretensions and claims for being the foremost "defender of Negro rights," they played the same anti-Negro game as all other whites did in Hollywood. Yet every Negro left-winger was called upon to shed tears when the notorious purge ousted the "Hollywood Ten" writers from the industry. Of these ten writers at least half were Jewish, which is a reflection of the fact that Jews had won group cultural status in the dominant media of mass communications along with other kinds of whites. Negroes, of course, missed the point completely when they raised questions of Hollywood "discrimination," but it was deeper than mere discrimination. It was (and is) merely a question of who owns the mass communications media and for what purposes. It is also a question of group power struggle for a share of the propaganda facilities the mass media allow. All of this is what I hoped to eventually get into when I wrote the review of "Call Me Mister," but it was a naive hope.

It was not until my two theater reviews appeared ("Josephine Baker" and "Green Pastures") that the Communist bigwigs began to writhe uncomfortably and question my "cultural ideology." Their general response was a serious blow to my blooming critical ego. At first, I found their attitudes incomprehensible, but they soon became clear. In the case of Josephine Baker, I was simply responding out of an historical appreciation of Baker's unique and exceptional career, and also my North African war experience. Young Negroes coming of age around 1941 and influenced by Harlem's cultural and theater history could not have helped but heard about Josephine Baker and her legendary career. However, no one of my generation had ever seen her because she migrated to Paris during the Harlem Renaissance of the twenties, became a French citizen, and became also a household word not only in France, but in the French colonies of North Africa. She was born in St. Louis and by 1921 was already recognized as a comedienne of the first rank as the top performer in Sissle and Blake's famous musical "Chocolate Dandies," in which she was billed as "the highest-paid showgirl in the world" (at $125 per week). Of all the great Negro stars who found greater social acceptance and financial rewards in Europe than in their native America, Josephine Baker became the most outstanding.

Knowing all of this, I had one of the memorable episodes of my North African war experience when I saw and heard Josephine Baker perform as an entertainer for the Allied Armies in 1942–43. Not long after the fall of Oran, Casablanca and Algiers, news got around that Josephine Baker had migrated to Morocco, escaping the Nazis as they overran all of Southern France. She was reported dangerously ill in Marrakech and for many weeks rumors of her whereabouts and condition were published by the Army newspaper *Stars and Stripes*. Then news came that the great Baker was rising from her sickbed to tour the Allied Armies as a performer. The heroic nature of this gesture was not fully appreciated until one saw her perform, an emaciated ghost of her former self, thin as a supple reed, but as dynamic as any young star in her first bid for fame. Josephine Baker was electrifying as she sang her most famous song, the song that best symbolizes her career, "J'ai Deux Amours—Mon Pays et Paris" (Two Loves Have I —My Country and Paris). I know that the American people (both black and white) will never have the opportunity to know the aching nostalgia that all the American exiles of the twenties carried in their souls. They had all run away from a country they had really tried to love but found incompatible. Baker was one, and it is certain that no amount of success she won in Europe really compensated for the thing she really wanted—fame and fortune in New York, Chicago, Boston, Philadelphia, Los Angeles, etc. I realized this profoundly when I saw her in North Africa. And so it was that when she made her first postwar visit to New York in 1951, I hastened to the Broadway theater to hear and meet her again. The result was my review—"Salute to Josephine Baker, Magnificent Negro Artist."

With the appearance of this review, ominous grumblings were heard below the delighted murmurings of some of the readership of the *Daily Worker*. The mumble of disapproval came from none other than the Negro Communist leadership from Harlem, led by Benjamin J. Davis, Jr., who objected, claiming that it was politically erroneous to praise Baker in the party press because of her pro-Gaullist sympathies during World War II! In this way cold water was dashed on my most enjoyable writing assignment up to that moment. I was outraged and appalled at this stupid political narrowness coming from the Negro leadership, most of whom had been too old to spend enough time in the Army to be rejected at the induction station.

The rejection of this review was only one on a long list of rebuffs I had been getting on account of my views. I argued and fought, rebelled and sulked, and became embittered, especially when one of the favorite inner-circle party reviewers came out with another article on Baker in Paul Robeson's *Freedom* newspaper sometime later. It was the party's bureaucratic clique mentality in operation. This power clique actually resented the outsider projecting anything resembling an authoritative critique on any aspect of cultural affairs. However, it was impossible at that moment to dislodge me from my post on the *Daily Worker*, inasmuch as the staff of this paper also represented a semi-independent power center in party affairs. But now I discerned very clearly that my days were numbered, and I knew I would be dropped at the first opportunity once the party machinery got into high gear against me.

The next ideological clash came over my two-part review of the play "Green Pastures." This time the criticism came from James E. Jackson, who, next to Harry Haywood, was then considered to be the important Negro Marxist theoretician. In Jackson, who is still around, the Communists have the Marxist-Negro Integrationist par excellence, who is also theoretically inclined. This is rare, although Jackson is somewhat limited in theoretical scope simply because he *is* an integrationist. (Marxism is superfluous to the integration movement since integrationists don't need the Marxists to achieve what limited integrationist aims the system allows.) Jackson's theoretical limitations were evident when he impatiently criticized my review on the grounds that *it paid too much attention to the creative and historical aspects of Negro folklore*. What he wanted was a brief statement which made short shrift of the play as an anti-Negro stereotype that should be banned. My response was that such an approach was not only narrow and simplistic but also critically vulgar. Such cultural inventions as "Green Pastures" should be criticized with an eye towards educating the readership on the many problems of dealing creatively with elements of Negro folklore material, else of what value is criticism as a cultural tool? Jackson would have none of that, and revealed an attitude that I immediately recognized as that of a Marxist political bureaucrat who was fundamentally anti-cultural in his training and reflexes. Through him I saw deeper into the problem of why Marxism failed to relate itself to the uniqueness of Negro cultural complexities in America. The deadhand of Russian-inspired Socialist Realism had insinuated its tenets into all areas of Marxist intellectual thought, thereby stifling and distorting not only the use of these culturally-oriented expressions but also a constructive critical approach to cultural ingredients. I haven't the slightest doubt that anyone reading my review of "Green Pastures" in 1968 could honestly object to its critical premises. After eighteen years, I am not ashamed of it.

Not long after my "Green Pastures" review my Communist Party career ended. It is not necessary to relate the manner of my departure except to say that it was "in the cards." I then discovered that I had never been, since Army discharge, actually "rehabilitated to civilian life." Belatedly I began this rehabilitation. It appalled me to realize that from 1941 to 1952 I had been regimented, first militarily and then socially and politically. I found individual freedom a grand personal experience. For about five years, I read and wrote, but published nothing until "An Afro-American's Cultural Views" was accepted by the magazine *Présence Africaine* in 1957. This started a new phase of my long career in wrestling with cultural problems. In the late 1950's my ideas began to mature as I approached the definitive cultural critique I strove for. From then on, under the prodding of the new civil rights trends among students, my ideas developed at a rapid rate as I tried to think out the cultural-political implications of these new trends.

Présence Africaine is the official publication of the Society of African Culture (SAC), established in the late 1940's and located in Paris. The magazine is called the *revue culturelle du monde noir* (cultural review of the black world). In 1958 an American branch of SAC, the American Society of African Culture (AMSAC), was established and I transferred my cultural loyalties in that direction.

The reader will note that in this article I used the designation "Afro-American," in contrast to my use of "Negro Intellectual" in the book title. I used Afro-American mostly in deference to the Africans with whom I was dealing in my negotiations with *Présence Africaine*. I frankly do not favor the term Afro-American at all, because as a writer I find the term cumbersome and awkward despite the claims made for its "ethnic" accord with our African origins. I frankly consider the objections to the word Negro intellectually childish and based on subjective motivations which have little relevance to the hard facts of American Negro existence. This, of course, is only an opinion, since I have never in my life suffered from any sense of a loss of black identity. I have always known exactly who I am as a person of African descent, and never lost sight of that reality even when deeply mired down in the frustrations of interracial politics and cultural life. I don't believe a change of word or title changes the content of anything —including people who are called Negroes. However, I cannot speak for others on this question, and therefore when I write, I use "Negro," "Black," or "Afro-American" as the spirit strikes me.

In the case of my article "An Afro-American's Cultural Views," I ran afoul, not of the Communists this time, but of the Negro intellectual establishment of whom Mr. J. Saunders Redding, the novelist-critic, was the chief critical spokesman. I think perhaps Mr. Redding was incensed not only over the term "Afro-American" but also over the article's content. At any rate, not long after this piece hit the articulate circles of the black establishment, I heard through the academic grapevine that a certain black intellectual of some repute in and around Howard University had responded to my article thusly: "I'm going to take care of this bird" (meaning the author, me). This demonstrated to me that despite all the furor made over party labels, Negro integrationism is the same thing, whether it emanates from the NAACP, the Urban League, SNCC, CORE, SCLC, the Communist Party, Howard University, or in this latter instance the American Society of African Culture. My article caused quite a stir among the Paris Africans and also among the AMSAC "Afros" in New York. None of the American Afros in AMSAC liked my article, and pitted J. Saunders Redding against me in a debate. This debate was ill-timed and ill-prepared and, thus, inconclusive. But it revealed that AMSAC was not of a mind to implement the Paris parent body's cultural program among American Negroes. That was clear. The Paris SAC's idea was to bring Africans and people of African descent in the Western world into one cohesive cultural community through the intellectual disciplines of history, literature, art, science, politics, etc. But the integrationist philosophy of the black intelligentsia in America foredoomed that plan to utter failure. After ten years AMSAC is moribund.

In the May, 1960, issue of the *New Leader*, J. Saunders Redding, the AMSAC spokesman, attacked my article in the following words:

Certainly there is no question at all of an Afro-American culture as against an Anglo-American culture. Harold W. Cruse, in his essay in *Présence Africaine* for January, 1958, was not only wrong but wrong-headed. The American Negro people are not a *people* in Cruse's sense of the word. When he complains rather petulantly that [there has been no] ... "rebirth of the culture of the American Negro," the proper answer to his complaint is that what has never been born cannot have a rebirth. And when he goes further not only to link but to equate the American Negro's struggle for full citizenship with the African Negro's struggle for political independence as the ultimate goal of race nationalism, one can only stand appalled at Cruse's total blindness to the truth.[2]

2 "Negro Writing In America," pp. 8–10.

The Negro Marxist Integrationists, such as Davis and Jackson, could never have dared to state their opposition to my views in such blunt terms, with such candor, and with such brazen ignorance of what brooding racial sentiments lay hidden in the minds of the up-and-coming generations. The Negro Marxists know too much about other Negroes to brush away the realities of "race nationalism," even though they must stop short of pursuing its implications vis-a-vis the African emergence. But a J. Saunders Reddings is truly appalled both at the clear and present fact and also at the implications. With a Redding there is no connection between Africans and Afro-Americans at all, be it political, cultural, aesthetic, literary, or whatever. As for literature, Redding asserts: "Negro American literature will continue in a direction quite different from the direction it is ardently hoped Negro African literature will take." Elsewhere: "In American Negro writers, the American outlook prevails . . ." Such writers as Langston Hughes, Frank Yerby, Richard Wright, Ann Petry, and James Baldwin, have, says Redding: ". . . sought a complete identification with white America, sometimes even to the extent of denying their Negroness." One cannot deny a critic like Redding the inviolate right to his literary opinions but, considering the writers named, one has to wonder how aware Redding was that he was speaking mostly for himself. In 1960, J. Saunders Redding could not have envisioned the popularity of Frantz Fanon's ideas among the young black generation of 1968.

During my AMSAC period I discovered to my grief that integrationists such as Redding present a greater liability in terms of an intellectual renaissance in black thought than the Marxist integrationists. The latter, at least, try hard not to stand still even if their social (and creative) logic runs a somewhat elliptical course, hardly ever in a progressive line. The Reddings stand still, afraid of the risks incident to pushing forward into the virgin territory of black and white relations in literature and art. In a new organization such as AMSAC was in 1960, the Reddings are handicaps out of a traditionalist past that persevered in its own way but was never able to break the custom barriers to any kind of originality. Thus, inadvertently, out of a certain conviction, they smother and choke each new conception that arises. Thus was AMSAC choked off. I did not include J. Saunders Redding in my book because of space. But as a man of letters, Redding is an important figure in Negro literature despite the personal and ideological brushes I had with him. In fact, Redding is Negro literature's only claim to any luster in literary criticism qua criticism. That he doesn't shine brilliantly like Edmund Wilson is nobody's fault but his own—he apparently is simply afraid to shine.

After the AMSAC interlude came my trip to Castro's Cuba, which served as part of my introduction into the lively 1960's. This new phase was represented by the article "Revolutionary Nationalism and the Afro-American," which was extracted from an unpublished essay of some ninety pages. This essay attempted to deal in a comparative manner with the nationalist content in Castro's movement and the black movement in America. This piece represented the first theoretical projection of the implications of nationalism within the new black American civil rights trends. "Negro Nationalism's New Wave" was also a part of this projection. In the meantime, beginning with 1961, two new publications appeared on the civil rights scene—*Freedomways* and *Liberator*, both of which I dealt with in my book. I chose to write for *Liberator* because I considered it free of the political control of the Old Left. I used this magazine to further develop many of my cultural views from earlier articles that needed more development and qualification. What followed were the articles "Rebellion or Revolution?," "Marxism and the Negro," and "The Economics of Black Nationalism." For the first time since 1951–52, I was able to deal at some length with my political, economic, and cultural conceptions of the black experience. Brief as this period was, I felt highly satisfied in my *Liberator* role, but it was short-lived because of certain ideological conflicts that were bound to develop within the staff over editorial policy.

In 1964, during hospitalization after an ulcer attack, I quit *Liberator*, finally convinced that only a lengthy book would allow me to elaborate fully on my views. When William Morrow & Company read the first draft and came through with the first contract I had ever succeeded in getting from a publisher, the final result was *The Crisis of the Negro Intellectual*. This book was, of course, no mere cumulative result of a critical line of reasoning. In writing this book, I had to submit myself to a subjective reappraisal and a psychological purgation in order to achieve the impact I wanted. Actually there were *two* books written—the first draft which was almost completely discarded, and a second book based on the edited remains of the first. I forced myself to go back almost twenty years and review all of my accumulated research notes and somehow incorporate them into the work.

When the book was finished, I did an article for Sartre's and de Beauvoir's *Les Temps Moderne*, in which I slanted my views to accommodate what I perceived the French philosophical mind-set to be. They titled the article "Les Noirs et l'idée de Révolte." I can't get over the notion that as conversant as foreigners might be with American developments, they have a distorted consensus on black and white relations. Finally, to round out this representative collection for *Rebellion or Revolution?*, I decided to include at least one unpublished essay—"Behind the Black Power Slogan," which was a paper prepared for the Socialist Scholars' Conference of 1967. Although my views are in conflict with those of the official Marxists in America, I was forced to argue for my own theoretical conclusions by falling back on the use of Marxian ideas and concepts. This was necessary because most Socialists are Marxists. Circumstances prevented me from attending this conference. But even before I decided I could not attend, the conference steering committee had refused to allow the paper to be presented, so I had no real motivation for attending in any event. It all added up to another of a long series of misadventures with the Marxists, with whom I am forever at odds.

In sum, these articles and essays were all derived from my great need to interpret what I perceived as a unique interplay of political, economic, and cultural factors at work behind the various freedom-seeking fronts of the black movement—factors which needed what Albert Camus once called a "theoretic frame." My pressing need to accomplish this was closely connected with creative impulses I had for other kinds of literature which are neither forensic nor theoretical nor polemical. The literature of theoretical sociology and the literature of artistic creativity are seldom compatible urges within the same consciousness. They get in the way of each other; polemics spoil poetry and poetry usually abhors the rational wit. In devoting all these years to the task of what I judge to be a rational inquiry into certain disputed facts of our reality, I persevere in the hope that I have helped to make the future of poetry and the other arts more relevant and secure. I believe that the only antidote to the present irrational thrust toward social oblivion is more rationality. I grant the right of the confirmed existentialist to dispute such a claim, but it is only through new forms of social engineering (programming) that the irrational drift towards chaos can be reversed.

In this regard, an advance review of this collection from the Kirkus Service, a book review services, says, "This book conforms to Kirkus' Law: the tendency to collect and publish one's odds and ends in the wake of a success . . . But mainly [Cruse] sifts the ashes of straw men instead of building the new radical theory he calls for." The Kirkus Service did not know, of course, that it had been the publisher's plan to publish these articles first, a situation which certainly upsets Kirkus' Law. The reason this collection was not published before the first book is that at the time I could not have written an introduction such as this—the first attempt in 1965 kept expanding because I had too much to say. And on the question of a "new radical theory," the reader should be advised that certain other readers have already perceived the outlines of a new radical theory in *The Crisis of the Negro Intellectual* which the Kirkus Service reviewer did not perceive.

This raises a crucial question as to whether members of the established white American radical movement would even recognize a new radical theory if they saw it. This is especially true when and if such a new radical theory emanates from the black direction. We are dealing here with a peculiarly American problem of a gulf between the social perceptions of whites and blacks who usually do not see and interpret the same phenomena the same way. Social psychology can explain this, but I have already mentioned earlier in this Introduction the deep biracial cultural impasse that exists in America and has so many unexplored ramifications. One of the ramifications is that there can be no new social theory of a radical nature developed in America until this gulf in perception is breached with the aid of a new cultural theory. But the most difficult concept for the white radical mind in America to understand and accept will be precisely such a cultural theory. The very profound reasons for this will be explained, I hope, in another book—if there is still time. As I said in my first book—the crisis of black and white is also *a crisis in social* theory.

HAROLD CRUSE

1

Purblind Slant on Africa

DAILY WORKER, NEW YORK, NOVEMBER 29, 1950

(*King Solomon's Mines,* an MGM production starring
Deborah Kerr, Stewart Granger and Richard Carlson.
Now showing at Loew's Warfield Theater, San Francisco).

Countee Cullen, the Negro poet, now dead, once wrote a long
and beautiful lyric called "Heritage." It began like this:

> What is Africa to me:
> Copper sun or scarlet sea,
> Jungle tar or jungle track
> Strong bronzed men, or
>   regal black
> Women from whose loins
>   I sprang
> When the birds of Eden sang?
> One three centuries removed
> From the scenes his
>   fathers loved,
> Spicy grove, cinnamon tree,
> What is Africa to me?

But to Hollywood's MGM, Africa was and still is the "dark
continent" of cannibals on the one hand, or docile primitives
always on hand to make up safaris for some English thrill-
seekers slumming in the jungles.

King Solomon's Mines, thus, is old-time stuff dressed up in
technicolor with wild animals killing nobody but Africans.

There is, of course, the white professional hunter who is
unwilling or unable to ever return to dear old England. He
is, unlike his traditional prototype, Trader Horn, a handsome

lout so that he can fall in love with the pretty Englishwoman
from London who came to Africa on the trail of her husband
who disappeared searching for the legendary King Solomon's
Mines chock full of diamonds. She brings her brother along
for interest.

Strange things happen in this fantasy which tries hard to
be a travelogue. The ferocious animals, this time, are not hun-
gry and don't often attack the white members of the safari,
and when they do they always go after the woman from
London—even spiders and snakes.

You would have thought an expert in animal psychology
had been through the jungles ahead of them. There were more
narrow escapes than were seen in the old "see next chapter"
serials.

Imperialist Touch

The film is adapted from a novel by H. Rider Haggard,
English barrister turned novelist and an agent for British imperialism during the annexation of the Transvaal in Africa in
1877. The faithfulness of the adaptation of the novel which
bears the same title as the film is unimportant. At best it has
all the earmarks of the type of stories which have served for
decades to foster romanticized ignorance of the vital and turbulent history of the continent of Africa.

Other writers, like Albert Schweitzer, a humanitarian, but
a supporter of European domination in Africa, gave better
accounts of African facts during the close of the nineteenth
century which saw European nations, chiefly England, fasten
their grips on African labor and resources.

Thus, the rich stakes in Africa are still being pursued and
the imaginary riches of King Solomon's Mines could only be
termed piddling compared to the real wealth of Africa. They
used to say that imperialism followed the flag, but in the face
of American economic penetration into Africa and other colonies, Hollywood can perform better than anybody's flag.

The time and setting of *King Solomon's Mines* was 1897,

but what does Hollywood care about African history? What does it matter that while Curtis, a privileged class Englishman, was seeking a fabled mine, the Abyssinian ruler Menelik and his army had, only a few months before in 1896, inflicted a decisive defeat on the Italian invaders at Adowa to preserve Ethiopian independence?

Or that the Beni peoples of the Gold Coast resisted British armed invasions from 1897–1899 until finally subjugated? Or that practically the entire African continent was being subjugated to bloodbaths, land confiscation, disruption of tribal life, famine, and a host of other calamities as direct results of European annexations, chiefly British.

Unconcerned

Or would Hollywood concern itself with the civilizations and cultures existing in Africa dating from centuries back, surviving the slave raids and internal wars, to stand as monuments to civilized achievements, like Dahomey, Yoruba, Ashanti, Benin, Mandingo, Timbuktoo, and others?

The very idea of African culture is repugnant to this contemptible lie factory which has become so degenerate that it can't even keep up with the times by inventing new lies. It must stick its hands into the ashcans for worthless and dated scriblings for its scenarios. Those who shot this film on location must have been instructed to wear blinkers lest they saw too much that might suggest how worthless and stupid their project was.

But let us not believe that there was not method to this filmic madness. Allan Quatermain (Stewart Granger) the professional hunter comes across a member of the Watussis people. He says: "I don't like him, he's too arrogant." This Watussi comes from a people whose history and origin ethnologists have not fully explained. These people grow to heights of eight and nine feet, have facial characteristics resembling those seen in pictures on the walls of Egyptian tombs. Their dress, hairdress, ornaments suggest an affinity to ancient Egypt as do their long horned, well-groomed cattle. Quatermain, the hunter, has contempt for the proud and stately Watussis people whose tribal dance is a thing of unsurpassed beauty.

This is as dangerous a bit of film poison imaginable in the face of the hard realities of present-day African struggles for independence from foreign domination.

2

Negro Soldier Sequences Censored
in "Call Me Mister"

DAILY WORKER, NEW YORK, FEBRUARY 2, 1951

Call Me Mister, the musical hit of Broadway, 1946, which glorified the army men and women, and set their overseas experiences and their post-war dreams to fancy steps and facile lyrics and music, has been to Hollywood and back.

The original had some meaty, progressive social content, but most of it has been purged. The film version at the Roxy is an ineffectual ghost of its former self.

From this reviewer's point of view the only sequence that had any vitality was the satire on the army air corps which did manage to wake up the audience with its originality. As for the rest, it just didn't jell one way or the other.

Betty Grable and Dan Dailey try hard and as far as the latter is concerned, it didn't seem worth his efforts for the screen production didn't begin to approach the level of his dancing talents.

As for Betty Grable, it appeared that Hollywood made more use of her personality as cheesecake for the GIs than for anything else. There was a creditable but dated comic stint by Danny Thomas. The setting is in Japan after V-J day and one of the early sketches showing Miss Grable in the dance lead with a chorus of Japanese women dancers eulogizing the American GI had a distasteful tone of Western chauvinism which won't sit well with the Japanese today.

The supporting troupers seemed as if their hearts weren't in the thing, and after all who could blame them. *Call Me Mister* was originally the product of a short-lived era of promises, optimism and high hopes for the post-war world. But look at us now! No doubt half the cast or more are on the verge of being drafted which is more than just irony.

But there is a deeper significance in the manner in which *Call Me Mister* has been watered down. The original version dealt more thoroughly with the Negro Soldier, but this has been censored except for the "Goin Home Train" sketch.

Even here the Negro singer was not a Negro GI portraying a Negro GI but a porter on a train with white GIs. Everybody was "Goin Home" but the Negro. Gone was the sketch, the symbol of the Negro GI's outstanding achievements in France. Gone was the scathing derision of Senator Burble, the personification of Bilbo, Rankin, and Eastland.

It must be pointed out here that the dropping of the Negro sequences from this film version, from this musical, amounts to more than just denying Negro actors, singers, dancers, etc., much needed work and pay which is an issue big enough in itself.

What is involved here, in the crassest manner, is cultural robbery on the one hand, coupled with a denial of the right of Negro artists to participate in expressing before the nation and the world as equals in precisely that which the Negro people have contributed to the total store of American culture.

The tap dance sketch performed by the Dunhill Dance Team is a good example. This dance routine was originated in Harlem over a decade ago, and the stages of the Apollo Theater and the Harlem Opera House were among the first to see the expression of this tap dance variation. It is a Negro art form, but how many Negro dancers will Hollywood employ in its musicals? A token number, if any, and at intervals few and far between.

And so in keeping with the times, the former spirit which infused *Call Me Mister* is dead. What remains is an anachronism, flabby, weak, inept. The dead hand of Hollywood has crushed the life out of it and what is flashed on the screen is a chauvinist testimony to Jimcrow.

3

Salute to Josephine Baker, Magnificent Negro Artist

DAILY WORKER, NEW YORK,

WEDNESDAY, MARCH 14, 1951

The name of Josephine Baker when mentioned has always conjured up many facts, real and imagined, relating to the career of this famous Negro artist of the international entertainment world.

To those in the United States who knew her personally, she is a friend, fellow artist, colleague. Between them there exist close bonds that have endured twenty years or more and are yet as strong as ever in spite of the fact that she, long, long ago, became a citizen of France. Her first appearance in France was in the 1925 Folies Bergère. To others in our country who never knew her personally, and they are many thousands, Josephine Baker has always been a legend flavored by sights and sounds and visions of Paris where she has reigned supreme. To most Negroes she is the outstanding example of a native daughter who made good far, far from home.

This reviewer remembers hearing of the personality of Josephine Baker so many years ago that it would be impossible to say just when. But it was not until the years of 1942–1943 that it was my pleasant good fortune to see and hear this marvelous woman.

It was during the North African campaign of World War II that the name of Josephine Baker found its way into consciousness of many soldiers, Negro and white, who had never heard of her. After working in the French underground resistance movement during those first years of the German Occupation, she had escaped to North Africa and was reported living in Marrakech, Morocco.

Rumor had it that she was at first ill, seriously ill, even dead. The Army newspaper *Stars and Stripes* carried many stories about her and then finally reported that she was not dead but had recovered from a serious illness and would be around soon on an entertainment junket. And so one starry night near the edge of the great Sahara, Josephine Baker sang and performed for my regiment. For this reviewer it was a never to be forgotten experience.

She was, at that time, thin and wasted from her illness, but so vibrant and vital, that her physical condition was soon lost sight of. She sang several American and French songs, one of which was the famous, "J'ai Deux Pays" (Two Loves Have I: My Country and Paris). The GIs swooned and she was the topic of conversation for many, many, months after.

And so for this reviewer, seeing Jo Baker again at the Strand was in the nature of a second triumph, a repeat performance, even better than the one seven years ago. It is an experience that surpasses anything describable in mere words. What she sings, what she says in words, expresses in movement of body, in dance motions and pantomime, constitute an art of such magnificence and individuality that it is not enough to talk about it. She must be seen.

She must be seen, not merely for the splendor of lavish gowns designed by Balenciaga, Dior, Dessès, and Madame Schiaparelli and Jacques Fath which alone would make a fashion show. She must be seen to partake of what she communicates across the boards to an audience. She creates an atmosphere alive with quiet and then audible wonder; tense and then vocal appreciation, an electric charge of spontaneous endearment. And you become lost in a rapport that centers around this personality, captivated by this Negro Woman who personifies an institution in France.

A little note in *The New York Times*, May 10, 1943,

quoted Josephine Baker as saying that she would never return to the U.S. but would return to France as soon as the war was over. One need not go into the reasons why she made that statement. No doubt she has expressed the same sentiments many times before and since.

Rather, it is a tribute to this artist who adopted another country, that she did not thereby become a rootless, declassed cosmopolitan spurning forever the tap-source of her talents—The Negro Cultural Idiom. So her return to this country is truly a triumph.

A triumph for herself and a triumph for the American Negroes who were drawn to the Strand by the magic mention of this fabulous personality. And there is a logic in all this, for the road that leads an individual to fight with resistance forces of a mother country against an invader is not the road that leads one away from one's nativity.

And this is the fine thing about Josephine Baker. That is the persistence of her native Negro idiom which she never lost and which predominates what she does artistically. Rather, it has enriched, and has been enriched by an acquired French and Latin flavor. When she sang the famous "J'ai Deux Pays" in French and English it was symbolic of a woman who, while having achieved integration on a high level, has never lost her touch.

This is how one must view Josephine Baker, and it is wished that American audiences, particularly white audiences, could grasp the full meaning of the story behind this statuesque Negro woman.

For here is a story of life, art, fame and fortune, that America, Jo Baker's native home, would not offer. There is, then, a real irony in the fact that Americans must know her by virtue of newspaper notices that speak of a fame she fashioned in another country. Her native countrymen's children will never speak the name of Josephine Baker with the fond familiarity that French children speak of her in France and in

French colonies where her name is practically a household word.

I wonder if the audience at the Strand comprehended what was happening when she stood on the stage and with consummate art reached out through the haze of American "show me" attitude at the beginning of her show, and clasped the reluctant ones to her person. Caressed them, indulged them in their lukewarm unfamiliarity, fondled them out of their standoffishness, then having won them, electrified them and sent them home after resounding applause agreeing with each other that they had just experienced something extraordinary.

Throughout her performance this reviewer's mind kept going across the sea to North Africa and back again to the Strand setting, linking up the two events over the span of years.

After the performance I waited at the stage door with several other admirers for her appearance. Her manager appeared finally and said that she was too tired for any more interviews for the night. However, when she did emerge she stopped to exchange greetings with the group that waited for her.

It was then that I approached her and asked her to remember a certain performance she gave in North Africa to a certain Negro regiment at a certain place. With a light of recognition she clasped my hand and said, "Oh, how well I remember that. North Africa? How could I ever forget!"

This is part of the story of a world figure who since returning to these shores has not shrunk from a consistent fight in her field of work and art against discrimination. She made history when recently in Miami, Florida, at the Copa City Club, a rule of no Jimcrow was enforced and her audiences were Negro and white. She has recently turned down other offers for appearances which did not promise a non-discriminatory policy. She also spoke out sharply against the legal lynching of the Martinsville Seven.

Let us all salute Josephine Baker, Negro woman, artist, soldier fighter against discrimination, former lieutenant, French Resistance Army, and a citizen of the world.

4

"Green Pastures" Twenty Years Ago and Today

DAILY WORKER, NEW YORK,
FRIDAY, MARCH 30, 1951. PAGE 10,
AND MONDAY, APRIL 2, 1951, PAGE 11

Twenty years after the first heavenly hosts of Marc Connelly's *Green Pastures* were introduced to the theater public and world at large, we find the Broadway Theater in 1951 emphasizing its steady descent into the lower regions of barrenness and uncreative sterility by inflicting on us again this dramatized collection of fables on alleged Negro religious folklore.

Green Pastures is based on a book of fictionalized "folk stories" by Roark Bradford, a southern white writer, entitled *Southern Sketches, Ol' Man Adam an' His Chillun.*

The fact that *Green Pastures* makes much of the theme of heavenly virtues as opposed to the sinful world does not alter the fact that angels have been called upon to do the dirty work of Satan. The play won the 1930 Pulitzer prize.

Newspaper files reveal that audiences of the 1930s were so affected by the "simple folk charm" of this glorified pageant that it ran for eighteen solid months in New York, then toured the south and Canada. During all this time Negroes did not support the play in any noticeable numbers. This notwithstanding the fact that its celebrated cast was entirely Negro and big. More than that, it is a play which no Negro theater group has ever performed off Broadway or Main Street.

Some interesting facts about the first run of *Green Pastures* are as follows: It was produced by a Wall Street financier after three well-known producers had turned it down. Religious circles questioned Marc Connelly's motives for writing the play. The play was condemned by the Washington, D.C., NAACP as a fraud, and barred by the National Theater of Norway. Hungary also banned any performance of it. Introduced in England, it resulted in a heated debate in the House of Commons. The *Reader's Digest* for May, 1936, said: "For five years *Green Pastures* became a quasi-religious, semi-public institution."

The current revival presents an opportunity for some serious evaluating of this play. For 1951 is not 1930 and it is safe to say that this revival won't be swallowed for too long. The America of 1951 is thinking too deeply about fundamental problems of a very earthly if not earthshaking nature to be long bothered with Marc Connelly's fraudulent message of folk whimsy from heaven by a cast of Negro actors and singers who, in order to work, have no alternative but to perform in what is offered, namely: plays like *Green Pastures* which have no relation whatsoever to life as they know and experience it.

Also the present cast of *Green Pastures* is one which has a radically different attitude towards its play material. Thus, there is evident in the performances of the actors a different quality of interpretation, not only in the portrayal of the lead roles like the "Lawd" and Gabriel but in the supporting roles and the group scenes.

So those of us who are opposed to the rehashing of such beautifully garnished inedibles as *Green Pastures* must, in order to be constructively critical, view the play within the context of the two main and conflicting trends which are historically operative within the development of the Negro Theater movement. This involves the whole complex of Negro actors, Negro themes and concretely the problems of dramatic treatment of true Negro life plus the very crucial question of work.

Green Pastures reflects dual trends in that it has Negro actors performing with great and genuine talent that is striving for democratic integration into the American Theater in roles depicting real Negro and everybody's life. This integration however must and can only be achieved through the medium of a National Negro theater where Negro dramatic talent can be trained and developed. Such a theater would be the ultimate logic of the positive trend in the Negro theater movement and would bring to bear on the American theater all that is national (Negro) in content in its highest form.

In the case of *Green Pastures* there is represented a distortion common to the American stage wherein the positive trends in the Negro theater movement are blocked by a play that continues to this day a negative trend that has its origin in the emergence of the minstrel shows during the 1830s and later in the sentimental plantation school of literature of the 1880s. These trends still distort and frustrate honest literature on Negro life and history. Roark Bradford and Marc Connelly are modern representatives of this trend.

The play is divided into two parts and seventeen scenes encompassing assorted places on earth, in heaven and points in between. It manages to cover all these places and still be out of this world. It is easy to be beguiled by its beauty, inasmuch as it has attracted unto itself much of the earthly treasure of Broadway's dollar reserve to the extent of expensive and imaginative settings, lighting and stage effects. This from a theater monopoly which would not proffer a punctured copper cent for an honest drama drawn from the experience of the Negro people in America.

Yes, verily, it's true, the millions of acres of pasturelands in the United States may be green in color but have never in the South run over with milk and honey, nor fishfries. More often than not they have been red with the blood of Negroes or soaked with Negro sweat when not eroded and depleted as a consequence of the southern plantation system. And this is the material basis from whence comes American Negro folklore, true folklore.

The Green Pastures, thus, has little in it that is true Negro folklore. Rather, it is the conception of paternalistic anti-Negro writers and folklorists of the South of what they would prefer Negro folklore to be. The old slave owners and their descendants did not want to hear and were not told folk stories revealing what Negroes really thought. If they had, the South would have been a doubly armed camp.

Thus Roark Bradford's *Ol' Man Adam an' His Chillun* (Children to you) cannot be accepted as folklore representative of Negro experience in the South, now or before. A Negro preacher might have told Sunday school children Bible stories in this fashion but Negro life in general was never so idyllic.

Marc Connelly writes as a foreword to his script:

"The Green Pastures is an attempt to present certain aspects of a living religion in the terms of its believers. The religion is that of thousands of Negroes in the Deep South. With terrific spiritual hunger and the greatest humility these untutored black Christians—many of whom cannot even read the book which is the treasure house of their faith—have adapted the contents of the Bible to the consistencies of their every-day lives."

Sterling A. Brown, Negro professor of English and a leading folklorist at Howard University, says this in an article on Negro folklore:

"Mythological tales explain the origin of the ocean, where the hurricane comes from, why the wind and waters are at war, why the moon's face is smutty. Others enlarge material from the Bible. Ingenuity is especially exercised on filling in gaps in the creation story. . . . Religion is treated freely, even irreverently, but not to the degree of Roark Bradford's *Ol' Man Adam an' His Chillun*, which is synthetic, not genuine folkstuff." See *Phylon* magazine, Atlanta University Review of Race and Culture, fourth quarter, 1950, page 325.

On page 318 of the same issue of *Phylon* magazine Professor Brown says:

"For a long time Uncle Remus and his Brer Rabbit tales stood for the Negro folk and their lore. One thing made clear by the resurrection of Uncle Remus in Walt Disney's *Song of the South* is the degree to which he belonged to white people rather than to the Negro folk. . . . In any consideration of American Negro folklore expression it is important to realize that even before Joel Chandler Harris revealed the antics of Brer Rabbit to America, John Henry was swinging his hammer in the Big Bend Tunnel on the C. & O. Road."

This last quoted reference applies also to Roark Bradford, Marc Connelly and the *Green Pastures*.

In the meantime much is being done today in the field of American Negro folklore in the way of re-evaluation of Negro folk traditions which have existed for decades watered down and distorted by the literary trends of the Southern sentimental and chauvinistic school of writers and researchers, pioneered in the 1880s by Joel Chandler Harris and continued by Marc Connelly's play.

Thus the dual trends in the interpretation of Negro folklore are as important here as the dual trends of Negro development in the American theater. These trends must be resolved soon so that Negro life and real folklore can find honest expression on the American stage.

On the positive side comment must be made on the way in which the present cast has changed and toned down most of the offensive elements in the original. Reading the original script produced in the 1930s it is discovered that many words, phrases, and references insulting to Negroes have been deleted or changed, except for the murder and the gambling scenes.

Thus this production has more formal dignity than the original. The group scenes, particularly around the ark, the night club and Pharaoh's throne room have much of the new spirit sophistication which Marc Connelly never intended.

This is all to the good, since it is not possible to deal with the problem of the Negro actor in a vacuum. It is plain that more is being achieved by direct participation of some of our best Negro talents in the play than would be achieved by remaining outside of it.

The "Lawd" of today portrayed by William Marshall is not the "Lawd" of the 1930's. He's really angry with the world and in a different manner. He walks the earth with tolerance and dignity that befits a great man. The first person he meets is the young Negro woman, Zeba (Vinie Burrows), strumming a ukelele. He rebukes her for carousing on the Sabbath. She is the only woman character in the play treated with any delineation, but she is an immoral person of disrepute. Marc Connelly will protest that this is a fable, that this is harmless entertainment based on the "simple" beliefs of a childishly simple people, meaning Southern Negroes. Which means ultimately all Negroes.

Fables concocted out of an anti-Negro conception could not conceivably take into account the earthly degradation heaped upon a million and more Zebas in the South's pasturelands. Marc Connelly, perhaps, wouldn't know about this, but it doesn't alter the fact that fables take on the qualities of real life and affect the same. Thus one Ralph Barton, critic, could write in the magazine, *U.S. Theatre*, back in the 1930s of *Green Pastures:*

"Only a simple race of people with medieval minds . . . is capable of forgetting hell and giving heaven an occasional thought. Such a race exists right under our noses."

* * *

If no such vileness is evident in today's reviews of *Green Pastures* it is because we live in times when fables are losing ground to the inexorable pressure of facts.

And more than that because William Marshall portrayed the "Lawd" like a man really concerned with the problems of a real world, and Gabriel (Ossie Davis) was no grinning comic, or Pharaoh (John Bouie) no buffoon but a ruler. Eve (Milroy Ingram) was beautiful in modern terms. The whole enormous cast of men, women and children have created the best possible in dramatic and dignified values that is possible in this distorted fable. A choir under Hall Johnson's direction highlighted the production with twenty-five spirituals.

5

An Afro-American's Cultural Views

For Africans at home and abroad, the cultural situation of the American Negro might seem vague and incomprehensible amidst the general civil rights struggle in this country. For the simple reason that American Negroes are part of the colored peoples of the world, it is easy for one to make the error of assuming that we Negroes here in the United States have a cultural outlook in terms of race, nationality, history and traditions similar in racial uniqueness to other colored nations the world over who are rising out of colonialism to national independence. When one speaks of a culture in the creative sense, one thinks of art, literature, music, drama, dance, language, skills and crafts, architecture, etc., and when one thinks of the liberation of oppressed peoples, one assumes a rebirth and a flowering of that people's native "culture" as a corollary of the rise to independence. Thus, in keeping with what is happening to colored peoples elsewhere, one might expect that in the United States the increased activity on the part of Negroes to achieve full citizenship, equality, and civil rights under the law would be accompanied by an increase in the quantity and quality of their "cultural" activities. Unfortunately, this is not the case. Why is this?

For colored peoples abroad, especially Africans, it will be necessary in many cases to readjust their racially influenced views on the American Negro in order to get him into proper focus in the racial scheme of things. The American Negro's cultural situation cannot be understood unless it is made clear what the American Negro truly is and what he is not. What some of us Negroes here hope he *might* become is another question. It is the real situation today in Negro thought that is disturbing for us who are conscious of the need of "culture." The Negro in the United States who writes books, plays, music, poetry; who dances, sings, paints, acts or performs, designs or creates in any way; who is a critic or a student of history—all of these are today faced with a great racial dilemma. The very fact that we stand today on the threshold of more democracy and freedom has posed a cultural problem of a very complex nature. Put in its simplest terms, the problem is this: As Negroes of Afro-American descent, and as writers, artists, creative individuals, whose culture do we develop and uphold—an Afro-American culture or an Anglo-American culture? No one in this country of Afro-American descent has answered this question. Recently a new book was published called *The Negro in American Culture* by Margaret Just Butcher, based on the collected writings of the late professor Alain Locke. This book was long awaited and long overdue, but when it appeared I found it greatly disappointing because it did not answer the question at all. The book was not even properly reviewed or discussed, and most of our alleged Negro thinkers and leaders completely ignored the book publicly. These are the days of "racial integration" among our leaders, professionals and intellectuals, and anything that smacks of "racial culture" or "nationalism" is strictly taboo. I will attempt to throw some light on the reasons for this situation.

The American Negro cannot be understood culturally unless he is seen as a member of a detached ethnic bloc of people of African descent reared for three hundred years in the unmotherly bosom of Western civilization. With regards to the African motherland, the American Negro is not an African, not even remotely. Not only have three hundred years separated him culturally from Africa; so have several thousand miles of geographical distance cut him off from any kind of real communication with Africa. As a detached offshoot of African peoples he is isolated, cut off, and has been subjected to racial intermingling in the process; today he is a racial mixture of African, Indian and Caucasian. Writers like sociologist William E. B. Du Bois claim that only a small percentage of American Negroes can be classified as pure "African."

There are many American Negroes who condemn the use of the word "Negro" as being a synonym for inferiority, and we have a weekly newspaper which does not print the word "Negro" anywhere in its pages. It uses the word "colored" instead. Some Negroes prefer the hyphenation, Afro-American, to correspond not only to our actual historical origin, but to the social status of other national and ethnic groups such as the Irish-American, Jewish-American, Italian-American, etc. Such Negroes feel that Afro-American would lend more dignity to the meaning of our racial heritage and would also raise the American Negro as a racial minority to political and social equality with other American minorities, at least nominally. There are other Negroes who do not like the term Afro-American since they especially eschew any affinities with Africa, either by color or culture. Clearly then, we American Negroes do not agree on what we actually are or even on what we shall call ourselves.

Without intending to deny the obvious—that is, our African antecedents—we must keep in mind that three hundred years of rearing in the United States has separated us from Africa in ways more insurmountable, culturally speaking, than time gaps of centuries—if the present attitudes of our Afro-American intellectuals and artists are any indication. It must be clearly understood that our racial and cultural experience as a group is distinctly American. The African languages, customs, religions, and traditions of our "American" forebears were discouraged and eventually destroyed by the necessities of the slave system. This de-Africanization process began at the point of landing of slaves on American shores. There, slaves were detribalized almost immediately, destroying any means of unity and communication. There began the process of westernization. We adopted the Caucasian's language, English—his religion, and as many customs as conditions permitted, including the eight-toned musical scale brought from Europe to America. Most slaves who learned to read English learned it from the Holy Bible. Emancipation from chattel slavery brought on by the Civil War between the northern and southern states (1861–1865) marked the beginning of a long, bitter struggle on the part of Afro-Americans for political, social and economic equality, objectives which are still far from being fully achieved. During slavery and for several decades after emancipation it was possible for one to say that Afro-Americans had a distinct culture, although there is much contention on this claim by both scholars and laymen. Nevertheless, Afro-Americans produced a distinct body of social art embodied in music, song, dance, folklore, poetry, formal literature, craftsmanship, mores, and even their own variant of Christian religious expression and experience. Much of this culture was of the "folk quality," more sophisticated expressions of this culture developing along with our rise in social status after emancipation. We produced novelists, poets, journalists, historians, a few dramatists, painters, sculptors. In the music field we have been outstanding, both in quantity and quality of musical creativity. American Negro jazz music and its concomitant dance patterns have given America its unique musical complexion and have influenced the Western world. The character of the American musical theater is so indebted to American Negro creative genius in music and dance that today our music and dance have been fully incorporated into what is called being "American." In the theater we have had notable successes of a certain kind due chiefly to our pioneering abilities in music, song and dance; but this must be accepted with certain serious reservations for reasons which will be considered further on in this article. It can be seen then, that despite our separation from the ways of Africa, Afro-Americans produced a culture that is distinctly our own and, for the most part, American in general milieu. It would then be assumed that because of our rise over the years in social, economic and political status, our Afro-American cultural heritage would find higher, fuller, more creative, more profound, more classical, more influential, more universal expression for all its uniqueness in the western world. For we are unique in the sense that we are a rather large non-white racial bloc of a stature of internationally strategic importance in the West. Yet it must be said that what we should be achieving "culturally" as Afro-Americans is not being achieved and is not in the immediate offing.

What then can be said culturally of the American Negro apropos of the international cultural problems of those of African descent at home or abroad? (The reader will note that "Afro-American" and "American Negro" are used interchangeably here. It is done because both terms are of common usage and acceptance.) To repeat, this writer, as an Afro-American, an aspiring novelist and dramatist, must, in all honesty, say that culturally speaking we Afro-Americans have sunk to a dismal low point in creative productivity, rapport, and inspiration in every creative field but jazz music. From the standpoint of our Afro-American cultural heritage we are living in a veritable cultural desert, caught in the no-man's land between two opposing racial and cultural identities—the Afro-American and Anglo-American. We stand before the world scene viewing the unprecedented rise of colored peoples to national independence and burgeoning identity not realizing or feeling who we are. This writer does not intend to foster illusions about Afro-Americans or pander to the international prestige-seeking of certain Afro-American leaders in politics, religion, education or what have you. Neither does this writer, most of all, intend to waste time in self-delusion about certain alleged advances in economics and politics made possible by the great material wealth of America. In times of prosperity even slaves receive more generous supplies of crumbs from the masters. The slave might, at the same time, be induced to sell his soul in times of prosperity for more crumbs, only to discover in leaner days that he is without soul, crumbs or the master's protection. The soul of a race, nation, people or nationality is its culture, its art, its literature, its poetry, drama, music, religion, philosophy, traditions, etc. If our Afro-American soul is to be felt and sought through, let us say, our output of creative literature, then it must be said our soul has lost its power of communication; for in the last ten years what novels, plays or essays can we point to as major works of art? Literary creations of any serious worth by Afro-Americans can be counted on the fingers of one hand. Offhand one can mention novels by Ralph Ellison, James Baldwin, John Killens, Ann Petry, and Chester Himes which deal with the American Negro scene. Leaving aside any attempt here to evaluate these novelists critically, it remains to be said that from the standpoint of quantity and social impact our literature is not impressive. The Supreme Court Decision of May, 1954, which struck a legal blow against racial segregation in public schools, gave a new impetus to the cultural and creative fields. But there has been no cultural upsurge commensurate with our stepped-up struggle for political and social equality. Hence it behooves Africans at home and abroad, when speaking of Afro-American "culture" in the United States, to first examine and understand the philosophy which Negro leaders have adopted and applied to our fight for full citizenship.

Today our struggle for complete racial equality in all areas of American life is summed up in the rallying slogans of "racial integration" or "full integration." Racial integration is the guiding outlook and philosophy of the National Association for the Advancement of Colored People (NAACP) and the Urban League, both leading American Negro pressure groups for civil rights. Racial integration is the racial philosophy of certain individual leaders and race spokesmen such as Martin Luther King, Jr. and a long list of public figures. The implications of the philosophy of "racial integration" vis-à-vis the idea of a legitimate Afro-American racial culture in the United States is a subject which is not being publically debated and clarified. Yet it lingers beneath the surface of a choppy sea of racial and interracial events like a powerful unseen social tide, inexorably flowing despite the agitation and clamor above. Let us now explore some of these implications.

When one speaks of the Afro-American and "culture" one has to be certain what one means. This writer is a member of the National Association for the Advancement of Colored People. On the back of my membership card there are listed six objectives having to do with educating Americans on Negro rights, wiping out lynching, securing the franchise, securing protective legislation against prejudice, etc. Item number five in this list of objectives reads: "To stimulate the cultural life of Negroes." This can mean many things to many people, depending upon what is meant by "cultural life." Does it mean the stimulation of Afro-American cultural expression as a thing in itself? Or does it mean the stimulation of Negro activity in the broad avenues of general "American culture"? For one to say that it means simply the participation of Afro-Americans in all-embracing "culture" which is an amalgam of all the racial and national minorities in the United States including that of our prime human stock, the Anglo-American, is much easier said as an oversimplification of American realities than done, inasmuch as this idealistic amalgamation of races, and nationalities in the United States does not exist. The proposition "To stimulate the cultural life of Negroes" has posed a question which has not been answered. Africans at home and abroad to whom this is addressed can hardly expect a forthright answer from us Afro-Americans, since we have not been able to answer it for ourselves.

This inability to find an appropriate answer has caused us

to lapse into a state of the most unbelievable intellectual confusion, immobility, and lassitude in matters of art, literature and cultural creativity. We are in a severe cultural crisis! This is true at a time when political pressures at home and abroad have forced most adamant upholders of white supremacy in this country to make concessions to us in political and economic spheres. Today, in New York City, which has been called the most liberal city in the United States on questions of race; which contains the largest concentration of Negroes in the entire country, namely Harlem; which has been called, among other things, "the cultural capital of the Negro world," we Negroes do not operate a single theater dedicated to Afro-American cultural traditions in drama, dance, or other performing arts. There exists much interest in acting, playwriting, the dance, directing, and all branches of dramatic arts on the part of Negroes; yet Negroes have no theater institutions. What then means "To stimulate the cultural life of Negroes"? The answer lies deep in the recesses of the Afro-American's racial outlook these days. It is a question of racial identity. The bulk of our intellectuals and artists of Afro-American background do not identify with Afro-American traditions in a group sense. On the part of Negro actors there is a grand obsession for Anglo-American (white) traditions and values in the theater. The concept of the "Negro theater" or the "Negro play" is actively or subtly resisted. The Negro playwright who writes on Negro themes cannot count on the support of Negro actors, even though the bulk of Negro actors, like the playwright, are struggling in an economic-cultural system which does not support the artistic development of either. Playwrights do not receive economic support from Negro sources. If they are fortunate enough to obtain funds for a production, it comes from white people. Negro participation in theatrical arts, then, is usually a result of philanthropic gestures on the part of liberal Caucasians. There have been efforts on the part of certain Negroes in the theater to become producers and directors. However, invariably it has been observed that rather than pioneer with original plays written by Negroes on Negro life, these aspiring producers will revive plays written by white authors for white characters and put them on stage with Negro casts. Here we have a strong manifestation of the imitation complex for white values. Culturally speaking this trend subscribes to the philosophy of "racial integration" in art. This philosophy attacks racial discrimination in social, economic and political areas, but when carried over into the social domain of racial culture, group psychology, aesthetics, and the historically created uniqueness of a people, it becomes a palpable flying into the face of history and the fallacious foundations of the entire doctrine stand exposed.

Culture is the mirror of true progress. Where culture is dying, weak and evanescent, there is something wrong with its roots. The root of the Afro-American's problems in the cultural fields is a debilitating sickness whose diagnosis is Caucasian idolatry in the arts, abandonment of true identity, and immature childlike mimicry of white aesthetics. Many Afro-Americans express this trend willingly, as a matter of choice, as a way of life based on class origins, skin color and personal affinities. Many others are being asked or compelled to accept it as a sacrifice or a price for full racial equality or "full integration." In the theater one hears such talk as this: "I am an actor, not just a Negro actor," or "I am interested in theater, not just Negro theater," or "Negroes should be writers, not just Negro writers." This is the verbalization of the idea that to be a "Negro actor" or a "Negro writer" or to espouse a "Negro theater" as an institution is self-proscribing and self-segregating. Whatever one might think of such artistic views, the realities of the American cultural scene have proven these views to be self-defeating, because most of this talk is heard during the long stretches of unemployment experienced by Afro-Americans, particularly the actors, who are trying to make a living and perfect their craft. Moreover, when work is available, Negroes are not hired just as "actors" to play any kind of a role on Broadway, television or in films. They are hired to portray Negro characterizations as Negroes in stories or plays usually written by whites. The dream of many Negro actors who wish to be hired to portray "any role," which actually means "white" roles, remains merely a dream. As for Negro writers, it is even more ridiculous for people to say "Negroes who write should be universal, not just Negro writers." Perhaps Negro writers should write "universally"; but Negro writers produce little enough literature of quality about the life they know (or should know best). It remains a puzzle to this writer how Negroes can be expected to develop to be "universal" when they avoid the wealth of racial literary material "in their own backyard." In any event little appears from our writers—racial or otherwise.

The intellectual and cultural impasse which the Afro-American finds himself in, the Negro press has played a leading role in creating. The Negro press, along with its weekly accounts of the progress of "racial integration" in various sectors of life, seeks "To stimulate the cultural life of Negroes" in this fashion. Here is an excerpt from a theatrical column which appeared in the Pittsburgh *Courier*, a Negro weekly, January 26, 1957. It was written by Izzy Rowe, a Negro woman writer who presents weekly a column on theater news and society gossip. The subject of this column was discrimination against Negroes in the Broadway theater, a topic which the press tackles periodically with renewed vigor. In this column the current views of Negro artists on racial integration in the arts are well represented:

. . . In the last few months this writer has gone over many plays, but nowhere could be found a description of the color of the person to play this or that role. For that reason, it is my belief that without bias any good actress or actor could be selected to play the role . . .

. . . Ever so often these barriers have been cast aside and great

performers like Frank Silvera get an opportunity to play an important role like the father in "Hatful of Rain" . . .

[Note: The actor, Frank Silvera, is so lightskinned only those
who know him personally, or are told so, recognize that he is
a Negro.]

. . . As it stands the race is without a big name-star in the world
of the legitimate theater . . .

. . . You can't call it anything but discrimination when such
great performers as Ethel Waters, Fred O'Neal, Leigh Whipper,
Lena Horne—among others who can't get a foothold in the Broadway spotlight . . .

. . . Sure, ever so often there comes to the boards an allcolored
this or that, and a few of them are used. Notwithstanding, from
where I sit, *this sort of show is just as biased as the lily-white ones
and both should be broken into by the unions and SCAD* . . .

[Note: Italics are the author's. SCAD stands for the New York
State Committee Against Discrimination, a state government
agency.]

In these excerpts one can see the ambivalence that haunts
the Negro mind on the questions of racial identity and artistic and cultural values. These are the ideas which dominate
Negro thinking in the arts these days. In the face of this, the
Negro theater is a lost cause and the aspiring Negro playwright a nonentity unless, as I have said, the playwright is
fortunate enough to get financial assistance from whites to
stage his plays. When he does, certain Negro actors will con-
sent to act in the play not because of any love or zeal for
furthering a racial dramatic art as such, but because the play
represents a "showcase" which might further their dreams of
racial integration on Broadway, in Hollywood, film or television. The Afro-American writer, actor, artist, etc., has suc-
cumbed almost completely to middle-class values of art, living,
and thinking. The Afro-American middle class has no real
love for art, racial or otherwise. When Negro individuals
enter the arts, particularly the performing arts, art becomes
in most cases a stepping stone to middle-class living which
involves adopting the white artistic standards in the fields in

which they aspire, the better to cross the racial bridge. Hence, racially conscious writers, actors, directors, dancers, painters, etc., can expect no financial support from the Afro-American middle class in furthering racial art in any form. These aspects—class and economic—of Afro-American culture—suggest an approach that has not been given serious study, although the way has now been cleared by the appearance of E. Franklin Frazier's brilliant study of the Negro middle class and its role in Negro life.* It is hoped that a re-evaluation of Negro culture will appear in the very near future, for the Afro-American needs at this time to regain a new grip and a reorientation on his identity.

Many rank and file Negroes have recently remarked to this writer that the Negro is a "lost race," that "the white man has destroyed the Negro's ability to think for himself," that "he is free in body but enslaved in mind," that "he is not really making progress in spite of all the noise about civil rights," that "he has no philosophy of his own," "the Negro has no unity," etc. This is the outlook of the Negro masses; but the racial integration philosophy has gripped the outlook of the Negro middle-class. It is a philosophy which is meant to further their own class aims, and the aspirations of the masses only incidentally. Middle-class Negroes do not identify with the masses nor with the cultural needs of the masses, and every rationalization is used by the middle-class to justify its views. Take for example this excerpt from a column on "Integration" by P. L. Prattis in the Pittsburgh *Courier* of July 28, 1956. He says:

. . . American Negroes who know no other culture or civilization but this and must make their future in this country, regard integration as most desirable. By way of integration, they want to overcome the handicaps the white man put on them through slavery and segregation. Integration looks good to the American Negro . . .

. . . But what about others? How about to the Bantus in the

* Frazier, *Black Bourgeoisie* (Glencoe, Illinois: The Free Press, 1957).

Union of South Africa? . . . If you put integration to a vote among these people, the chances are that they would reject it. They have their own culture, their own way of life with which they are satisfied . . .

. . . How about the Arabs in North Africa? What do they think of integration? For 126 years, the French have been trying to integrate [assimilate] the Algerian Arabs, to make Frenchmen out of them. These Arabs don't want to be Frenchmen. They don't want integration. They have fought integration in every way they could. They want their own culture, their own religion, their own language . . .

. . . It is ironic indeed that in the United States twelve million Negroes who live in the southern part of the United States should be fighting for integration, whereas eight million Arabs who live in the northern part of Africa are fighting [with their lives] against being integrated . . .

. . . American Indians never showed much disposition to integrate with the foreigners who had come here to and robbed them of their lands. However it is pertinent to ask: "Where are the American Indians now?"

. . . Integration is a must with us if we are to continue to live successfully alongside this white man and help him in the time when the tide of war and civilization may change . . .

On the same page that this column appeared is a weekly cartoon feature by J. A. Rogers called "Your History," which publicizes the achievements, past and present, of Afro-Americans!

The confusion of the Negro middle-class mind on this question of racial integration is best exemplified in the remarks of Martin Luther King, Jr., who has achieved national and international fame as the young leader of the Montgomery, Alabama, public bus boycott. In the first quarterly 1957 issue of *Phylon* magazine, a cultural publication sponsored by Atlanta University, an all-Negro school, Dr. King published an article entitled "Challenge of a New Age." Speaking of the colonial peoples and their new upsurge for liberation, he said of Egypt:

... They have broken loose from the Egypt of colonialism and imperialism, and they are now moving through the wilderness of adjustment toward the *promised land of cultural integration*. As they look back they see the old order of colonialism and imperialism passing away and the new order of freedom and justice coming into being ...

[Note: Italics are the author's.]

This reference to "cultural integration" has a familiar ring to those who know the workings of the mind of the Afro-American bourgeois intellectual on questions such as "culture." Only an Afro-American racial integrationist could make such a statement, revealing such fundamental misconceptions of the nature of colonial revolutions. Egypt is not struggling to become "culturally integrated" with anybody. Dr. King left the statement hanging; he did not suggest with whom Egypt is going to "integrate." But the implication is quite clear. It has been said by writers and sociologists like E. Franklin Frazier, author of the recent *Bourgeoisie-Noire*, a sociological study of the Negro middle class, that the Afro-American middle class knows little of culture, art, politics and world events, so involved is it in seeking personal status as close as possible to the middle-class white world and its values. Through some strange process of intellectual sleight-of-hand, Dr. King has managed to view the Egyptian revolution in the mirror of our own Afro-American middle-class "revolution" here in the United States. If such were the true state of affairs in Egypt, I would say "God help the Egyptians!" For it is not the Egyptians who are out of step with their own revolution; it is we Afro-Americans who are out of step with the rest of the colonial world. They are seeking their identity while we are endeavoring to lose ours in exchange for a brand of freedom in a never-never-land of assimilated racial differences—the great dream of the integrationists, but hardly visible on the horizons of reality. Dr. King says further on:

... In the new age we will be forced to compete with people of all races and nationalities. Therefore, we cannot aim merely to be good Negro teachers, good Negro doctors, good Negro ministers, good Negro skilled laborers. We must set out to do a good job, irrespective of race, and do it so well that nobody could do it better . . .

Now here we have platitudes par excellence! Can one seriously consider this kind of talk of any consequence in crucial times like these? One wonders what the ordinary Negro worker has been doing all of these decades *but* competing on the labor market with people of all races and nationalities and doing an excellent job of maintaining himself in the face of discriminations, not only from the owners of industry, but from certain labor unions as well. I recall not many years ago when it was vociferously argued by the middle-class professionals of our race that a Negro had to be twice as good as a white man in order to get ahead in his chosen profession. Now the integrationists come along and say "not twice as good" but "just as good" (if not better), because race in the future will not count. Are we going backwards or forwards? It will not be difficult for Africans at home and abroad to understand what Negroes mean when they say, "We American Negroes have no real leaders." It requires neither intellect, education, nor morality these days to howl for civil rights; but it does require some profundity of insight and honesty in racial matters to know what to do with civil rights after they are achieved.

The present upsurge of the American Negro, then, is political and social, with certain economic overtones growing out of the present prosperity of the Negro middle class. It is a movement for civil rights, political and social equality, the enforcement of the 14th and 15th Amendments to the U.S. Constitution which involve rights of citizens to equal protection under the laws, due process of law, and the right to vote. The present level of Negro struggles for full citizenship was given impetus by the Supreme Court decision of May, 1954, which outlawed the separation of the white and Negro races in public schools. The political, social, racial and economic implications of this court ruling are of tremendous national and international scope in view of the racial practices prevalent in the United States and our government's position of eminence and leadership in world affairs. However, from the Negro's side of the civil rights struggle, the racial integration movement is being led by the Negro middle class, composed of lawyers, professionals, educators, ministers, public office holders, politicians, etc. For the middle classes the civil rights drive is aimed at achieving much more than mere "civil rights" for the masses. The prime motivations of the bourgeois leaders of this movement are selfish class interests, because the main objective of the Negro middle class is a status and a social position approximating as closely as possible that pre-eminence enjoyed by the great Anglo-American middle class. Practically everything in Negro life today is being subordinated to that aim, including ideas on art and culture (such as they are). Therefore, unlike the revolutions of rising nations in the colonies, our "revolution" is not a cultural rebirth effected through any renaissance of racial art, literature, philosophy, etc. Herein lies the great difference. The question is: Can this fundamental difference in content of our liberation movement be viewed as historically logical or justified in the light of our peculiar racial development in the Western world? Whatever the case might be, the issue is not being discussed.

Regarding the Negro in the theater, this particular branch of cultural art is of strategic importance as an area for the study of current trends in Negro thought on culture and integration. This is so because of our outstanding cultural fluency in music, dance, and the interpretive arts. The Afro-American never reached the eminence in the dramatic arts prophesied by certain whites like the dramatist Eugene O'Neill thirty years ago. It is also a fact that our level of participation in the theater is far below what Negroes knew thirty years ago, and we have not yet produced a single outstanding dramatist. It is easy to attribute all this to racial discrimination in the American theater, as the Negro press continues to do; but this approach does no more than cover up a dismal record of racial irresponsibility on the part of Negro artists, intellectuals, leaders and educators in the necessity "To stimulate the cultural life of Negroes." Too long has the Afro-American acquiesced to Anglo-American paternalism and exploitation in theatrical endeavors. Outstanding Negro stars have come and gone, made names for themselves while having known varying degrees of wealth, without leaving a single dramatic school or a theater bearing their names or their efforts to increase the participation and prestige of their race in the theater. A case in point is the present plight of singer-actress Ethel Waters after forty-one years in show business. An article on Miss Waters appeared in *Ebony* magazine in February, 1957, entitled "Theater's First Negro Lady Is Broke and Bitter at 56." The article says:

> . . . Over the span of a generation she has watched with rising horror what she calls the American Negro's retreat from the reality of his racial integrity. "So many Negroes today are ashamed of their past, their background, traditions, culture and history," she notes sadly. "Not all, but many. Me, I'm crazy about my color. I love my race, all Negroes should . . ."

It appears Miss Waters is rather late coming to this conclusion about race and culture—forty-one years late, to be exact. Like most Negro theatrical stars, Miss Waters has spent the greater part of her career satisfying the taste of American white audiences. Money and middle-class status have always been more important to Negro stars than racial and cultural integrity in the arts. They come to the end of their days having been used for pay by whites. These stars complain about the lack of decent roles offered them in the theater, or the lack of roles altogether. However, this article does not reveal any attempt on the part of either Miss Waters or *Ebony*'s editorial staff to draw the necessary conclusions from Miss Waters' career—that Afro-Americans as a race would have been much better off in the arts today if we had not prostituted our racial art to the prejudiced tastes of the great American white audiences. The race has nothing to show for Miss Waters' career and neither has Miss Waters. She, by her own admission, is debt-ridden and cast aside for younger Negroes who, for the most part, are doing the same thing as she—seeking stardom as individuals on practically the same terms. Yet it is a fact, that no matter how long we delay it, no matter what the sacrifices made in the way of individual desires, in the long run, we Afro-Americans will have to start from the bottom and fashion a national school of our own standards in theater, literature, acting, the dance, and so on. We will have to write a new philosophy of art, the basic principle of which must be to please ourselves first and others secondly. Today, the only Negro artist who approaches this attitude is the jazz musician, and he has more respect from the whites for this integrity. The jazz musician is the one artist we have who whites try to imitate. Everyone respects true originality. Artists like Miss Waters, who started out as singers with true originality in their art, changed into actors who failed to find ways and means of creating originality in the theater. The Negro actor, playwright, director, choreographer, stage designer never found common ground for collaboration. We are a race of a long list of stars without a theater they could call their own. It is the tragedy of Afro-American culture in the United States. The roots of these failures go deep into our own racial outlook. In writing about her early life in her autobiography * Miss Waters says:

. . . I just ran wild as a little girl. I was bad, always a leader of the street gang in stealing and general hellraising. By the time I was seven I knew all about sex and life in the raw. I could out-curse any stevedore and took a sadistic pleasure in shocking people . . .
My mixed blood explains this, partly, I think.
My paternal great-grandfather was Albert Harris, a native of

* Waters, *His Eye Is on the Sparrow*, ed. by Charles Samuels (New York: Doubleday, 1951).

India. My great-grandmother was a slave, but very fair, and Albert Harris had to buy her from her owner before he could marry her. That made their five children freeborn, according to law . . .

It seems that Miss Waters' pride in her racial background, traditions, and culture came much too late.

From all this it is clear that assimilation tendencies in the outlooks of Afro-American intellectuals, artists, writers, etc., have made our cultural problem a very complex one. It is for this reason I believe the Negro problem in the United States to be primarily a cultural question—yet it is precisely the cultural side of the question which is most overlooked and neglected. On the cultural plane of our American existence we find keys to questions of identity, cultural values expressed in group institutional forms, standards for judgment in literature, art, music, dance, drama, poetry, and racial historiography. It seems to me that the Afro-American cannot take a firm grip on his own destiny in the United States until there comes a wholehearted effort on his part to essay a cultural rehabilitation and refurbishing of his entire racial outlook. This in no way implies that politics and economics are unimportant; it does mean that all things in life are relative. In the United States, the Afro-American can never dominate politics or economics. Being a racial minority without an ownership class, all that he has to offer in economics are labor and purchasing power; he is not a producer and his economic fortunes are tied to the rise and fall of American productive prosperity as a whole. In politics, his lack of economic controlling power renders his political bargaining power effective only during presidential elections when his vote is sought after numerically. However, smaller racial minorities in the United States wield infinitely greater political and economic power than we. Progress for the Afro-American, then, demands the strongest kind of racial unity and cooperative endeavor. But racial unity cannot be had in the face of the extreme racial and cultural diffidence toward our heritage which is evident in our racial outlook these days. It is for this reason that I believe our problem is fundamentally a cultural one. The entire question is broad and complicated and requires intensive study. What has been said here is purely one Afro-American's attitude to things seen and felt on the surface of our community life. The whole question involves separate treatment of many different trends, institutions and personalities in Negro cultural life; for example: the future of Negro music, the problem of the Negro novel and play, liberal and Communist influences in Negro cultural forms, the economic and class aspects of Negroes in art, the question of Paul Robeson as a major cultural figure, etc. It is hoped that an opportunity will be found to present some views on these different aspects sometime in the very near future.

6

Negro Nationalism's New Wave

During the past fifteen years, there has been more noise in the United States about the Negro's changing status than actual changes in that status. At the same time, the social changes taking place in the colonial world—especially in Africa and Latin America—have been more revolutionary than anything the American Negro has experienced since the post-Civil War period. By comparison with colored peoples elsewhere, Negroes in America have found that their own advance toward fuller freedom is lagging. And an uncomfortable awareness of the discrepancy has given rise to a new set of political and cultural values which, taken together, have come to be called "Afro-Americanism."

Most of the young generation of Negroes who articulate these values are beset with a compelling problem of self-identification. They are plagued by an obsessive search for identity in a predominantly white society which has its own problems of self-identification, both at home and abroad. The rise in the fortunes of colonial self-determination has intensified many an American Negro's sense of alienation and isolation in the West. For those who adopt it, Afro-Americanism serves the purpose of placing them in close rapport with the content and spirit of the world revolution.

The first publicized demonstration of the new position took place at the United Nations shortly after the murder of Patrice Lumumba, while the Security Council was debating the Congo crisis. It involved more than fifty Negroes who had been seated in the gallery, and forced the Council President to call a half-hour recess. The general reaction to what was considered the worst disorder in UN history was a mixture of surprise, shock, and indignation. Reporters went scurrying up to Harlem to determine the causes of the UN row. The result was a series of factual but superficial surveys on the temperament of Harlem.

The New York Times, for example, ran two articles under the heads, NEGRO EXTREMIST GROUPS STEP UP NATIONALIST DRIVE and NEGROES SAY CONDITIONS IN U.S. EXPLAIN NATIONALISTS' MILITANCY. Now the presence of "nationalism" among United States Negroes may come as a surprise to some whites, but it has existed a long time. Americans will have to learn to cope with it, for as adapted by Afro-Americans it is an increasingly popular ideology.

Americans have long believed that this country was never a "colonial" power. This is true, in the strictest sense of the word. Moreover, the crasser aspects of economic colonialism do not show through the mores of race relations; as a nation we are so rich that we can boast of rich Negroes in Georgia and rich Indians in Oklahoma. But from the nationalist viewpoint, the nature of economic, cultural and political exploitation common to the Negro experience in the U.S. differs from pure colonialism only in that the Negro maintains a formal kind of halfway citizenship within the nation's geographical boundaries.

The difference in social status between an American Negro and a Black African in South Africa, it is felt, is one of degree, not kind. Thus Negro nationalism in the United States has its roots in the same kind of soil as the nationalism of the African colonies proper. Or, to use a frequently heard analogy related to American minority politics, Negro nationalism can be likened to Jewish nationalism (Zionism) in motivation, although, of course, their histories and social causes are dissimilar.

In this light, it is easy for the nationalists to show that the American Negro suffers a more insuperable kind of subjugation than would be true under pure colonialism: He cannot sever his ties with his rulers and go his own way. This is why Negro nationalism will become the foremost political issue in future American race relations. It is even conceivable that a domestic counterpart of this country's foreign policy toward African nationalism will have to be adopted. Not all Afro-Americans, however, are really traditional Negro nationalists. The genuine nationalist ideology stems from the economics of Negro ghetto existence and a pride in black African heritage which often borders on chauvinism. It is defensive in posture and, because it feels trapped and overwhelmed, strident in tone. Its stridency is disturbing to both moderate Negroes and liberal whites, who insist that American racial democracy will prove itself viable.

Most traditional Negro nationalists simply have no faith in the democratic promises of whites. They believe that the American Negro will get only as much racial democracy as his economic power can buy on Wall Street or in Congress. They have less respect for liberals and left-wingers than for conservatives of the Barry Goldwater type. The latter, they believe, at least honestly expresses real white attitudes on economics, politics and race relations. White liberals, nationalists feel, do Negroes a disservice because they conceal the true character of American mass attitudes on race from the impressionable young Negro. "The best friend a black man has in the U.S.," I once heard a veteran Negro nationalist say, "is a reactionary Southern cracker, because that cracker will look a black man in the face and tell him, 'I think you're inferior to a white man. If you ain't inferior, goddammit, prove it.'"

This fits in with the nationalist belief that second-class citizenship is largely the result of the Negro's lack of economic control over services and consumer products in the segregated Negro community. It is not the segregation which rankles as much as the fact that Negroes themselves have no control over the ghetto exchequer; hence, the typical Negro nationalist economic slogans—"Buy Black," "Don't Buy Where You Can't Work," "Build Negro Business," etc.

The Negro nationalist ferment has been working at various levels of intensity in the Negro ghetto ever since Marcus Garvey's "Back to Africa" movement went into eclipse back in 1927. Its eclipse gave rise to the new Afro-American trend of the younger generation. But Afro-Americanism is not so much a traditional nationalist movement as it is a unique fusion of conflicting ideas. It is critical of the National Association for the Advancement of Colored People (NAACP), the Congress of Racial Equality (CORE), Martin Luther King, Jr., the Democrats and the Republicans; contemptuous of white liberals; ambivalent toward Marxist factions; and shy of the extreme position of Muslims and other old Negro nationalist groups. Yet the Afro-Americans are much indebted to the original nationalists, who kept the embers of hope for African freedom alive at a time when most Negro intellectuals were ashamed of their African heritage.

The zeal of the Afro-Americans is often frighteningly self-righteous and often contradictory. They consider themselves revolutionaries, but the new movement has emerged from a social situation which has provided no philosophy suitable to its needs or relevant enough to guide its eclecticism. In the face of the realities of Negro development in the United States, it is surely an almost impossible task to reconcile nationalism and integrationism. Yet this is precisely what the Afro-Americans are trying to do. They disdain the legalism of the NAACP because the organization is not sufficiently militant in its fight for integration. They refuse to accept the hard reality that integration, if it is ever to achieve its aims, has to be gradual.

Afro-Americans consider the Freedom Riders a revolutionary phenomenon (which in actuality it is not). They reject, in principle, the passive resistance of Martin Luther King, Jr.,

and the CORE group as a negation of the revolutionary essence of the Freedom Riders. Confusing protest with revolution, they equate being more demonstrative and militant than
the NAACP with being more revolutionary. This is the position of James Baldwin and others like him when they talk
about the "intriguing" problems of integration, as Baldwin
did in a *Harper's* article on Martin Luther King, Jr., not long
ago.

In his article, Baldwin unwittingly revealed Afro-Americanism's major weakness: an almost complete lack of historical
perspective. Writing about Booker T. Washington, he shows
little understanding of the man or his period. In another article on nationalism in Harlem, which appeared in *The New
York Times Magazine* after the UN demonstration, Baldwin
was unable to explain those tendencies of Negro nationalism
which run counter to racial integration. He could not cope
philosophically with the Black Muslims' almost complete
rejection of every aspect of white society. Clearly, his difficulties reflect the split intellectual personality of the Afro-
American. Interestingly, neither the traditional Negro
nationalist nor the NAACP-King-CORE position on integration is inconsistent; each group is true to its own logic. The
nationalists are for complete or nominal separation of the
races; the NAACP, King and CORE are for complete, un-
qualified integration.

Afro-Americanism, by its very nature, must plant itself
solidly in both the Negro community and in the international
politics of African liberation, else it can have no real meaning
beyond a certain social or racial symbolism. Over the past
fifteen years, however, the trend toward integration has favored the eradication of the Negro community as a symbol
of segregation. And proponents of integration frown on any
kind of racial togetherness among Negroes, be it economic,
cultural or political. Long in vogue among Negro intellectuals, the tendency to seek assimilation among whites has mili-
tated against the cultivation of a strong sense of racial

identification within the Negro community, as well as between the Negro community and Africa. Consequently, Afro-Americanism has no established social base other than the original Negro nationalist organizations. But considering the old nationalists too extreme, while at the same time disdaining the moderation of the NAACP, the Afro-Americans are finding themselves pulled by political gravity toward the far left. Here they are fighting hard not to become absorbed in the dead-end politics of American Marxism, which has lost its relevance to the realities of Negro existence.

Despite all their inadequacies, inexperience and lack of any historical sense of Negro life, the Afro-Americans are here to stay. In the future, they will undoubtedly make a lot of noise in militant demonstrations, cultivate beards and sport their Negroid hair in various degrees of la mode au naturel, and tend to be cultish with African- and Arab-style dress. They will probably not frown upon interracialism, if only to prove that nationalism must be made acceptable to whites in their own terms. The intellectuals will read more Western philosophy than has been their custom. Today it is not uncommon to see Albert Camus' *The Rebel* protruding from the hip pocket of a well-worn pair of jeans among the Afro-American set.

Already they have a pantheon of modern heroes—Lumumba, Kwame Nkrumah, Sekou Toure in Africa; Fidel Castro in Latin America; Malcolm X, the Muslim leader, in New York; Robert Williams in the South; and Mao Tse-tung in China. These men seem heroic to the Afro-Americans not because of their political philosophy, but because they were either former colonials who achieved complete independence, or because, like Malcolm X, they dared to look the white community in the face and say: "We don't think your civilization is worth the effort of any black man to try to integrate into." This to many Afro-Americans is an act of defiance that is truly revolutionary.

7

Revolutionary Nationalism
and the Afro-American

Revolutionary Nationalism and Western Marxism

Many of Western Marxism's fundamental theoretical formulations concerning revolution and nationalism are seriously challenged by the Cuban Revolution. American Marxism, which, since World War II, has undergone a progressive loss of influence and prestige, is challenged most profoundly. For while most American Marxists assert that the Cuban Revolution substantiates their theories of nationalism, national liberation and revolution, in fact the Cuban success is more nearly a *succes de circonstance*. Orthodox Marxists were unable to foresee it, and indeed opposed Castro until the last minute. One would hope that such a development might cause American radicals to re-evaluate their habitual methods of perceiving social realities; but in the spate of written analyses of the Cuban Revolution one looks in vain for a new idea or a fleeting spark of creative theoretical inspiration apropos of the situation in the United States.

The failure of American Marxists to work out a meaningful approach to revolutionary nationalism has special significance for the American Negro. The Negro has a relationship to the dominant culture of the United States similar to that of colonies and semi-dependents to their particular foreign overseers: the Negro is the American problem of underdevelopment. The failure of American Marxists to understand the bond between the Negro and the colonial peoples of the world has led to their failure to develop theories that would be of value to Negroes in the United States.

As far as American Marxists are concerned, it appears that thirty-odd years of failure on the North American mainland are now being offered compensatory vindication "ninety miles from home." With all due respect to the Marxists, however, the hard facts remain. Revolutionary nationalism has not waited for Western Marxian thought to catch up with the realities of the "underdeveloped" world. From underdevelopment itself have come the indigenous schools of theory and practice for achieving independence. The liberation of the colonies before the socialist revolution in the West is not orthodox Marxism (although it might be called Maoism or Castroism). As long as American Marxists cannot deal with the implications of revolutionary nationalism, both abroad and at home, they will continue to play the role of revolutionaries by proxy.

The revolutionary initiative has passed to the colonial world, and in the United States is passing to the Negro, while Western Marxists theorize, temporize and debate. The success of the colonial and semicolonial revolutions is not now, if it ever was, dependent upon the prior success of the Western proletariat. Indeed, the reverse may now be true; namely, that the success of the latter is aided by the weakening of the imperial outposts of Western capitalism. What is true of the colonial world is also true of the Negro in the United States. Here, the Negro is the leading revolutionary force, independent and ahead of the Marxists in the development of a movement towards social change.

The American Negro: A Subject of Domestic Colonialism

The American Negro shares with colonial peoples many of the socioeconomic factors which form the material basis for present-day revolutionary nationalism. Like the peoples of the underdeveloped countries, the Negro suffers in varying degree from hunger, illiteracy, disease, ties to the land, urban and semi-urban slums, cultural starvation, and the psychological reactions to being ruled over by others not of his kind. He experiences the tyranny imposed upon the lives of those who inhabit underdeveloped countries. In the words of a Mexican writer, Enrique Gonzales Pedrero, underdevelopment creates a situation where that which exists "only half exists," where "countries are almost countries, only fifty percent nations, and a man who inhabits these countries is a dependent being, a sub-man." Such a man depends "not on himself but on other men and other outside worlds that order him around, counsel and guide him like a newly born infant."

From the beginning, the American Negro has existed as a colonial being. His enslavement coincided with the colonial expansion of European powers and was nothing more or less than a condition of domestic colonialism. Instead of the United States establishing a colonial empire in Africa, it brought the colonial system home and installed it in the Southern states. When the Civil War broke up the slave system and the Negro was emancipated, he gained only partial freedom. Emancipation elevated him only to the position of a semi-dependent man, not to that of an equal or independent being.

The immense wealth and democratic pretensions of the American way of life have often served to obscure the real conditions under which the eighteen to twenty million Negroes in the United States live. As a wage laborer or tenant farmer, the Negro is discriminated against and exploited. Those in the educated, professional, and intellectual classes suffer a similar fate. Except for a very small percentage of the Negro intelligentsia, the Negro functions in a subcultural world made up, usually of necessity, of his own race only. This is much more than a problem of racial discrimination; it is a problem of political, economic, cultural, and administrative underdevelopment.

American Marxists, however, have never been able to understand the implications of the Negro's position in the social structure of the United States. They have no more been able to see the Negro as having revolutionary potentialities in his own right, than European Marxists could see the revolutionary aspirations of their colonials as being independent of, and not subordinate to, their own. As Western Marxism had no adequate revolutionary theory for the colonies, American Marxists have no adequate theory for the Negro. The belief of some American Marxists in a political alliance of Negroes and whites is based on a superficial assessment of the Negro's social status: the notion that the Negro is an integral part of the American nation in the same way as is the white working class. Although this idea of Negro and white unity is convenient in describing the American multinational and multiracial makeup, it cannot withstand a deeper analysis of the components which make American society what it is.

Negroes have never been equal to whites of any class in economic, social, cultural, or political status, and very few whites of any class have ever regarded them as such. The Negro is not really an integral part of the American nation beyond the convenient formal recognition that he lives within the borders of the United States. From the white's point of view, the Negro is not related to the "we," the Negro is the "they." This attitude assumes its most extreme expression in the Southern states and spreads out over the nation in varying modes of racial mores. The only factor which differentiates the Negro's status from that of a pure colonial status is that his position is maintained in the "home" country in close proximity to the dominant racial group. It is not at all remarkable then that the semi-colonial status of the Negro has given rise to nationalist movements. It would be surprising if it had not. Although Negro nationalism today is a reflection of the revolutionary nationalism that is changing the world, the present nationalist movement stems from a tradition dating back to the period of World War I.

Negro nationalism came into its own at that time with the appearance of Marcus Garvey and his "Back to Africa" movement. Garvey mobilized large sections of the discontented urban petit-bourgeois and working-class elements from the West Indies and the South into the greatest mass movement yet achieved in American Negro history. The Garvey movement was revolutionary nationalism being expressed in the very heart of Western capitalism. Despite the obvious parallels to colonial revolutions, however, Marxists of all parties not only rejected Garvey, but have traditionally ostracized Negro nationalism.

American Marxism has neither understood the nature of Negro nationalism, nor dealt with its roots in American society. When the Communists first promulgated the Negro question as a "national question" in 1928, they wanted a national question without nationalism. They posed the question mechanically because they did not really understand it. They relegated the "national" aspects of the Negro question to the "black belt" of the South, despite the fact that Garvey's "national movement" had been organized in 1916 in a northern urban center where the Negro was, according to the Communists, a "national minority," but not a "nation," as he was in the Southern states. Of course, the national character of the Negro has little to do with what part of the country he lives in. Wherever he lives, he is restricted. His national boundaries are the color of his skin, his racial characteristics, and the social conditions within his subcultural world.

The ramifications of the national and colonial question are clear only if the initial bourgeois character of national movements is understood. According to American Marxism, Negro movements do not have "bourgeois nationalist" beginnings. American Marxists have fabricated the term "Negro Liberation Movement"—an "all-class" affair united around a program of civil and political equality, the beginnings of which they approximately date back to the founding of the National Association for the Advancement of Colored People in 1909. True, the NAACP was, from its inception, and is still, a bourgeois movement. However, it is a distortion to characterize this particular organization as the sole repository of the beginnings of the Negro bourgeois movement. Such a narrow analysis cannot explain how or why there are two divergent trends in Negro life today: pro-integration and anti-integration. That is to say, it does not explain the origins of the nationalist wing, composed of black nationalists, Black Muslims, and other minor Negro nationalist groupings, as an outgrowth of basic conflicts within the early bourgeois movements (circa 1900), from which also developed the present day NAACP-Martin Luther King-student coalition. Furthermore, the Marxian version of the NAACP's origins does not explain why the nationalist wing and the NAACP wing oppose each other, or why the overwhelming majority of Negroes are uncommitted to either one. There is widespread dissatisfaction among various classes of Negroes with the NAACP's approach to racial problems. On the other hand, in recent years the nationalists have been gaining support and prestige among uncommitted Negroes. This is especially true of the Muslims, the newest Negro nationalist phenomenon.

The rise of free African nations and the Cuban Revolution have, without a doubt, stirred up the latent nationalism of many Negroes. The popular acclaim given Fidel Castro by the working-class Negroes of Harlem during his visit in the fall of 1960 demonstrated that the effects of the colonial revolutions are reaching the American Negro and arousing his nationalist impulses. Many Negroes, who are neither nationalists nor supporters of the NAACP, are becoming impatient with the NAACP-Martin Luther King-student legalistic and "passive resistance" tactics. They suspect that the long-drawn-out battle of attrition with which the NAACP integration movement is faced may very well end in no more than Pyrrhic victories. They feel that racial integration, as a goal, lacks the tangible objectives needed to bring about genuine equality. After all, social and racial equality remain intangible goals unless they are related to the seizure and retention of objectives which can be used as levers to exert political, social, economic, and administrative power in society. Power cannot be wielded from integrated lunch counters, waiting rooms, schools, housing, baseball teams, or love affairs, even though these are social advances.

There emerges from this dilemma a recognizable third trend, personified in the case of Robert F. Williams. Williams was forced to take an anti-NAACP position, but he was not a nationalist and was critical of the Marxists. As a rebel, Williams' objectives were the same as those of the NAACP; he differed only in his approach. His seemingly "revolutionary" stance is thwarted by the same lack of substance that makes a program of racial integration unsatisfactory to many Negroes. Williams resorted to arms for defense purposes; but arms are superfluous in terms of the objectives of racial integration, and to the seizure of actual centers of social power. The adherents of this third trend—young social rebels who are followers of Williams' Monroe Movement—are faced with this predicament. They are neither avowed nationalists nor NAACPers. They consider themselves "revolutionary," but do not have revolutionary objectives. However, they are not yet a force, and their future importance will rest, no doubt, upon how much influence the nationalist wing will exert in the Negro community. The main trends in Negro life are becoming more and more polarized around the issues of pro- and anti-integration.

Integration vs. Separation: History and Interpretations

Negro historiography does not offer a very clear explanation of how the American Negro has become what he is today. As written, Negro history appears as a parade of lesser and greater personalities against a clamor of many contending anonymous voices and a welter of spasmodic trends all negating each other. Through the pages of Negro history the Negro marches, always arriving but never getting anywhere. His "national goals" are always receding.

Integration vs. separation has become polarized around two

main wings of racial ideology, with fateful implications for the Negro movement and the country at large. Yet we are faced with a problem in racial ideology without any means of properly understanding how to deal with it. The dilemma arises from a lack of comprehension of the historical origins of the conflict.

The problem is complicated by a lack of recognition that the conflict even exists. The fundamental economic and cultural issues at stake in this conflict cannot be dealt with by American sociologists for the simple reason that sociologists never admit that such issues should exist at all in American society. They talk of "Americanizing" all the varied racial elements in the United States; but, when it is clear that certain racial elements are not being "Americanized," socially, economically, or culturally, the sociologists proffer nothing but total evasion, or more studies on "the nature of prejudice." Hence the problems remain with us in a neglected state of suspension until they break out in what are considered to be "negative," "antisocial," "antiwhite," "antidemocratic" reactions.

One of the few attempts to bring a semblance of order to the dominant trends in the chaos of Negro history was made by Marxist historians in the 1930's and 1940's. However, it proved to be a one-sided analysis which failed to examine the class structure of the Negro people. Viewing Negro history as a parade from slavery to socialism, the Marxist historians favor certain Negro personalities uncritically while ignoring others who played vital roles. Major figures, such as Booker T. Washington and Marcus Garvey, who do not fit into the Communist stereotype of Negro heroes are ignored or downgraded. In the process, Marxist historians have further obscured the roots of the current conflict in racial ideology. Under the aegis of other slogans, issues and rivalries, the pro-integration vs. anti-integration controversy first appeared at the turn of the century in the famous Booker T. Washington-W. E. B. Du Bois debate. Washington's position was that the

Negro had to achieve economic self-sufficiency before demanding his political rights. This position led Washington to take a less "militant" stand on civil rights than did other Negro leaders, such as Du Bois, who accused Washington of compromising with the racists on the Negro's political position in the South. It is not sufficient, however, to judge Washington purely on the political policies he advocated for the Negro in the South. For Washington gave voice to an important trend in Negro life, one that made him the most popular leader American Negroes have had. The Washington-Du Bois controversy was not a debate between representatives of reaction and progress, as Communist historians have asserted, but over the correct tactics for the emerging Negro bourgeoisie.

From the Reconstruction era on, the would-be Negro bourgeoisie in the United States confronted unique difficulties quite unlike those experienced by the young bourgeoisie in colonial situations. As a class, the Negro bourgeoisie wanted liberty and equality, but also money, prestige, and political power. How to achieve all this within the American framework was a difficult problem, since the whites had a monopoly on these benefits of Western civilization, and looked upon the new aspirants as interlopers and upstarts. The Negro bourgeoisie was trapped and stymied by the entrenched and expanding power of American capitalism. Unlike the situation in the colonial area, the Negro could not seize the power he wanted nor oust "foreigners." Hence he turned inward toward organizations of fraternal, religious, nationalistic, educational and political natures. There was much frustrated bickering and internal conflict within this new class over strategy and tactics. Finally the issues boiled down to that of politics vs. economics, and emerged in the Washington Du Bois controversy.

In this context, it is clear that Washington's program for a "separate" Negro economy was not compatible with the idea of integration into the dominant white economy. In 1907 Du Bois complained of Washington that:

He is striving nobly to make Negro artisans business men and property-owners; but it is impossible, under modern competitive methods, for workingmen and property-owners to defend their rights and exist without the right of suffrage.*

Yet Washington could not logically seek participation in "white" politics in so far as such politics were a reflection of the mastery of whites in the surrounding economy. He reasoned that since Negroes had no chance to take part in the white world as producers and proprietors, what value was there in seeking political rights immediately? Herbert Aptheker, the leading Marxist authority on Negro history, quotes Washington as saying:

Brains, property, and character for the Negro will settle the question of civil rights. The best course to pursue in regard to a civil rights bill in the South is to let it alone; let it alone and it will settle itself. Good school teachers and plenty of money to pay them will be more potent in settling the race question than many civil rights bills and investigation committees.**

This was the typical Washington attitude—a bourgeois attitude, practical and pragmatic, based on the expediencies of the situation. Washington sought to train and develop a new class. He had a longer-range view than most of his contemporaries, and for his plans he wanted racial peace at any cost.

Few of the implications of this can be found in Marxist interpretations of Negro history. By taking a partisan position in favor of Du Bois, Marxists dismiss the economic aspects of the question in favor of the purely political. This is the same as saying that the Negro bourgeoisie had no right to try to become capitalists—an idea that makes no historical sense whatsoever. If a small proprietor, native to an underdeveloped country, should want to oust foreign capitalists and

* Du Bois, *The Souls of Black Folk* (Chicago: A. C. McLurg, 1907).
** E. Davidson Washington, *Selected Speeches of Booker T. Washington*, Doubleday, New York, p. 6.

take over his internal markets, why should not the Negro proprietor have the same desire? Of course, a substantial Negro bourgeoisie never developed in the United States. Although this fact obscured and complicated the problems of Negro nationalism, it did not and does not change the principles involved. Washington sought to develop a Negro bourgeoisie. He failed. But his failure was no greater than that of those who sought equality through politics.

Washington's role in developing an economic program to counteract the Negro's social position is central to the emergence of Negro nationalism, and accounts for much of his popularity among Negroes. Yet Aptheker makes the error of assessing Washington purely on political grounds. On this basis, of course, Aptheker finds him not "revolutionary" or "militant" in the fashion that befits a Negro leader, past or present. He rejects the historic-economic-class basis of Washington's philosophy, although these are essential in analyzing social movements, personalities, or historical situations. Aptheker has not seen Washington in the light of what he was: the leading spokesman and theoretician of the new Negro capitalists, whom he was trying to mold into existence. All that Aptheker has to say about Washington is summed up by him as follows:

Mr. Washington's policy amounted objectively to an acceptance by the Negro of second class citizenship. His appearance on the historical stage and the growth of his influence coincided with and reflected the propertied interests' resistance to the farmers' and workers' great protest movements in the generations spanning the close of the nineteenth and the opening of the twentieth centuries. American imperialism conquers the South during these years and Mr. Washington's program of industrial education, ultra-gradualism and opposition to independent political activity and trade unionism assisted in this conquest.*

Thus is the Marxian scheme about the "Negro people" pro-

* Herbert Aptheker, *A Documentary History of Negro People in the United States* (New York: Citadel Press, 1951).

jected back into history—a people without classes or differing class interests.

It is naive to believe that any aspiring member of the bourgeoisie would have been interested in trade-unionism and the political action of farmers. But American Marxists cannot "see" the Negro at all unless he is storming the barricades, either in the present or in history. Does it make any sense to look back into history and expect to find Negroes involved in trade unionism and political action in the most lynch-ridden decade the South has ever known? Anyone reading about the South at the turn of the century must wonder how Negroes managed to survive at all, let alone become involved in political activity when politics was dominated by the Ku Klux Klan. According to Aptheker, however, the Negroes who supported Washington were wrong. It was the handful of Negro militants from above the Mason-Dixon line who had never known slavery, who had never known Southern poverty and illiteracy, the whip of the lynch-mad KKK, or the peasant's agony of landlessness, who were correct in their high-sounding idealistic criticism of Washington. These were, Aptheker tells us, within a politically revolutionary tradition —a tradition which in fact had not even emerged when Washington died!

After the Washington-Du Bois debate, Du Bois went on to help form the NAACP in 1909. Washington died in 1915. The controversy continued, however, in the conflict between the NAACP and the Garvey movement.

In 1916, Marcus Garvey, the West Indian-born nationalist, organized his "Back to Africa" movement in the United States. Garvey had, from his earliest years, been deeply influenced by the racial and economic philosophies of Booker T. Washington. Adopting what he wanted from Washington's ideas, Garvey carried them further—advocating Negro self-sufficiency in the United States linked, this time, with the idea of regaining access to the African homeland as a basis for constructing a viable black economy. Whereas Washington had earlier chosen an accommodationist position in the South to achieve his objectives, Garvey added the racial ingredient of black nationalism to Washington's ideas with potent effect. This development paralleled the bourgeois origins of the colonial revolutions then in their initial stages in Africa and Asia. Coming from a British colony, Garvey had the psychology of a colonial revolutionary and acted as such.

With the rise of nationalism, Du Bois and the NAACP took a strong stand against the Garvey Movement and against revolutionary nationalism. The issues were much deeper than mere rivalry between different factions for the leadership of Negro politics. The rise of Garvey nationalism meant that the NAACP became the accommodationists and the nationalists became the militants. From its very inception, the Negro bourgeois movement found itself deeply split over aims, ideology, and tactics, growing out of its unique position of contending for its aims in the very heart of Western capitalism. Neither the nationalist side of the bourgeois movement nor the reformist NAACP wing, however, were able to vanquish the social barriers facing Negroes in the United States. The Garvey movement found its answer in seeking a way out—"Back to Africa!" where the nationalist revolution had elbow room, where there was land, resources, sovereignty—all that the black man had been denied in the United States.

The Garvey era manifested the most self-conscious expression of nationality in the entire history of the Negro in the United States. To refrain from pointing this out, as Aptheker does in his essays on Negro history, is inexcusable. In his essay, "The Negro in World War I," Aptheker says: "What was the position of the Negro People during the years of Wilson's 'New Freedom'?" He then mentions the activities of the NAACP, the National Race Congress of 1915, and the formation in 1915 of the Association for the Study of Negro Life and History. But in discussing the racial unrest of the time, Aptheker fails to mention the Garvey movement, despite the fact that it had organized more Negroes than any other organization in the three years following its establishment in 1916. The causes for these omissions are, of course, apparent: orthodox Western Marxism cannot incorporate nationalism into its schema.

With the NAACP and the Garvey movement growing apace, the "Negro People" had two "Negro Liberation Movements" to contend with. Never was an oppressed people so richly endowed with leadership; the only difficulty was that these two movements were at bitter odds with one another. Furthermore, within the Negro community, prejudice about lighter and darker skin coloring also served as a basis for class stratification. Thus, when retaliating against Du Bois' criticisms of his movement, Garvey attacked him on the basis of his skin color, and assailed the assimilationist values of the upper-class Negro leadership. In addition, the Garvey "blacks" and the NAACP "coloreds" disagreed as to which was the true "motherland"—black Africa or white America.

During the period when the Communists looked upon the Negro question as a national question, some Communist writers perceived the positive, as well as the negative, aspects of Garvey's appeal. Harry Haywood, for example, wrote that the Garvey movement "reflected the widening rift between the policies of the Negro bourgeois reformism and the life needs of the sorely pressed people." He sees in Garvey's "renunciation of the whole program of interracialism" a belief that the upper-class Negro leadership was "motivated solely by their desire for cultural assimilation," and that they "banked their hopes for Negro equality on support from the white enemy." Haywood sympathized with this position, seeing in the "huge movement lead by Garvey" a "deep feeling for the intrinsic national character of the Negro problem."

In 1959, the Communists withdrew the concept of "self-determination" in the black belt, and sidestepped the question of the Negro's "national character." Instead, they adopted a position essentially the same as that of the NAACP. Their present goal is to secure "with all speed" the "fullest realization of genuinely equal economic, political and social status with all other nationalities and individual citizens of the United States"—this to be accompanied by "genuinely representative government, with proportionate representation in the areas of Negro majority population in the South." This position is essentially no different from that supported by the NAACP.

Thus, it is not surprising that it is difficult to understand the present conflict within the Negro movement; the roots of the conflict have been obliterated. While most historians do not attempt at all to bring order to the chaos of Negro history, those who have—the Marxists—find it convenient from a theoretical standpoint to see Negroes in history as black proletarian "prototypes" and forerunners of the "black workers" who will participate in the proletarian revolution. This Aptheker-Communist Party mythology, created around a patronizing deification of Negro slave heroes (Denmark Vesey, Nat Turner, Sojourner Truth, Frederick Douglass, etc.), results in abstracting them from their proper historical context and making it appear that they are relevant to modern reality. Of course, there will be those Marxists who will argue that their inability to come to terms in theory with Negro nationalism does not arise from an error in their interpretations of the role of the Negro bourgeoisie, of Washington, or of Du Bois. They will defend all the historical romanticism and the sentimental slave hero worship of the Aptheker Cult. They will say that all this is past history and has no bearing on the "new situation." But if one takes this position, then of what value is history of any kind, and particularly, of what value is the Marxist historical method? The flaws in the Marxist theoretical approach lead to the inability to cope with the implications of Negro nationalism.

Negro Nationalism and the Left

To the extent that the myth of a uniform "Negro People" has endured, a clear understanding of the causes of Negro nationalism has been prevented. In reality, no such uniformity exists. There are class divisions among Negroes, and it is misleading to maintain that the interests of the Negro working and middle classes are identical. To be sure, a middle-class NAACP leader and an illiterate farmhand in Mississippi or a porter who lives in Harlem all want civil rights. However, it would be enlightening to examine why the NAACP is not composed of Negro porters and farmhands, but only of Negroes of a certain type.

What we must ask is why these classes are not all striving in the same directions and with the same degrees of intensity. Why are some lagging behind the integration movement, and still others in conflict with it? Where is the integration movement going? Into what is the integration movement integrating? Is the Negro middle class integrating into the white middle class? Are integrated lunch counters and waiting stations commensurate with integration into the "mainstream of American life"? Will the Negro ten percent of the population get ten percent representation in the local, state, and national legislatures?—or ten percent representation in the exclusive club of the "power elite"? Why are some Negroes anti-integration, others pro-integration, and still others uncommitted? Why is there such a lack of real unity among different Negro classes towards one objective? Why are there only some 400,000 members in the NAACP out of a total Negro population of some 18 to 20 million? Why does this membership constantly fluctuate? Why is the NAACP called a "Negro" organization when it is an interracial organization? Why are the Negro nationalist organizations "all Negro"? Why do nationalist organizations have a far greater proportion of working-class Negro membership than the NAACP? Finally, why is it that the Marxists, of all groups, are at this late date tail-ending organizations such as the NAACP (King, CORE, etc.), which do not have the broad support of Negro workers and farmers? To attempt to answer these questions we must

consider why the interests of the Negro bourgeoisie have become separated from those of the Negro working classes.

Tracing the origins of the Negro bourgeoisie back to the
Booker T. Washington period (circa 1900), E. Franklin
Frazier, a Negro sociologist and non-Marxist scholar, came
to the enlightening conclusion that "the black bourgeoisie
lacks the economic basis that would give it roots in the world
of reality." * Frazier shows that the failure of the Negro to
establish an economic base in American society served to sever
the Negro bourgeoisie, in its "slow and difficult occupational
differentiation," from any economic, and therefore cultural
and organizational ties with the Negro working class. Since the
Negro bourgeoisie does not, in the main, control the Negro
"market" in the United States economy, and since it derives
its income from whatever "integrated" occupational advan-
tages it has achieved, it has neither developed a sense of association of its status with that of the Negro working class,
nor a "community" of economic, political, or cultural interests conducive to cultivating "nationalistic sentiments." Today, except for the issue of civil rights, no unity of interests
exists between the Negro middle class and the Negro working
class. Furthermore, large segments of the modern Negro bourgeoisie have played a continually regressive "non-national"
role in Negro affairs. Thriving off the crumbs of integration,
these bourgeois elements have become de-racialized and de-
cultured, leaving the Negro working class without voice or
leadership, while serving the negative role of class buffer between the deprived working class and the white ruling elites.
In this respect, such groups have become a social millstone
around the necks of the Negro working class—a point which
none of the militant phrases that accompany the racial integration movement down the road to "racial attrition" should
be allowed to obscure.

The dilemma of the Negro intellectual in the United States
results from the duality of his position. Detached from the

* Frazier, *Black Bourgeoisie* (Glencoe, Illinois: The Free Press, 1957).

Negro working class, he tries to integrate and to gain full membership in a stagnating and declining Western society. At the same time, failing to gain entry to the status quo, he resorts to talking like a revolutionary, championing revolutionary nationalism and its social dynamism in the underdeveloped world. But this gesture of flirting with the revolutionary nationalism of the non-West does not mask the fact that the American Negro intellectual is floating in ideological space. He is caught up in the world contradiction. Forced to face up to the colonial revolution and to make shallow propaganda out of it for himself, the American Negro intellectual is unable to cement his ties with the more racial-minded segments of the Negro working class. For this would require him to take a nationalistic stand in American politics—which he is loath to do. Nevertheless, the impact of revolutionary nationalism in the non-Western world is forcing certain Negro intellectuals to take a nationalist position in regard to their American situation.

Although Frazier does not delve into the nature of nationalism or connect the rise of nationalism with the failure of the Negro bourgeoisie to establish the "economic basis" of which he writes, it can be seen that the sense of a need for economic self-sufficiency is one of the causes for the persistence of nationalist groupings in Negro life. The attempt to organize and agitate for Negro ascendancy in and control of the Negro market is expressed in such racial slogans as "Buy Black." The Negro nationalist ideology regards all the social ills from which the Negroes suffer as being caused by the lack of economic control over the segregated Negro community. Since the nationalists do not envision a time when whites will voluntarily end segregation, they feel that it is necessary to gain control of the economic welfare of the segregated community. Moreover, many Negro nationalists, such as the Black Muslims, actually believe that racial separation is in the best interests of both races. Others maintain this separatist position because of the fact of the persistence of segregation.

When Communists and other Marxists imply that racial integration represents an all-class movement for liberation, it indicates that they have lost touch with the realities of Negro life. They fail to concern themselves with the mind of the working-class Negro in the depths of the ghetto, or the nationalistic yearnings of those hundreds of thousands of ghetto Negroes whose every aspiration has been negated by white society. Instead, the Marxists gear their position to Negro middle-class aspirations and ideology. Such Marxists support the position of the Negro bourgeoisie in denying, condemning, or ignoring the existence of Negro nationalism in the United States—while regarding the reality of nationalism in the colonial world as something peculiar to "exotic" peoples. The measure of the lack of appeal to the working classes of the Marxist movement is indicated by the fact that Negro nationalist movements are basically working-class in character while the new Negroes attracted to the Marxist movement are of bourgeois outlook and sympathies.

Ironically, even within Marxist organizations Negroes have had to function as a numerical minority, and have been subordinated to the will of a white majority on all crucial matters of racial policy. What the Marxists called "Negro-white unity" within their organizations was, in reality, white domination. Thus the Marxist movement took a position of favoring a racial equality that did not even exist within the organization of the movement itself. Today, the Marxist organizations which advocate racial integration do not have a single objective for the Negro that is not advocated by the NAACP or some other reform organization. It is only by virtue of asserting the "necessity of socialism" that the Marxist movement is not altogether superfluous. It could not be otherwise. For Marxism has stripped the Negro question of every theoretical concern for the class, color, ethnic, economic, cultural, psychological, and "national" complexities. They have no program apart from uttering the visionary call for "integration plus socialism" or "socialism plus integration."

When Marxists speak of socialism to the Negro, they leave many young Negro social rebels unimpressed. Many concrete questions remain unanswered. What guarantee do Negroes have that socialism means racial equality any more than does capitalist democracy? Would socialism mean the assimilation of the Negro into the dominant racial group? Although this would be "racial democracy" of a kind, the Negro would wield no political power as a minority. If he desired to exert political power as a racial minority, he might, even under socialism, be accused of being "nationalistic." In other words, the failure of American capitalist abundance to help solve the crying problems of the Negro's existence cannot be fobbed off on some future socialist heaven.

We have learned that the means to the end are just as important as the end itself. In this regard, Marxists have always been very naive about the psychology of the Negro. It was always an easy matter for Marxists to find Negro careerists, social climbers, and parlor radicals to agree with the Marxist position on the Negro masses. However, it rarely occurred to Marxists that, to the average Negro, the means used by Marxists were as significant as the ends. Thus, except in times of national catastrophe (such as in the Depression of the 30's), Marxist means, suitable only for bourgeois reform, seldom approximated the aspirations of the majority of Negroes. Lacking a working-class character, Marxism in the United States cannot objectively analyze the role of the bourgeoisie or take a political position in Negro affairs that would be more in keeping with the aspirations of the masses.

The failure to deal adequately with the Negro question is the chief cause of American Marxism's ultimate alienation from the vital stream of American life. This political and theoretical deficiency poses a serious and vexing problem for the younger generation who today have become involved in political activity centered around the defense of Cuba. Some accept Marxism; others voice criticisms of Marxist parties as being conservative or otherwise limited in their grasp of present realities. All of these young people are more or less part of what is loosely called the "New Left" (a trend not limited to the United States). It is now the responsibility of these new forces to find the new thinking and new approaches needed to cope with the old problems. Open-minded whites of the New Left must understand that Negro consciousness in the United States will be plagued with the conflict between the compulsions toward integration and the compulsions toward separation. It is the inescapable result of semi-dependence.

The Negro in the United States can no more look to American Marxist schema than the colonials and semi-dependents could conform to the Western Marxist timetable for revolutionary advances. Those on the American left who support revolutionary nationalism in Asia, Africa, and Latin America must also accept the validity of Negro nationalism in the United States. Is it not just as valid for Negro nationalists to want to separate from American whites as it is for Cuban nationalists to want to separate economically and politically from the United States? The answer cannot hinge merely on pragmatic practicalities. It is a political question which involves the inherent right accruing to individuals, groups, nations and national minorities; i.e., the right of political separation from another political entity when joint existence is incompatible, coercive, unequal, or otherwise injurious to the rights of one or both. This is a principle that must be upheld, all expedient prejudices to the contrary.

It is up to the Negro to take the organizational, political, and economic steps necessary to raise and defend his status. The present situation in racial affairs will inevitably force nationalist movements to make demands which should be supported by people who are not Negro nationalists. The nationalists may be forced to demand the right of political separation. This too must be upheld because it is the surest means of achieving Federal action on all Negro demands of an economic or political nature. It will be the most direct means of publicizing the fact that the American government's policy on underdeveloped areas must be complemented by the same approach to Negro underdevelopment in the United States.

It is pointless to argue, as many do, that Negro nationalism is an invalid ideology for Negroes to have in American life, or that the nationalist ideas of economic self-sufficiency or the "separate Negro economy" are unrealistic or utopian. Perhaps they are, but it must be clearly understood that as long as racial segregation remains a built-in characteristic of American society, nationalist ideology will continue to grow and spread. If allowed to spread unchecked and unameliorated, the end result can only be racial wars in the United States. This is no idle prophecy, for there are many convinced Negro nationalists who maintain that the idea of the eventual acceptance of the Negro as a full-fledged American without regard to race, creed, or color, is also utopian and will never be realized. Can it be said, in all truth, that nationalist groups such as the Black Muslims are being unrealistic when they reject white society as a lost cause in terms of fulfilling any humanistic promises for the Negro? For whites to react subjectively to this attitude solves nothing. It must be understood. It must be seen that this rejection of white society has valid reasons. White society, the Muslims feel, is sick, immoral, dishonest, and filled with hate for non-whites. Their rejection of white society is analogous to the colonial peoples' rejection of imperialist rule. The difference is only that people in colonies can succeed and American Negro nationalists cannot. The peculiar position of Negro nationalists in the United States requires them to set themselves against the dominance of whites and still manage to live in the same country.

It has to be admitted that it is impossible for American society as it is now constituted to integrate or assimilate the Negro. Jimcrow is a built-in component of the American social structure. There is no getting around it. Moreover, there is no organized force in the United States at present capable of altering the structural form of American society. Due to his semi-dependent status in society, the American

Negro is the only potentially revolutionary force in the United States today. From the Negro himself must come the revolutionary social theories of an economic, cultural, and political nature that will be his guides for social action—the new philosophies of social change. If the white working class is ever to move in the direction of demanding structural changes in society, it will be the Negro who will furnish the initial force.

The more the system frustrates the integration efforts of the Negro, the more he will be forced to resolve in his own consciousness the contradiction and conflict inherent in the pro- and anti-integration trends in his racial and historical background. Out of this process, new organizational forms will emerge in Negro life to cope with new demands and new situations. To be sure, much of this of necessity will be empirical, and no one can say how much time this process will take to work itself toward its own logical ends. But it will be revolutionary pioneering by that segment of our society most suitable to and most amenable to pioneering—the have-nots, the victims of the American brand of social underdevelopment.

The coming coalition of Negro organizations will contain nationalist elements in roles of conspicuous leadership. It cannot and will not be subordinate to any white groups with which it is allied. There is no longer room for the revolutionary paternalism that has been the hallmark of organizations such as the Communist Party. This is what the New Left must clearly understand in its future relations with Negro movements that are indigenous to the Negro community.

8

Rebellion or Revolution?–I

For the first time since the 1930's Americans of more than ordinary social insight are openly discussing the possibility of social revolution in the United States. We know that during the 1930's "revolution" implied the overthrow of capitalistic institutions—a real threat which the more enlightened wing of American bourgeois wealth successfully defeated by the implementation of the various New Deal policies. But unlike the 1930's, when it was reported that some of the idle rich were so fearful of revolution that they had their yachts readied in the harbor for a fast getaway just in case, the talk of revolution today has little to do with conflicts in labor-capital relations or the imminent collapse of the capitalist system. It has to do with the present state of American race relations which some people (hopefully or fearfully) describe as the "Negro revolution."

There is no need to mention the obvious—that the racial crisis reflects broad and profound discontent within the American Negro minority. However, when one goes so far as to say that this racial discontent contains the seeds of social revolution in America, this immediately calls up a flock of other questions concerning the present outlook of the American state of mind which, when considered side by side with the possibility of a Negro revolution, has a very sobering, if not disturbing, effect on such speculations. Without a doubt it must have been the influence of such considerations which prompted President Kennedy to counsel, some time ago, apropos of the racial question, that the revolution be a peaceful one.

Considering the social, historical and political background of twentieth-century revolutions thus far, the talk about Negro revolution also demands that all segments of the Negro movement in America be examined very closely. In doing so, we will note that none of the leadership corps of any segment, be it the NAACP-King-CORE students-Urban League-Muslims, etc., is anti-capitalist. The same can generally be said for the followers of these leadership factions. If the Negro movement, then, is revolutionary, it must be revolutionary in a sense which is uniquely different from the characteristics and aims of all other revolutions of our century.

The speculations about the Negro revolution have also inspired the usual suspicions that the integration movement is Communist-inspired. In answer to such charges one could again point to the very conservative and loyal pro-capitalist sentiments of Negro leadership. But still this would not explain very much about the Negro revolution. We know very well that Communists and other Marxist factions, such as Trotskyites, Independent Socialists, etc., are very much in support of the Negro movement in one way or another. One has only to read the Marxist-oriented press to see this. The truth is, however, that the Marxist factions are trailing very eagerly behind the Negro movement in search of issues for their programs. Marxists are no longer able, as they once were, to initiate any movements among Negroes. Moreover, what is not generally understood by those who raise the issue of Communism is that the integration movement, by its very nature, has rendered the Marxist movement superfluous and irrelevant, since Marxists qua Marxists are not needed in the integration struggle. The character of the integration struggle cuts the ground from under Marxist parties since they cannot beat the NAACP or CORE at their own game, nor can Marxist theories about revolution cope with a Negro movement that is pro-capitalist to the extent of demanding no more than an equitable share of the abundance of capitalist democracy. Yet people express the feeling that there is a revolution in the air. There is tenseness abounding as reports of racial strife become more and more a common occurrence. Instinctively we sense that America is preparing itself for great social changes of some kind and the idea of revolution is the first that comes to mind. But to conjure up the idea of Negro revolution under the present conditions in America also calls for a definition or redefinition of what one means when one says "revolution" or "revolutionary," because in highly industrialized America it is not possible to use such terms as freely as one could in describing social conditions in, let us say, Latin America and still make sense.

People who use the term "Negro revolution" loosely are unwittingly adding fuel to the flames of racial crisis which can lead to more racial chaos instead of racial solutions because such people are not helping to explain exactly what the Negro is up against in his struggle to win racial equality in America. Winning racial equality in America could very well require revolutionary methods, and very probably will; but then we will have to understand *why* a revolution and *how* the Negro could possibly make one. The why and the how are important considerations because the racial crisis does lay down an indirect challenge to the American capitalist status quo while the Negro leadership, at the very same time, seeks integration into the status quo with no professed desire to alter it. This creates for the Negro movement a highly contradictory situation which is also a dangerous one. It is dangerous because Americans, of all people in the world today, are the least amenable to, adaptable to, or desirous of any far-reaching changes in their social structures. It is also dangerous because Negro leadership has been instrumental in creating a situation which has implications far beyond its limited range of program. Taken as a whole, Negro leadership does not measure up to the demands of the racial crisis—a crisis which developed because the Negro movement has now transcended the moderate limits established by its leadership.

The Negro movement represents an *indirect* challenge to the capitalist status quo not because it is programmatically anti-capitalist, but because full integration of the Negro in all levels of American society *is not possible within the present framework of the American system*. If this sounds categorically absolute one can only say that the time has come for blunt appraisals of reality: The United States cannot and never will solve the race problem unless Americans change the economic, political, cultural, and administrative social organization of this country in various sectors. Any superoptimism concerning the race question based on a lesser assessment or hope for a neo-liberalistic American revival is heartening but hardly realistic. Is this the same thing as saying that in order to solve the racial crisis what is needed is a revolution? Again the question is: What do we mean by "revolution"?

Social change in any society can be either revolutionary or evolutionary depending on what organizational methods are pursued and who directs the organizational methods. In the United States the capitalist system in all of its major and minor levels of economic administration is owned, controlled, and directed by whites of various classes. Even white labor of the trade union type can be said to have a stake in white ownership of capital either by racial identification with the unions or with a bureaucracy with a capitalist mentality to match its capital investments. Racial discrimination growing out of the racist ideology of the dominant whites of the capital-labor alliance in America has traditionally excluded Negroes (both bourgeois and working-class) from equal participation in either the industrial or trade union fields or administration in the capital-labor alliance. Hence, if the Negro movement is revolutionary or has revolutionary potential, how can the Negro movement have the power in and of itself to enforce structural and administrative changes in this capital-labor combination in order to make room for the democratic participation of the Negro as an American equal? Essentially, this is what is implied in the word "integration" as projected by the Negro bourgeoisie—or at least that portion of the black bourgeoisie that supports integration. But since the integration program does not demand alterations in the structural forms of American society; since the white capital-labor alliance does not desire such changes and would further cement their alliance to block such changes; and since the Negro movement must have such changes in order to achieve its aims—where does this leave the Negro movement? From this analysis—which admittedly is oversimplified for the purpose of illustration—we have to conclude that the Negro movement at this moment is not a revolutionary movement because it has no present means or program to alter the structural forms of American institutions. It is pure political romanticism, at this point, to call the Negro movement the "Negro revolution." It is more properly called the "Negro rebellion" against the American racial status quo.

There is a great difference between rebellion and revolution—two conceptions which some people insist on confusing. This confusion is what led, for example, to the outcome of the situation in Monroe, North Carolina, involving Robert Williams. The American Marxists of certain tendencies—and Marxists are incurable romantics—tried to make a revolutionary out of Robert Williams, who was not a revolutionary but a rebel. The Monroe movement was but a small, local manifestation of the growing Negro rebellion which some Marxists and others mistook for the revolution in the making. One can say that the final outcome of the adventurous happenings in Monroe was unavoidable due to the tense racial situation in America. Nevertheless, this does not excuse incorrect and superficial assessments applied to the Negro movement in whole or in part. A rebellion is not a revolutionary movement unless it changes the structural arrangements of the society or else is able to project programmatic ideas toward that end. The Negro movement does not have the latter, and in America neither arms nor demonstrations nor protest marches mean very much without such ideas. The question that follows is: If indeed a revolution is required to achieve Negro aspirations of whatever class stratification in America, how is it possible to change the Negro movement from a rebellion into a revolutionary movement? Again this is predicated on whether or not social changes to come in America will be revolutionary or evolutionary. This has not yet been determined. It is a dialectical question. However, prior to making any rash, or let us say, unscientific predictions, let us get a clearer conception of the American capitalistic status quo and the American Negro's relationship to that status quo.

What all of us Americans, black and white, are facing today is a racial crisis which is composed in part of the accumulated results of white liberal lying and dishonesty about race, caste and class in this country. On the other hand, it is also due to the superficial and intellectually empty racial propaganda projected over the years by Negro middle-class moderation policies on civil rights. The liberal New York *Post* which has for years been catering to the NAACP and later to Martin Luther King, Jr., was forced to admit, through Stan Opotowsky, one of its reporters, that the class of Negroes that revolted in Birmingham and transformed King's "orderly" protest movement into a race riot had nothing to hope for, no benefits to anticipate from whatever integrated gains King's properly behaved passive protesters would achieve. The liberal New York *Post* is very late in admitting what many of us voiceless Negroes have been saying for years in criticism of white liberalism that caters to the aims and aspirations of the middle-class Negro. Belatedly the liberals have discovered a class of Negroes in Birmingham which Opotowsky described as "lost men." If these disprivileged Birmingham mavericks *are* lost then we are all lost—for the Negroes cited by Opotowsky represent the majority of American Negroes. The majority of Negroes cannot be restrained or contained within the legalistic, gradualistic, passive-moderation approach any longer. The civil rights movement has moved from NAACP protest to broad and general rebellion. It is a rebellion which cannot be put down; a rebellion which, if not handled with the highest order of internal statesmanship, will lead to racial and social chaos.

Opotowsky came to the wrong conclusion about Birmingham's "lost men." While it is true that the integration movement offers the majority of Negroes very little, it is far from proving that the majority of Negroes are lost, i.e., lost to social history and eternity. If we are that lost there is nothing left but to join the Muslims or some other like movement for repatriation or separation. On the contrary, what the Negro rebellion is proving in its own as yet inconclusive manner is that the United States, the greatest and most advanced of the capitalist nations in the Western combine, is not at all exempt or immune from the forces of social change that are sweeping the world today. Unhappily, this is a fact which American whites will find most difficult to comprehend. Americans think they are a very special and privileged people as they peer uncomprehendingly beyond their ocean beaches into a world wracked and seething with revolution, discontent, and political turmoil. Americans have been lulled into a deluded fog of complacency by America's ability to maintain long-term stability. This expertly controlled stability is why there is so much perplexity, desperation, fear, and resentment shown by whites all over the country as the Negro protest movement moves into open rebellion. These attitudes are but a reflection of the uncomfortable fact that America, at present, has no clear answers to the problems emerging out of the racial crisis. President Kennedy voiced this fact right after the Birmingham crisis when he said, "The fires of frustration and discord are burning in every city, North and South, where legal remedies are not at hand." This is the bitter truth which the NAACP et al. could not admit. For to admit there is no legal remedy for full integration means that the integrationist leadership is out on a limb.

We American Negroes are not a "lost" ethnic minority in America. We must admit, however, that the very widespread psychology of alienation from American civilization noted among many younger-generation Negroes could lead to the pessimistic conclusion voiced by Muslims and others that there is no hope for black people in white society. Add to this the negative attitudes of most whites, plus the incompetence and obsolence of liberal remedies, and it is difficult for many not to believe with the Muslims that white civilization is a sinking ship. The flaw for us in the sinking ship forecast is that we are more or less doomed to sink with it. The American Negro, caught in a social situation from which he cannot readily depart, retreat, or easily advance, resembles Jean Paul Sartre's existential man who is "condemned to be free."

The American Negro must stand up and fight his way out of the social trap in which Western civilization has ensnared him. But he can no longer struggle with the old methods alone. Protest actions of whatever nature are no longer enough. The Negro must now develop and begin to use a set of new ideas. What we are up against is the fact that Western civilization is intellectually, spiritually and morally bankrupt. It is a civilization that is no longer able to originate creative ideas in social thinking—and America is no exception to this creative decline that is sapping the vitality of the Western world. In this sense, white America has inherited a racial crisis that it cannot handle and is unable to create a solution for that does not do violence to the collective white American racial ego. The racial crisis in America is more than a question of what white Americans are going to do about their subclass of exploited Negro wards. It is also a broader question: which way is America going as a nation, up or down? Beyond that, it is a question of which way is white civilization going? How do white people, Americans included, propose to accommodate themselves to an emerging world of non-white peoples over whom whites no longer have the right of unilateral dispensation? The racial crisis in America is an internal reflection of this contemporary world-wide problem of readjustment between ex-colonial masters and ex-colonial subjects. The so-called "democratic heritage" of the American tradition has served as historical camouflage to hide the fact that America participated in colonialism through its peculiar institution of slavery. Although a very special kind of colonialism, as we shall elaborate later, slavery was an organic offshoot of European subjugation of Africa and the New World. After the Civil War, the Negro was transformed into a semi-colonial people no different from any other semi-colonial people in South Africa or parts of Latin America.

The historical development of the relationship between the races in America has cultivated a strange and unique pattern of intergroup psychologies between Negro and white of various castes and classes. Many Negroes, especially those who aspire to leadership of one form or another, and the majority of whites have shown a very perverse tendency to overlook or deny exactly what America is as a nation. America never was the all-white nation that the national psychology pretends. America is and always was multi-racial, multi-national, and culturally pluralistic. People who try to deny this fact with talk about Americans all speaking the same language or sharing the same "customs" are merely propagating the myth about "assimilated Americanism." America shares the English language with Canada but they are two nations. The universality of Spanish in South America did not prevent the formation of several independent republics on that continent. If language has failed to break down the racial fences or assimilate the various American ethnic minorities, why cite the American language as proof of an Americanized ideal which America has never achieved? (And let us not mention the Indians.) Either we accept without further delusions that America is pluralistic and democratically adjust our economic, political, cultural, and administrative institutions to fit what is the human living fact and cease believing in the mythology of assimilated Americanism based on the dominant white Protestant Anglo-Saxon ideal, or the racial crisis will be more and more exacerbated. This would be the approach to an evolutionary path for social change in America.

It is possibly too late for this approach. It would require voluntary social planning and governmental intervention into the economy—the great bugbears of the free enterprise economic religion. America has grown up planlessly and chaotically, leaving her racial and ethnic minorities to shift for themselves while she cultivates the idea that America is an all-white Anglo-Saxon nation. This is a totally false image. A psychology, whether individual or national, that tries to deny the essential facts about its social origins is lying to itself and to the world. Such a psychology, individual or national, cannot deal effectively with social reality. America in its national psychology lies to itself that Anglo-Saxon and North European racial ingenuity plus the resources of a virgin continent built American capitalist democracy. America lies to itself that it was always, from the beginning, a democratic nation when its very constitution sanctioned and upheld chattel slavery. Moreover, America conveniently forgets that the first capitalist "free enterprise" banks and stock markets in the land were made possible by accumulated capital accrued from the unpaid labor of Negro slaves. But it would be too much to expect contemporary America to go back over its own history and reassess all these racial facts. Americans are not historically minded and the capitalistic free-enterprise mentality only looks to the future in terms of monetary profits. A program of socially administered evolutionary changes in our economic, political, and cultural life seems very remote. A racial "New Deal" would cause more of an outcry than Roosevelt's reforms, even though these reforms were evolutionary methods to ward off revolutionary threats.

If the realities of the American way of life lead us to rule out the possibilities of voluntary evolutionary social change along racially or ethnically democratic lines, we are then faced with the other alternative: revolutionary ideas and methods. But here we encounter a very unique and complex set of problems. For to transform the Negro rebellion into a movement with revolutionary approaches, ideas, and appeals is an immense intellectual and organizational problem. Moreover, it poses what amounts to a new question in America: What, precisely, is revolutionary in form and content? This is not a simple question to answer because the only concept of social revolution that has come out of Western thought since the nineteenth century is the revolutionary overthrow of capital by the combined forces of labor. This is ruled out of our considerations because of the reality of the American capital-labor alliance. To speak, then, of social revolution in the United States from the Negro point of view means a reinterpretation of the meaning of social revolution for our times. This may appear a startling statement but it is, in all evidence, quite true. In investigating this problem, we American Negroes must not lose sight of one fact about the Western world and its intellectual traditions: New social frontiers do not cease to be simply because Western philosophers have no more answers for the problems of the world. Still, we Afro-Americans who have always been excluded to the fringe world of Western society can learn a lot from Western philosophers and pick up where they left off. In this regard, the theories of social revolution thought up by Western philosophers such as Marx and others are bankrupt, passé, and irrelevant in Western society today. Socialism has not come to the Western world through the revolt of the working classes of white nations. As a result, the whole Western world is in serious trouble because social revolution is today the prerogative of the colored peoples. Despite the fact that Western white Marxists may attempt to cast colonial and semi-colonial revolutions in their own Marxian image, it is a fact that these revolutions are all indigenous, original, autonomous and unique in themselves. Marx did not invent social revolution but, at the same time, this does not mean that we cannot learn many things from Marx. The failure of the Marxist revolution in Europe and America has led many intellectuals, especially in Europe, to attempt to reinvestigate and reinterpret social revolution. The Negro intellectual must do the same if the Negro rebellion is ever to become a revolutionary movement in its own right. The Negro rebellion can learn much from other Western critics of revolutionary theory and arrive at its own answers for its own situation. Albert Camus, discussing rebellion and revolution, had this to say:

Rebellion is, by nature, limited in scope. It is no more than an incoherent pronouncement. Revolution, on the contrary, originates in the realm of ideas. Specifically, it is the injection of ideas into historical experience, while rebellion is only the movement that leads from individual experience into the realm of ideas. While even the collective history of a movement of rebellion is always that of a fruitless struggle with facts, of an obscure protest which involves neither methods nor reasons, a revolution is an attempt to shape actions to ideas, to fit the world into a theoretic frame.*

These words were written by a man who died relatively young, who had become increasingly disturbed and alarmed by the steady deterioration of the political, moral and spiritual reality of Western Europe. Originally a French Marxist, Camus recoiled in the face of the obvious collapse and degeneration of the Marxian revolution between the two World Wars and after. For our purposes, we need not go into this very complex question as to why the working classes of European white nations failed to make the hoped-for revolution. Our immediate problem is not Europe but America, where we live. However, it is enough to point out that the white capital-labor alliance that has taken place in America has its parallel in Europe where the white Marxist "revolutionaries" became less and less revolutionary the more the European

* Camus, *The Rebel* (New York: Alfred A. Knopf, 1954), p. 106.

colonies became truly revolutionary. At the root of the whole question of the degeneration of Western Marxism in Europe was the colonial problem. It was not the Marxist plan that colored colonies should become liberated before white socialism came to Europe. The fact that this is what happened threw the European capitalists, and the Marxists as well, into a state of confusion and panic. The Marxists in Europe talked like revolutionaries but their internal politics became more and more geared to the necessities of preventing their own capitalist societies from collapse as a result of colonial losses. In Algeria, for example, where Camus was born, it is a fact that many French Marxists, when the racial showdown came, turned against the Algerian rebel forces. These facts, and many more, were not lost on Camus, who was an honest revolutionary defeated and confounded by the utter betrayal perpetrated by his own revolutionary tradition and the degeneration of Western morality.

From Camus we are able to learn the most precise difference between mere rebellion and viable revolution. More than that, we understand why the Negro movement, which is a rebellion, has its "revolutionary" limitations: It is a movement without any unique ideas of its own. The key to the question of "unique ideas" is lost in the confusion of ideas, or better, the lack of positive ideas, of what America really is as a nation and the true nature of the Negroes' intrinsic relationship to the American reality. This is a problem that has not been adequately or honestly explored in all of its sociological ramifications. It could not be because, as we have pointed out, the national psychology of the dominant white ideal prefers to project the image of America as an all-white nation. (Look at American films, television and the advertising media, etc.) More than that, since we are dealing with a society which, besides wanting to be called an all-white nation, is also the most extensively industrialized capitalist nation in the world, and also wants desperately to remain capitalistic in order to defend its "free" institutions by keeping Negroes excluded (white labor is not going to overthrow it), it behooves us to examine this American capitalism in order to determine just what kind of economic animal it is. What are its characteristics? What are its strong points? What are its weaknesses?

American capitalism is not the same as other capitalisms in the Western world because it developed according to its own peculiar geographical, social, racial, political, and cultural climate. Moreover, American capitalism helps to sustain and prop up other capitalisms. What is crucial for capitalism as an economic system is that beyond the United States capitalism has nowhere else to go in terms of development. America is the last hope of capitalism as a system. But in terms of revolutionary ideas, the Negroes' relationship to this American system is a unique one, since we are excluded, and also for other reasons not yet explored. One significant reason for this uniqueness is that social revolution today is a product of the underdeveloped sections of the world's colored populations where there exists no such highly industrialized social base. For the Negro, this presents a very novel situation; in fact, one of the most unique in world history.

We American Negroes exist in essentially the same relationship to American capitalism as other colonials and semi-colonials have to Western capitalism as a whole. Yet when other semi-colonials of the colored world rebel against the political and economic subjugation of Western capitalism, it is for the aim of having the freedom to build up their own native industrial bases for themselves. Our American Negro rebellion derives from the fact that we exist side by side with the greatest industrial complex the world has ever seen, which we are not allowed to use democratically for ourselves. Hence, while the Negro rebellion emerges out of the same semi-colonial social conditions of others, it must have different objectives in order to be considered revolutionary. In other words, we must locate the weakest sector of the American capitalist "free enterprise" front and strike there. Where is that weak front in the free-enterprise armor? It is in the cultural front. Or better, it is that part of the American economic system that has to do with the ownership and administration of cultural communication in America, i.e., film, theater, radio and television, music, performing and publishing, popular entertainment booking, management, etc. In short, it is that part of the system devoted to the economics and aesthetic ideology involved in the cultural arts of America. If the Negro rebellion is limited by a lack of original social, political and economic ideas to "fit the world into a theoretic frame," then it is only in the cultural areas of American life that such new ideas can have any social meaning. What is meant here is that the only observable way in which the Negro rebellion can become revolutionary in terms of American conditions is for the Negro movement to project the concept of Cultural Revolution in America. Why this is so we shall proceed to show by a historical, racial, economic, and cultural analysis of the American Negroes' many-sided relationship to the American system.

The Negro rebellion in America is destined to usher in a new era in human relations and to add a thoroughly new conception of the meaning and the form and content of social revolution. In order to make social progress the world as a whole must move toward unification within the democratic framework of a human, national, ethnic, or racial variety. A great stride toward this world ideal of unification through national variety has been achieved in the process of dissolution of colonial empires.

In America, however, we have an unsolved problem of a unique type of semi-colonialism. The Negro rebellion comes at this time to give voice to the long suppressed ethnic consciousness of the American Negro as he rises to the task to throw off his semi-colonial yoke. But this Negro rebellion, mistakenly called by some the Negro revolution, is not revolutionary because it projects no new ideas beyond what have already been ratified in the democratic philosophy of the American Constitution. These constitutional concepts about "freedom" are the heritage of a revolutionary movement ushered in by the industrial revolution of centuries past. Since our traditions of latter-day liberalism are unable to apply these concepts to the realities of race in America, social progress demands that new ideas of social revolution be introduced into the bloodstream of the American tradition. It goes without saying that these new concepts must be extracted from native American social ingredients.

Hence, we have projected the new concept of Cultural Revolution. We maintain that this concept affords the intellectual means, the conceptual framework, the theoretical link that ties together all the disparate, conflicting and contending trends within the Negro movement as a whole in order to transform the movement from a mere rebellion into a revolutionary movement that can "shape actions to ideas, to fit the world into a theoretic frame." What do we mean by Cultural Revolution? Stated simply, Cultural Revolution means an ideological and organizational approach to American social change by revolutionizing the administration, the organization, the functioning, and the social purpose of the entire American apparatus of cultural communication and placing it under public ownership.

What has this to do with the Negro's struggle for racial equality, and why should the American Negro assume the initiative for such a task? Because the American Negro is the only ethnic group in America who has the need, the motivation and the historical prerogative to demand such changes. Also because racial equality cannot be achieved unless the Negro rebellion adopts revolutionary tactics which can enforce structural changes in the administration of certain sections of the national economy. Since the alliance of white capital and labor obviates any challenge to the economic status quo where the production of basic commodities takes place, the Negro movement must challenge free enterprise at its weakest link in the production chain, where no tangible commodities are produced. This becomes the "economic" aspect of the Negro movement. However, it is the cultural aspect of this problem that is most important in terms of form and content in new revolutionary ideas.

The Negro concept of Cultural Revolution demands that both the American national psychology and the organization of American cultural institutions be altered to fit the facts of what America really is. Culturally speaking, America is a European-African-Indian racial amalgam—an imperfect and incompletely realized amalgam. Therefore, the American racial problem is a problem of many aspects, but it is essentially a cultural problem of a type that is new in modern history. Until this is intellectually admitted and sociologically practiced, chaotic and retrograde racial practices and conflicts will continue in American society. That the Negro question in America is essentially a cultural question has escaped the attention of the so-called theoreticians and practitioners of sociology and political and social theory. This is why the concept of Cultural Revolution becomes an intellectual means of introducing a new set of ideas into American social theory. A basic reason why the cultural aspect of Negro reality has been overlooked, dismissed, and neglected is that most articulate and intellectually inclined Negroes are beguiled to think of culture solely in terms of the white Anglo-Saxon ideal, which is the cultural image that America attempts to project to the world. The American national psychology prefers to be regarded as an all-white nation, and the American cultural arts are, therefore, cultivated to preserve and reflect this all-white ideal. Any other artistic expression is regarded as an exotic curiosity.

If we examine this cultural side of the race question in America very closely, we will find that, historically and culturally speaking, the white American Anglo-Saxon cultural ideal of artistic and aesthetic practices is false, predicated as it is on the myth of Western superiority in cultural tradition, and conceals the true facts of native American cultural development. What the white American creative artist or cultural critic is upholding as "superior" is the Western tradition of cultural creativity stemming from European sources to which the white American Anglo-Saxon (and those others who try to be such and are not) never truly added very much this side of the Atlantic. The statement often heard that "America has no real culture" is not far from the truth.

But to say that white America has not been culturally creative or original does not mean that America as a racial or cultural amalgam has not been culturally or artistically original. The historical truth is that it was the Afro-American cultural ingredient in music, dance and theatrical forms (the three forms of art in which America has innovated) that has been the basis for whatever culturally new and unique that has come out of America. Take away the Afro-American tradition of folk-songs, plantation minstrel, spirituals, blues, ragtime, jazz styles, dance forms, and the first Negro theatrical pioneers in musical comedy of the 1890's down to Sissle and Blake of the 1920's, and there would be no jazz industry involving publishing, entertainment, recording; there would have been no Gershwins, Rodgers and Hammersteins, Cole Porters or Carmichaels or popular song tradition—which is based on the Negro blues idiom; there would have been no American musical comedy form—which is America's only original contribution to theater; there would have been no foxtrot—which has formed the basis for American ballroom dancing (not to mention several other popular dance styles in the history of American dance). In other words, the Afro-American ingredients formed the basis of all "popular culture" as opposed to "classical culture" in America. We can see from this that "cultural" aspects of life in America are closely linked with the development of American racial mores. Moreover, since all of these popular art forms comprise those cultural commodities involved in multimillion dollar industries (which exclude or exploit Negroes as much as possible), there is an organic connection in American capitalism between race, culture, and economics.

Culturally speaking, the American intellectual community has arbitrarily dichotomized the national culture into exclusive divisions—"popular culture" and "classical culture." In American terms classical culture is the tradition of glorifying the artistic traditions of Western Europe in the seven arts and the desire to cultivate an American extension of this Western tradition. In this endeavor, Americans as a whole have not done very well. The white intellectual community of America is, and always has been, very painfully aware of this American deficiency. Hence, the recurrent complaint: "America has no real culture." What is meant is that America has no real tradition of a classical culture to match the ascendant European. This fact becomes glaringly noticeable today when America is called upon to demonstrate the cultural results of its "democratic heritage" to the world at large, which is amazed at how little this country has to offer. That the upper levels of the American cultural community is painfully aware of this was mentioned by the late C. Wright Mills a few years ago: "The United States is now engaged with other nations, in particular Russia, in a full-scale competition for cultural prestige based on nationality. . . . What America has abroad is power; what it does not have at home or abroad is cultural prestige." *

Despite the grievous lack of a classical culture in America, however, this country always has at its disposal a reserve cultural weapon and that is jazz music, the Afro-American cultural contribution to the national soul. In 1955, *The New York Times* carried a headline on its front page to the effect: "United States Has a Secret Sonic Weapon—Jazz." The article went on to say: "All Europe now seems to find American jazz as necessary as the seasons . . . American jazz has now become a universal language. It knows no national boundaries . . ." etc. The State Department is quite willing

* Mills, *Power Elite* (New York: Oxford University Press, 1959), p. 334.

to use jazz as a cultural weapon because it hasn't got much else. The problem posed here is that jazz, in the view of America's white cultural elite, is a "popular" mode of cultural expression and does not make up for the serious lack of American "classical" cultural arts. The question then is why was jazz music never cultivated by musical America into an American school of classical music in the same fashion that European folk-music was incorporated into the European classical music tradition? The answer to this question is also the answer to the question: Why does America have no real culture? American jazz was never seriously developed into an American classical school of musical creation because American composers and critics never really desired it. For to elevate jazz into a serious classical school would have demanded that the whole body of Afro-American folk-music also be elevated and glorified. This would also mean that the Afro-American ethnic minority which originally created this music would have to be culturally glorified and elevated socially, economically and politically. It would mean that the black composer would have to be accepted on this social, cultural, economic, and political level. But this the white American cultural ego would never permit. The inescapable conclusion is this: At the bottom of the whole question of the backward cultural development of America, the cultural banality, the cultural decadence, the cultural debasement of the entire American social scene, lies the reality of racism—racial exclusion, racial exploitation, racial segregation and all the manifestations of the ideology of white superiority.

This whole question of race and culture in America is imbedded in the social roots of the historical development of native American cultural standards and institutions. For this fundamental reason the Negro civil rights movement, at this late stage of its development, cannot go any further; it cannot transform itself into a movement with a revolutionary set of ideas unless it incorporates a cultural program along with its economic, social, and political platforms.

Such a cultural program, however, must be two-sided. It must be concerned not only with the aesthetics of the form and content of artistic creation in America but also with transforming the economic, institutional, business and administrative organizational apparatus that buys and sells, limits or permits, hires and disposes of, distributes or retains, determines or negates, and profits from the creation and distribution of cultural production in America. This is the meaning, for our purposes, of Cultural Revolution. We maintain that without such a revolution the Negro movement has no point of departure from which to compel the necessary social impact to effect structural changes within the American social system.

Moreover, it seems to be historically determined, if one seriously analyzes and examines the peculiarities of American capitalism, that it is precisely the economic spheres of cultural communications in America that must be revolutionized for more humanistic social use before such changes take place in commodity production, political organization or racial democratization. The theoretical reasoning behind this assumption is that, if the world revolution now in process emerges from the conditions of social underdevelopment, then social revolution in highly developed societies cannot have those same motivations. This would be particularly true for the United States, whose industrial development is greater than that of any other society. When we clearly observe that Western capitalism has cultivated the new class alliance between white labor and white capital in the face of colonial and semi-colonial revolutions, it becomes evident that the old Marxian formula of the revolutionary class struggle between capital and labor is passé and obsolescent. Hence any theory of social revolution must be modernized with a new set of ideas, coming not from the whites, since that is improbable, but from the colored races. This is why the African nations are involved in the cultivation of new social, political, cultural, and economic ideas to fit their respective needs. It is incumbent upon the Afro-American to do the same within his own social context.

What is the precise connection between the Negro rebellion and the African revolution? It is partially answered by saying that the connection is precisely cultural. It could not be anything else but cultural—which already implies "racial" or "ethnic." It certainly is not economic or even political in any serious dimension. What is the meaning of "Negritude," the aesthetic concept projected by the Paris group of African intellectuals sixteen years ago when they organized the Society of African Culture? One of the resolutions of that organizing congress describes the idea of Negritude very succinctly: "The imperious necessity for proceeding toward a rediscovery of historical truth and a re-evaluation of Negro cultures" in order to "revive, rehabilitate, and develop those cultures so as to favour their integration into the general stream of human culture." When Leopold Sedar Senghor met with some Negro authors in New York a few years ago, he told these authors that the American Negro should seriously study the question of the Negro aesthetic in American culture. Leopold Senghor, who is also a leading African poet, is one of the major African intellectuals on the question of Negritude. The unfortunate difficulty here is that Leopold Senghor, who is not an American Negro, understands the implication of Negro culture in American historical development better than any of the Negro writers with whom he discussed the matter. These Negro writers did not understand what Senghor meant, and have not discussed the matter since.

The American branch of the Society of African Culture (AMSAC), which was supposed to take up the question of Negritude as it relates to the American Negro, is run by a group of culturally white-oriented Negroes who did not believe that the African concept of Negritude really applies to the American Negro and heaped ridicule on Negroes in AMSAC who fought for the cultivation of the concept in

America. The real problem was that AMSAC's leadership did not know how to apply the idea. The failures of AMSAC on this aesthetic question of Negritude in America means that the theoretical link between the African revolution and the Negro movement in America has not been established in the politics of the Negro intellectual community in America. This link must be a cultural one for the basic reason that the exploitation practiced on Africans and those of African descent in the Western hemisphere has not only been economic, in terms of labor and natural resources, but it has also been cultural. In America the entire industry of popular music writing, publishing, and selling was established by white appropriation of the whole body of Afro-American folk music—the only original music in America with a broad human appeal. This music has been cheapened, debased and commercialized for popular appeal. The American music industry has been exploiting, cheating, stealing from, browbeating, excluding, plagiarizing Negro singers, jazz musicians, composers, etc., for decades and getting away with it. The cultural exploitation established by white America in the early years of the twentieth century by the white appropriation of Afro-American folk-music was the first great manifestation of the racist development in the economics of American culture. This racist cultural doctrine, once established in music, spread through the entire field of cultural expression in America. It has had its poisonous effect on American theater, both musical and dramatic, and a distorting influence on American dance. Today it is still rampant in the jazz fields.

The racial attitudes behind American cultural developments were the basic problem of cultural competition between white and Negro. The whites very quickly realized that from the lowly Negro in America came the only rich vein of untapped and completely original material for song, dance, music and theater. This was the motivation behind the creation of the blackface or burnt cork tradition by the whites. (Ironically, in the nineteenth century Negroes were forced to use blackface in order to compete with whites in the use of Negro theatrical material.) The economic benefits derived from the creative and artistic use of Negro cultural ingredients were reaped by the whites through the simple practice of cultural appropriation of aesthetic ideas not native to their own tradition. As a result there came into being a long line of white creative artists and performers who either enriched themselves or got their start by using Negro material—the Al Jolsons, the George Gershwins, the Amos 'n' Andys, Eugene O'Neill, Ridgely Torrence, Marc Connelly, and more, plus scores of plagiarizing white composers (including very big names). Booking agents and managers have for decades made millions by the shrewd exploitation and manipulation of Negro performers and creators over whom they held the life and death economic power to hire or fire.

We have only one Negro "cultural" spokesman today and that is James Baldwin. But he is not talking about culture. In fact, Baldwin does not believe in "race" and would rather not consider himself a Negro author, merely another American author who accidentally happens not to be white. This may sound very "modern" and "New Negroid" but it is negative in the extreme. Baldwin's literary power of expression exists precisely because he is black in America. For all of his gift of creative expression, Baldwin is another example of the process of negation visited upon the Negro intellectual who is overawed by the glitter and glamor of a steel-riveted and chrome-plated Western world in the last stages of cultural and spiritual decline. The tragedy of cultural negation inflicted on the Negro personality in America is that this process of negation induces the negated to negate himself.

Thus it is that the concept of Cultural Revolution brings together in America several seemingly separate and disparate historical trends and processes that started with the industrial revolution and lifted millions out of Europe and Africa and placed them in a fateful social juxtaposition in the New World. This revolutionary process has never really ceased.

It has merely halted for a spell of decades only to appear again in new forms with new aims for different peoples and nations. In the beginning the revolutionary leadership came from European whites who ushered in the modern world. But today the revolutionary leadership is the "browns," "blacks," and "yellows." Black revolution in Africa means black revolution in the United States because Africa and the United States are historically welded in that fateful juxtaposition of races which went into their national make-ups in the beginning. America is not immune from those social forces that are changing the world. No nation can step outside of history, and each nation must pay its just dues to historical demands at the proper time or decline.

The Afro-American must understand that he is Africa's cultural contribution to "the general stream of human culture" as defined by the Paris Society of African Culture. He must understand that his social revolution is nothing if it is not cultural in content. He must understand that all social revolutions are at once social, economic, political, cultural and administrative. But, depending on circumstances, each specific revolution is couched in different central demands. In the United States the only kind of revolution the Negro can make is a cultural revolution, because he represents the only ethnic group who has a political right to raise such a demand. The Negro revolution can be economic, social, political, administrative, or racial in form, but it must be cultural in content. If it is not cultural in content it is not revolutionary, but a mere rebellion without ideas "to fit the world in a theoretic frame." It is only the cultural needs of the Negro that coincide with or are complementary to the main humanistic need that goes unfulfilled in America despite this country's economic and administrative achievements—the need for a thriving, creative, humanistically progressive national culture.

Cultural Revolution brings, for the first time in Negro history, a new class of Negro leadership into the arena of public affairs with a national program for social change. This class or social stratum is the Negro writer, dramatist, poet, actor, painter, dancer, architect, designer, composer, arranger, film technician, sculptor, critic, etc. Heretofore, this class among American Negroes has been divided and compartmentalized along craft lines. There has been little or no conception among Negroes of the crucial need for artists of all crafts to work together within one organization comprising all the arts. This lack of cultural unity on the intercraft level existed because of the lack of a comprehensive cultural philosophy among Negroes in the arts. The present "cultural" work among Negroes consists of "integration in the theater," "integration in the films," "integration in this and that," etc. This amounts to an inconsequential and dead-end cultural approach to American arts. Integration in the arts ignores the racist premises upon which the whole institution of the cultural arts in America is based. American culture is predicated on racial exclusion and the glorification of the white cultural ego. The entire economic and administrative apparatus of cultural communication in America is geared to, dependent upon, and motivated by racial exclusion and the cultural negation of the Negro, and, having no democratic or humanistic role to play in society, becomes of necessity more and more commercialized and more and more unable to deal with the living truths of American social realities. It is a foregone conclusion that a film industry that is unable to deal with the social truths of race relations in America is certainly not about to integrate Negroes in any phase of film production. Therefore, it is the economic and administrative foundations of cultural communications in America that must be radically altered before the social role of cultural communications can be changed and democratized. Until this takes place in the cultural arts there will be no integration in the arts. It is the same thing as asking to join the dead and the dying at the gates of the graveyard of dead civilizations for any Negro to seek integration in American culture as it now stands. This is most certainly not our historical role in world culture. With all the indignities American culture has heaped on the Negro in the past with its blackface imitation, stereotypes, servant-role handouts, lazybone characterizations, the "Mammy" sagas, etc., we should now be embarrassedly particular about asking to be made more ludicrous by participation in the banalities of what passes for "cultural arts." For any Negro today to beg, with childlike and empty-minded mimicry, to have the Negro image further distorted by its inclusion in the whitefaced orgy of spiritual decadence that has corrupted and debased all the cultural arts in America, is to ask that the Negro participate with the whites in their senseless and insane debasement of every humanistic social value that ever came out of the Western cultural tradition. This tradition has come to a sorry end in America as practically the whole cultural outlook retreats from the social realities of America and the world at large into an idiotic ivory tower.

The time has arrived for the Negro creative artists to see that they have a special role to play in the Negro movement in terms of ideas relating to their respective arts, not as interim pinch-hitters for professional civil rights leaders. Rather, the Negro creative artist's role in America is the same as that already outlined by the Society of African Culture in its perspective for the African creative artist and intellectual:

The mission of Negro men of culture within the framework of S.A.C. is to: (a) assert, uphold and enrich their national cultures; (b) decide the sense of events and cultural works in the world according to the bearing of these on their own life and destiny; (c) bring about an increasing awareness of their responsibilities as men of culture; face to face with their national cultures; face to face with general culture.

With regard to the present active social class of Negro creative artists, however, we are up against a difficult ideological problem. The majority of this group (excepting jazz musicians) are pretty much a-racial in their artistic or aesthetic preferences. Most Negro actors do not believe in a specifically Negro theater. Many Negro writers do not like to be designated "Negro" writers. The ethnic dance forms of the Negro have been abandoned by most Negro dancers of the modern school. With the exception of the jazz musician there exists no specifically Negro school of aesthetics. The fact that such an a-racial attitude exists among the creative artists representing an ethnic minority of eighteen to twenty million people is to be deplored. Here it is shown that the concept of integration is negative, one-sided—a negation of the idea of the social meaning of art itself. "Universality" cannot be used to mean the negation of one's own ethnic origins or the art ingredients or the cultural qualities of those origins. For a Negro artist to take this position means, in effect, that he is accepting as his aesthetic model the white standard in art and aesthetics. The American cultural wasteland has nothing to offer the Negro who is so bent on integrating into nothing. The political task of the Negro artist, then, is to fight for the over-all democratization of the American apparatus of cultural communication in order to make a place for the unrestricted expression of his own ethnic personality, his own innate creative originality. In other words, the Negro must become nationalistic in terms of the ethnic and cultural attributes of his art expression.

These ideas on Cultural Revolution are merely exploratory and are meant to open the question for general discussion. We are seeking definitive answers to the question: What is social revolution in the United States? In doing so, we must seek to inject new ideas into the Negro movement. We believe Cultural Revolution to be a vehicle for the expression of a set of new ideas. The basic social problems implied in the concept of Cultural Revolution are by no means new problems. They emerged in the latter part of the nineteenth century in America and became potent social, cultural, and economic factors that shaped American race relations into what they are today. Cultural Revolution is a new concept only insofar as we believe it to be the first definitive attempt to conceptualize these basic social realities into an ethnic or cultural (or even political) philosophy. More must be said about this concept. Simply to present it also raises a score of other questions that must be discussed.

9

Rebellion or Revolution?–II

Despite many new features of the present-day Negro rebellion, this movement has its roots in the accumulated experiences of the past fifty-odd years. But most of the younger, articulate "radical" elements of Negro leadership imagine themselves to be inspired by ideals whose existential relationships to the here-and-now need no other rationalizations. Thus the movement, while having many historical carry-overs, is guided by individuals whose slogans reveal little awareness of historical ingredients that have gone into the making of such a complex social force as is the Negro movement today. As a result, the Negro movement's potential is compromised not only by the hard barriers thrown up by the establishment, but by a leadership whose views about American realities are extremely a-historical, limited and oversimplified.

This leadership outlook has been able to mobilize a great variety of direct mass-actions, some scattered, others concerted. But it has not been sufficient in comprehension to carry these actions beyond the great impasse of the March on Washington. There the great Freedom clamor was absorbed in the emptiness of a great void and the protests became like echoes in a canyon that bounce about in mocking repetition. The march led not to a victory but to a crisis, and many are asking: How could it happen that the voices of Freedom could echo with such a hollow sound?

Part of the answer is that the Negro movement suffers from the serious disease of "historical discontinuity." For example, since World War I a series of world-shaking events, social upheavals and aborted movements have intruded and sharply set succeeding generations of Negroes apart in terms of social experiences. The youngest elements in the Negro movement today are activists, of one quality or another, who enter the arena unfortified with the knowledge or meaning of many of the vital experiences of Negro radicals born in 1900, 1910, 1920, or even 1930. The problem is that too many of the earlier-twentieth-century-vintage Negro radicals have become too conservative for the 1940ers. Worse than that, the oldsters have nothing to hand down to the 1940ers in the way of refined principles of struggle, original social theory, historical analysis of previous Negro social trends or radical philosophy suitable for black people.

In the wake of the March on Washington one semblance of a radical idea did emerge out of the din of hollow protests— the Freedom Now Party as a vehicle for black political expression. But it is already evident from the discussions going on within this embryonic political movement that its leading voices are far from grasping the nature and scope of the problems inherent in the Freedom Now Party idea. The leadership of the Freedom Now Party inherits the peculiar disease of all Negro movements—historical discontinuity. This leadership would like to pick up the new banner across which is emblazoned "Political Action!" and go forward. But to what and where? How can the Freedom Now Party manage to fill the great void that greeted the March on Washington? The simple fact of raising the issue of a black political party does not mean that the views of those who raise it are any less compromised by historical discontinuity than those of others. For the problems facing the FNP are historically cumulative. It falls to the FNP to attempt to unravel the knot that binds Negro consciousness with the multiple strictures of ideological confusion and ethnic disorientation. A black political party that is going to mean anything in America has to be a party with an ideology that is persuasive enough to enable Negroes to cope with extremely difficult economic, political, and cultural problems peculiar to American society. But parties with such an ideology are not built overnight—as some of our superenthusiastic FNPers are prone to think. The Freedom Now Party comes into existence at the end of a fifty-year period whose experiences have, for all political intents and purposes, gone wasted.

Consider the fact that it has taken all these years, from 1910 when the NAACP was first organized to August, 1963 in Washington, to bring home the fact that NAACP methods (or variations thereof) are insufficient for achieving Negro aspirations in America. Did not Bayard Rustin, one of the leading generals of "marching" campaigns admit (*N.Y. Times*, 12/2/63): "The civil rights movement not only reached an impasse with its current tactics but also had retrogressed in many cities to conditions that existed before this year's upsurge."

Mr. Rustin said more than that. We quote:

Interviewed at Howard University . . . Mr. Rustin described the tactics of lying down in the streets to prevent the movement of trucks, and other forms of direct action, as "gimmicks." He said there was a danger that the civil rights organizations would become wedded to these gimmicks as ends in themselves.

The civil rights movement had gone as far as it could with its original approach and the time had come to broaden the movement which, he added, faces the danger of degenerating into a sterile sectarianism.

Heroism and ability to go to jail should not be substituted for an overall social reform program. We need a political and social reform program that will not only help the Negroes but one that will help all Americans. Only then can we win.

In *The New York Times* of November 12, 1963, other leaders were quoted:

"Direct action efforts have failed," said the leaders of New York City's civil rights organizations. "Picketting and work stoppages . . . . not the answer," said a Teamsters Union leader. "It's a political matter and it must be treated as a political matter."

Well, many of us black radicals knew this a long time before the March on Washington took place, but it was considered akin to racial treason to say so. The trouble is that leaders of Mr. Rustin's type have always been very late in waking up to the realities. When he advises Negroes to "shift tactics" he is tardy, because thousands of Negroes have already shifted to positions which it is very doubtful Mr. Rustin himself would take. And do you think that any of Bayard Rustin's co-strategists among the Big Six Rights General Staff (James Farmer, Whitney Young, Roy Wilkins, Martin Luther King, Jr., A. Philip Randolph, Bayard Rustin) will pay any heed to his late but sage advice? No! More marches are planned to state capitols and city halls and a proliferation of more "gimmicks." The great sit-in morality crusade will continue in a society predicated on immorality that breeds the pathological martyrdom of the jailhouse. The constant search will go on for new styles of "causes" with new martyrs and other Negro martyred personalities to romanticize in the left-wing press with new "defense" committees. This whole tragi-comedy of racial frustration is an indication that fifty years of protest has left the senior leadership bankrupt in terms of social and political imagination, trapped between the grave limitations of their philosophies and the crushing might of the establishment which they cannot dent.

There is no one leader or school of civil rights thought responsible for this state of affairs. It is the collective weakness peculiar to a class-a political disease endemic to the entire civil rights leadership. Except for an abundance of lawyers for the battle of attrition on the legal front, this class is not even technically equipped for reform. Who will replace E. Franklin Frazier and W. E. B. Du Bois in the social sciences? Where are the Negro economists, statisticians, etc.? Practically, the entire civil rights leadership reveals the propensity for loud protest and quiet status climbing; i.e. social opportunism. Thus Mr. Rustin's demand for "a political and social reform program" will fall on deaf ears and barren ground. What kind of social reform movement will come from a class which is characterized by a complete disdain for advanced social theory of any kind but has a strong affinity for the very social values of the establishment which it is alleged to be fighting against? Political and social reform Mr. Rustin demands. We wonder what Mr. Rustin will do to implement his own suggestion. The Freedom Now Party movement has to overcome fifty years of wasted experiences which have not left us a single school of social reform, radical or otherwise, to cure the crisis-ills of the civil rights movement. In order to advance towards Mr. Rustin's "political and social reform program" it is necessary to review history, because the seeds of the protest movement's failures lie hidden in the record of past decades. A movement that is not historically determined has little future.

All the evidence indicates that the roots of the current crisis of the Negro movement are to be found in the period between the end of World War I and the years of the Great Depression. This is what is meant by "historical discontinuity." For most of the social issues that absorb the attention of all the Negro radical elements today were prominently foreshadowed in these years. Yet the strands between the period called by some the "Fabulous Twenties" and the current Negro movement have been broken. The real implications of this historical discontinuity will not be appreciated unless one presents a panoramic view of that period. Consider what was happening.

In the early 1920's two of the great giants in the history of Negro leadership clashed in a bitter ideological conflict over the destiny of black people in the Western world—W. E. B. Du Bois and Marcus Garvey. The strange thing about this clash was that both of these personalities were strong advocates of two different brands of "Pan-Africanism" which neither one could cultivate in his own homeland. The West Indians did not back Garvey's nationalism in Jamaica, B.W.I., and Du Bois' first Pan-African Congress had to be sponsored by France—one of the leading imperialist powers—who turned over the Paris Grand Hotel. At home Du Bois was far from being a nationalist. At the time, he was editor of the NAACP's *Crisis* magazine, with a circulation of over 100,000 annually. The NAACP was then, as now, the leading integrationist organization among Negroes. But it is noteworthy that the word "integration" was not in vogue at that time as a synonym for "civil rights." Integration as a slogan appears to have gained wide usage during World War II and after because of the urgency of the campaign to integrate the armed forces.

The clash between Du Bois and Garvey was a bitter one. The former denounced Garvey as (to put it mildly) "bombastic and impractical" while Garvey scornfully relegated Du Bois to the Negro "cultural assimilationists" whom Garvey despised. That the Du Bois-NAACP philosophy and Garvey should so sharply conflict is understandable. But the fact that black nationalism should arise in the United States with such persuasive mass-potency raised many questions about the Negro movement in America which were not settled at that time or even understood. For the actions and reactions of both Du Bois and Garvey to black nationalism indicated that both were unable to deal with nationalist ideology purely within the American social framework where it is destined to play out its positive role. In this sense was the "Back to Africa" aspect of Garvey impractical and escapist in the same way as is the "Separate State" idea of the Muslims escapist. The tendency of Negro nationalism of all varieties to drift toward escapist solutions and ideals is the result of an inability to find the proper economic-political framework that has relevance to American realities. Truthfully, it would have been too much to expect the 1920 Negro radicals to be detached and objective enough to clarify the integrationist vs. nationalist tendencies and mold them theoretically into a political fusion. Dialectical processes have never really been understood in America. The two fundamentally basic trends behind Negro racial ideology in America, though sharply etched out in terms of organizational confrontation, got lost and went unresolved in the turbulence that seethed in American society during the "Fabulous Twenties."

World War I shook the very foundations of world capitalism in Europe and inspired liberating currents within the colonies. It sent Garvey to New York and Du Bois to Paris in search of "Pan-Africanism." It uprooted southern Negroes by the thousands for the great trek to the North to meet West Indians that many had never known existed. It sent Negro soldiers to France to fight for "democracy" and brought them back to march into a race war on the home front because the KKK had been revived again in 1915. The real semicolonial status of the Negro was grimly revealed as lynch-law raged across the country north, south, and west as black soldiers in uniform had to fight for their very lives, homes, and families. "We return. We return from fighting. We return fighting," said Du Bois' *Crisis* magazine as it echoed the temper of the times, and the NAACP opened up its great postwar protest campaign in 1919. Other organizations entered the crucial fray—the National Equal Rights League, the National Race Congress and the Commission on Interracial Cooperation, a Southern group. All during this time, more and more Negroes were streaming north.

Though the thunder of racial wars boomed ominously, it cannot be overlooked that the post-World War I turmoil in America dug deep into the national consciousness, churned it up, and threw onto the open stage of life everything that was sick and ailing in the nation; i.e., in American capitalism. Both black and white were profoundly agitated and, unlike the 1950's and 1960's, were openly saying so in every conceivable way. Today the only real agitation is black. A. Philip

Randolph's *Messenger*, "The only Negro radical magazine in America," preached "social revolution." A Harlem radical press evolved—*Challenge*, *The Crusader*, *The Emancipator*, etc. The Federal Government investigated "Radicalism and Sedition Among the Negroes . . ." The 1920's saw a genuinely serious questioning of the American national purpose, a great rash of individual quests for the relationship of man, the individual, to and in the collective badly shaken by world events. Sinclair Lewis' novel, *Main Street*, described the drab, dehumanizing effects of capitalism on American urban life which sent intellectuals by the scores escaping to emigré existence in Paris. Many a Negro soldier wished he had never returned. The twentieth-century revolution was continuing and it sent its currents into odd places.

Claude McKay, the West Indian poet and novelist, preceded Garvey in New York. He was uprooted and a poet-seeker on the move. So was Langston Hughes, out of Joplin, Missouri, who later worked his way to Africa in a romantic search for "lost identity." McKay found a literary home as associate editor of *Liberator* magazine, founded in 1919 by the leading white radicals of the time, one of whom was the famous John Reed, who had recently written *Ten Days That Shook the World*. Here McKay clashed with Michael Gold, who later became the main "cultural" commissar of the newly formed American Communist Party. McKay resigned. The white radicals on the *Liberator* staff made the first attempt to contact Garveyites in Harlem for an "alliance." They failed, and thus the incompatibility of Negro nationalism and white radicalism was first demonstrated. But McKay, too, rejected Garveyism and revealed that the black intellectual did not really understand what was happening and was forming the wrong alliances. The uprooted McKay, always the seeker, took off for Moscow to learn about the "new society" that was causing capitalist nightmares. He was well received, wined and dined, and much was made over the "American" Negro. He hobnobbed with the top leaders of the revolution at the Fourth Congress of the Communist International which he described as "The Pride and Pomp of Proletarian Power." * The black radical always has reasons to doubt. After touring Europe McKay returned *Home to Harlem* (his next book). Some left the United States and did not return for a long time. Josephine Baker, the famous singer-comedienne, came out of St. Louis, was briefly seen on New York stages in Negro shows, but left for Paris to become the famed attraction of the Folies Bergere and a household word in Europe. Some of us heard her perform in the North African desert in World War II, but didn't know her story then.

Creative things blossomed in the 1920's like flowers on a battlefield and the Negro, despite his economic and social disabilities, was going through another phase of his unique experience in the Western world. It was during the years of his harshest oppression on slave plantations that the most divine Negro spirituals were created. Similarly, during the post-World War I years when American racism reached its highest pitch in this century, Negroes again reached for another level of cultural attainment. For the 1920's ushered in the age of Paul Robeson, Countee Cullen, Charles Gilpin, Rose McClendon, and Jean Toomer, whose literary career was short but brilliant before he disappeared. The "New York Wits," a thriving literary movement composed of a blend of older and younger writers, won the critical spotlight for several years. Among them were James Weldon Johnson, mature and experienced, and the younger Wallace Thurman, Jessie Fauset, Rudolph Fisher, and others. Most of them were bitter, ironical and satirical.

Noble Sissle and Eubie Blake brought new stature to the musical theater with *Shuffle Along*, a sensation in 1921 which established a new vogue. Ethel Waters and the immortal Florence Mills sang and performed before thousands whose critical acclaim was boundless. The latter's career was cut short by her early death in 1927; the "peerless child artist" who

* McKay, *A Long Way from Home* (New York: Lee Furman, 1937).

became the "Little Blackbird" had sung a brief song. Florence Mills was the greatest, it is said, but she was representative of scores of Negroes of varying talents of that decade who appeared in search of fulfillment to light up the American cultural scene. Alain Locke, the scholar, chronicled that movement in his study of the Negro Renaissance, *The New Negro*.

American whites were also having a cultural revival and the process by which the whites intervened in the Negro revival, contained it, distorted it, and fastened the incubus of cultural paternalism on this Negro movement has not been told. The great symbol of this process was the folk-opera, *Porgy and Bess*—written by whites for whites who at first did not even think that Negroes were good enough to perform it. Its first recordings were by whites in "black-voice," and it represents the classic example of cultural exploitation practiced by whites on the Negro under capitalist culture. Its distorted social and aesthetic values have been projected ever since as the outstanding "American" musical accomplishment.

Briefly, this describes what the 1920's were like. The lynch mobs fought the Negro for his very life while the white aesthetes ran to Harlem and other places for the unique experience of warming their chilly souls and fingers by his cultural bloodstreams. White writers and aesthetes, such as Eugene O'Neill and Carl Van Vechten, the patron of Negro artists, discovered the creative power of the Negro "passion," hailed it, used it, exploited it, and sold it. The Communists and Michael Gold scolded the Negro artists for falling prey to Van Vechten's "bourgeois" corruption at the Harlem parties of the famous A'Lelia Walker, where white Bohemia from Greenwich Village and black Bohemia made "social" revolution. Of Van Vechten, Langston Hughes wrote: "He never talks grandiloquently about democracy. . . . But he lives it with sincerity and humor." * The Communists who did talk so much about "democracy" never understood the role of Negro art in capitalist society. Michael Gold, who was a great

* Hughes, *The Big Sea* (New York: Alfred A. Knopf, 1945).

admirer of Leon Trotsky (that is, before Stalin expelled him from Russia), had hailed Trotsky's book *Literature and Revolution* when it appeared a few years before. In this book Trotsky had said:

It would be monstrous to conclude that the technique of bourgeois art is not necessary to the worker. Yet there are many who fall into this error. "Give us," they say, "something even pockmarked, but our own." . . . Those who believe in a "pock-marked" art are imbued with contempt for the masses.

Michael Gold never believed this. The Communist white never understood real Negro proletarian art in the 1920's. It was the non-political whites who hailed "The Jazz Age" when the "real" Negro soul was revealed. One exuberant white music critic said that Negro music was an antidote to white "spiritual bankruptcy." But the roots of American spiritual bankruptcy were basically socio-economic, of which race was an ugly surface manifestation, and which was concealed by capitalism's booming prosperity. People could exist, if not really live in the full meaning of the word. Prosperity, especially in the North, made the newly formed Communist Party's appeal to white labor a one-sided dialogue between radical intellectuals and themselves. It was an oddly eclectic period when the elements of the melting pot boiled almost to the rims of the oceans. It was a decade of extreme poverty and riches, hopes, dreams, despair and disillusionment. Culture *did* boom. In fact, there were all the ingredients of "Cultural Revolution" in the making in America—the *real* American revolution of that time, which is yet unfinished. But the primitive Marxists of the 1920's did not comprehend that American capitalism's technological advances in mass cultural media —films, radio, and music records, etc.—was a new capitalistic feature to replace Marx's "religion" as the real modern opium of the people. Instead, in the intense debate on politics vs. art that was raging in the leftwing between John Dos Passos and Michael Gold of the *Liberator*, the Gold faction won out and subordinated the creative artist, who was already being crushed by capitalist culture, to the domination of a "politics" not even relevant to the American scene. Thus did the Marxist leftwing separate itself at the outset from the American mainstream; its influence was forever tangential. The Negro affinity with the leftwing during the 1920's was a mere flirtation and the nationalists went their own way. Radical artists and radical politicians split and went their own ways. As Genevieve Taggard, one of the leading radical poets of the time, put it in her book, *May Days:*

"It is the artist's fault because he is afraid of revolution. It is the propagandist's fault for giving the artist a job he cannot perform. . . . From now on, as long as this division holds our art will have no fertility."

This was written in 1925 as the poet reviewed what the *Liberator* radicals had accomplished before the magazine folded in 1924. And how true her prophecy had been for America! Claude McKay had already seen that Michael Gold's political position on the role of the radical artist was destructive and had resigned from the *Liberator*. The high watermark of the 1920's had been reached. Negro nationalism went into decline after Garvey was jailed in 1927. A. Philip Randolph's radical *Messenger* folded in 1928. Two years later the "Fabulous Twenties" disappeared in the catastrophe of the 1929 economic crash. And all the great issues, trends and expectations that agitated and moved Negroes of the time were left suspended and unresolved in the memories of those who first flourished in that decade.

In the devastating pall of the 1930's depression the great issue among Negroes was sheer survival, which lessened the ardor for nationalism, and "protest" took on other survival meanings. Thus all Negro ideology from the 1920's, whether nationalistic, integrationist, separatist, or cultural, fell under the influence of "New Dealism," or the expedient lure of the white labor movement, or the mystique of the Marxist left given prominence by hard times.

Came World War II and a new generation of Negroes was caught up in another crisis of world capitalism; but the "historical continuity" between them and their elders of 1917 was already broken. The 1930's produced a generation who spoke another language. It was not understood that though the setting for the world conflict that was brewing was on another plane and in another key, the fundamental issues would always be the same in this century. Hence, nationalism the world over would become a universal theme of liberation that one would have to listen to. And the Negro in America, born in 1920, 1930, or even 1940, would hear the echoes of the Du Bois-Garvey conflict over the meaning of nationalism come back to him through other voices from other platforms. Only this time the Negro in America must resolve the conflict between integration and nationalism in a positive way once and for all.

Black Nationalism in America lapses into romantic and escapist moods so long as it depends on emotional slogans, the messianic complex for a leader, or empty militant aggressiveness. Nationalism the world over is being expressed and must be expressed through economic, political, and cultural institutions to make them conform to nationalist aspirations. That these questions are not understood among Negroes is more than obvious. But the ability of the Negro movement to proceed beyond its present impasse depends on the solutions to these problems.

10

Marxism and the Negro

The fact that the Socialist Workers Party (Trotskyite) announced in *The New York Times*, January 14, 1964, that it had nominated a Negro, Clifton DeBerry, to run for President allows us the opportunity to discuss in depth a question that has long been agitating many individuals, friends and foes, concerning the relationship of Marxism to the Negro movement in America today. We emphasize "today" because some years ago it was impossible to be objective about this, inasmuch as the Marxist movement as represented by the Communist Party was so indissolubly linked with practically everything Negroes attempted to do, it was impossible not to find a Communist or two under the bed if one looked earnestly enough. Some very relevant issues about Marxism were thereby distorted and confused by a barrage of heated denials and accusations about the "Red Menace."

The relationship between the Negro movement and the Marxist movement has gone through a succession of qualitative changes on both sides. Today the Negro movement has developed to its highest level of organizational scope and programmatic independence in this century. In the meantime, the dominant trend in American Marxism, the Communist Party, had declined to the low status of a weak, ineffectual sect creating a vacuum in "revolutionary" politics which the Trotskyites are desperately trying to fill. The eclipse of Communist Party Marxism went hand in hand with the decline of labor union radicalism in America. White labor (as differentiated from black labor) went conservative, pro-capitalist and strongly anti-Negro. This created a serious and a practically insoluble dilemma for the Marxist movement because the theory and practice of revolutionary Marxism in America is based on the assumption that white labor, both organized and unorganized, must be a radical, anti-capitalist force in America and must form an alliance with Negroes for the liberation of both labor and the Negro from capitalist exploitation. No matter what the facts of life reveal to the contrary, no matter what the Marxists say or do in terms of momentary tactics, this is what the Marxists believe, and *must* believe or cease functioning as Marxists. For Karl Marx's dictum on this question was that "Labor cannot emancipate itself in the white skin where in the black it is branded." Today, the Trotskyites consider themselves to be the most "orthodox" of Marxists.

The fact that white labor in America today is clearly unsympathetic to the "emancipation" of either Negro workers or the "petit bourgeois" Negroes—or the "intellectuals," as the Marxists are fond of citing—poses, as was said, a serious dilemma for the revolutionary Marxists. On the other hand, the Negro movement's rise to the ascendancy as a radical force in America completely upsets Marxian theory and forces the Marxists to adopt momentary tactics which they do not essentially believe in. In short, they become opportunistic. Here we refer to the white Marxists. The black ones are another question which is currently personified in the case of DeBerry. The realities in America today force the Marxists to deal with the Negro movement as the *de facto* radical force, but this does not hide the fact that the Marxist movement is in a serious crisis. Moreover, the greater the Negro movement becomes as an independent force, the more the Marxists must strive to ally themselves with the Negro movement, and the deeper becomes the crisis for the Marxist movement itself. For the "alliance" it attempts to forge with the

Negro must be one in which the Marxists dominate in order not to be absorbed. This alliance is meant to build the Marxist party, *not* the Negro movement, in order to rescue the Marxists from their own crisis. In the Fall, 1963, issue of the *International Socialistic Review*, the Trotskyites, in discussing the "Freedom Now" Party movement, said:

The present tasks of the SWP in connection with the Negro struggle for liberation are:
(4) To expand and strengthen the party's cadre and forces in the Negro organizations and the civil rights movements, by: (a) recruiting revolutionary Negroes and helping to train them for leadership in the party and mass movements.

Elsewhere in the same issue the Trotskyites said:

In the same way the influence of the colonial revolution . . . upon vanguard elements of the Negro movement has helped prepare the emergence of a new radical left wing. In all these cases, it is the task of revolutionary Marxists to seek to win the best elements of this newly emerging vanguard to Trotskyism.

The *real* issue at stake here is: Who is destined to be the dominant and decisive radical force in America—black radicals or white radicals? And this is a question that will and must be settled outside the scope of any existing theory, Marxian or otherwise, because there is no theory that covers this development. Such an American theory (if it is ever written down) will have to come from blacks. Hence we have the most unprecedented situation yet seen in the Western world —a Marxist movement with a time-honored social theory which does not work out in life with a mass following, and a viable Negro movement of masses in movement which is stymied because it has no social theory or program to take it further. World historical trends have brought both the old Marxist tradition and the new Negro movement face to face on either side of a profound impasse. The Trotskyites, being the most astute of all Marxists, attempt to bridge the chasm by nominating a Negro for President! This desperate gesture

cannot cure the Marxian crisis by enlisting the Negro potential. Moreover, it is not the right remedy for what really ails
the Negro movement at this juncture. It is the same thing as
offering an impoverished man with a wife and ten children
a Palm Beach vacation with some political V.I.P.'s and all the
trimmings just "to get away from it all." What happens to the
man's family? These are some of the reasons why the SWP's
presidential announcement caused so much confusion, anger,
and suspicion within the ranks of the Freedom Now Party
movement concerning "white radical influence." For De-
Berry also linked himself with the Freedom Now Party without the party's permission to do so—a well-known Marxian
type of maneuver in Negro affairs.

As the Negro movement stops and gropes about for its
methods of entering its next stage, this question of Marxism's
influence will keep bobbing up in different situations. It is
therefore necessary for black radical "thinkers" (as opposed
to the "strugglers" or "street-men" as some proudly call themselves) to get a clearer understanding of why the Marxists
act the way they do and why they are in a crisis. The Negro
movement is also in a crisis despite its late achievements—a
crisis which is linked to world developments broader than our
own problems and with roots in events which predate us.

The crisis of Marxism in Europe and North America has
its roots in the confused events of the Russian Revolution of
1917. In the case of the Socialist Workers Party, it was Leon
Trotsky, its guiding revolutionary thinker, who first said that
a socialist revolution was even possible in Russia. This was in
1905 when none of the Russian Marxists agreed to that possibility (not even Lenin). Trotsky was denounced as a ridiculous visionary for saying this, but later won other Russian
Marxists over to his thinking. Thus Trotsky was actually the
theoretical father of the Russian Revolution and Lenin was
its chief architect and leader.

Marxism, as Marx himself developed it, did not foresee or
predict a socialist revolution in a backward agrarian country

such as Russia. According to Marx, the revolution he predicted had to come about in a highly industrialized nation which had necessarily created a large, industrial class of workers, well organized and well trained in the production skills of capitalist industry. The capitalist class of owners would get richer and more compact due to monopoly growths, and the working class would get poorer and poorer to the point where they would revolt and overturn the system and expropriate the owners. Recognizing full well that they were revising the original view of Marx, both Trotsky and Lenin then agreed that if a socialist revolution was possible in Russia —a large agrarian country with only a small degree of industrial development—then this revolution could not stand alone. It would have to be supported by simultaneous revolutions in the advanced nations of Western Europe.

Such did not happen. There *was* a revolution in Russia but it had to stand alone because supporting revolutions elsewhere did not succeed. The result was that the most important single event of the twentieth century was transformed into its gravest tragedy. Moreover, it put the Marxist parties in Western Europe, the United States and elsewhere in a serious dilemma —a dilemma which over the years has deepened into a series of crises. This is because every social revolution that has taken place since the Russian Revolution has also developed out of industrially backward, agrarian, semi-colonial or colonial conditions while the working classes of the advanced white nations became more and more conservative, pro-capitalist and *pro-imperialist*. Moreover, the very fact that the world revolutionary initiative had passed from white nations of the capitalist world to *non-white nations* of the colonial and semi-colonial world introduced another factor in revolutionary politics, the racial factor, which the Western Marxists never admitted should be a factor of any importance at all. Workers, in their opinion, regardless of race and national differences, should all think alike on the question of capitalism and imperialism. The Trotskyites still function under this grand illusion. This is why Clifton DeBerry, in the Socialist Workers Party's announcement in *The New York Times*, had to project his support of the Freedom Now Party on the basis that it is "a step toward independent political action by *labor* and Negroes." By this he means *white labor* and Negroes (emphasis ours). But the leaders of the Freedom Now Party never made any such pronouncement. The Freedom Now Party is a step towards *independent black political action.* Clearly, the Trotskyites do not really want this. Because Marxism is in a crisis in America, they must attempt to project the idea of the Freedom Now Party in their own Marxian image, with the old worn-out, discredited theme of Negro-labor unity.

The Trotskyist theoreticians realize very well that a truly independent black political party which functions irrespective of what white labor does or does not do will further deepen the already serious crisis of Marxist creed in the West. It could show that Marxian ideas about capitalism in advanced countries are not to be taken seriously. A whole raft of Marxian formulations would be further called into question. In any event, none of this would be the fault of the Negro. Rather, it would be the fault of the Marxists for being dishonest with themselves and misleading generation after generation of innocents about the true nature of the Russian Revolution. What was this revolution? What did it achieve? The Communists and the Trotskyites, twin branches of the same withering tree trunk of Western Marxism, have been attacking and accusing each other over these questions for almost forty years. Why?

Let the Trotskyites tell it—it was because Stalin and the bureaucracy "distorted" and "betrayed" the "socialist revolution." But the Trotskyites have only inherited a problem in socialist theory and practice that Trotsky made for himself. Who was it but Trotsky himself who first claimed that such a revolution was possible? All the facts reveal that Trotsky got the very kind of revolution he actually made and deserved and then disowned it because it wasn't really "socialist." He accused the Stalin bureaucracy of "terrorism," of "smothering democracy," of "suppressing the opposition," of taking away the political power of the workers' soviets (councils). But it was Trotsky himself who set such precedents by ordering the brutal suppression of the Kronstadt sailors' revolt of 1921 long before the Stalin bureaucracy set in.

The Russian Revolution logically turned out just the way it had to, considering how and where it was achieved and what the social objectives were it set for itself. Trotsky helped formulate these objectives. Nothing was betrayed—it was the Russian revolutionaries who betrayed themselves, and the Russian masses suffered. After Trotsky's revolution it was imperative that the Communists industrialize a backward country in as short a time as possible, because there can be no socialism until there is enough of an industrial base to socialize (i.e., nationalize). Hence, all the political conflicts between Russian factions centered around the great, pressing problem thrust on them by their own revolutionary seizure of power: How to plan and administer nationalized property, most of which had to be built before it could be administered. This was no ordinary task and the nature of the revolution itself brought to the fore just the type of individuals needed to perform the operation—Stalin and his Stalinists, single-minded, dictatorial, brutal and practical. Not the Trotsky type at all. Trotsky opposed this natural trend of his own revolution and was expelled from Russia.

According to a strict interpretation of Marxian formulations, Trotsky tampered very loosely with Marxian "laws" and reaped the whirlwind. This premise of course absolves Marx of responsibility for the tragic, anti-socialist aspects of the Russian Revolution. The intent is to argue that if Marx was right about the workings of "historical laws" and Trotsky was a Marxist, then something was wrong with Marx's "historical law" formulations. Either this or Trotsky was a Marxist who gravely misinterpreted the functioning of Marxian laws. But it was Marx himself who insisted: "One thing is certain: I am not a Marxist." Meaning what? Are we to take it to mean that because his prophecies about advanced capitalist societies—the white nations—did not materialize, we are entitled to say that Marx was wrong because he failed to properly interpret the very laws he is credited with being the first to discover? If this is the case we then have a strong premise for taking Marx at his own word. If he himself admits he was not a Marxist, then who really was a Marxist after he passed away? Whose claim to be a Marxist must anyone take seriously?

We pose these questions because the Trotskyite nomination of DeBerry for President grows out of the Marxists' belief that the "historical laws" have preordained the Negro movement in America to be used as a kind of transitional social phase leading to the Marxian revolution. In this instance we are to suppose that the Trotskyites are applying the "methods and principles of historical materialism," i.e., the "laws" correctly "before the fact." But even to grant the Marxists, for the sake of argument, the validity of their own Marxian premises, we have to say that their application of the method is no more Marxian than others that failed to bring, in their opinion, Marxian results. This assertion might surprise or even shock the Trotskyites, coming as it does from non-Marxist radicals of the Negro movement. However, it is not that we are prejudiced against "Marxism" per se. We study Marxism in the same way we study objectively all social science schools of thought which claim to be scientific. What we strenuously object to are the methods that the Marxists use.

Fundamental to all Marxist formulations is the *dialectical method of theory and practice*. Marx made it amply clear that his method was dialectical; hence any approach to social life which is not dialectical cannot be Marxian. We would tend to agree with many, such as the late C. Wright Mills, who said of Marx in his book *The Marxists*, "His *method* is a signal and lasting contribution to the best sociological ways of reflection and inquiry available." [Emphasis ours.] We make a distinction here between Marx's original *method* and the *applications* of his latter-day disciples, and we reject these applications precisely because they are not, in our opinion, arrived at by the dialectical method of reflection and inquiry.

How did Marx arrive at his conclusions about the role of the working class in capitalist society? Through the application of one of his prime laws of dialectics: *The law of the unity and conflict of opposites.* In Marxian dialectical processes social phenomena, e.g., classes, ideas, institutions, etc., are not static, but proceed through constant development and change. Capitalistic production creates capitalists and workers (opposites) who come into conflict because their class interests are not identical. Capitalists exploit workers by not paying them their full labor value. Capitalists seek the highest rate of profit through intensified exploitation of the working class. The conflict of interests generates "class struggle," e.g., strikes. Marx observed that the basis of class struggle lies in a contradiction between the methods of production and the social relations of production (private property). These contradictions can be resolved only by a social revolution wherein the working class overthrows or otherwise expropriates the capitalists. This description of dialectics, while simplified, explains why Marxists have considered it to be the historic role of the working class in capitalist societies to usher in the socialist era.

Marx came to these conclusions about the working class in Europe over a hundred years ago, and these predictions still have not been borne out in the advanced capitalist societies of Western Europe and North America. Yet it must be stated that according to his own dialectical premise of analysis Marx had every right to make such predictions. The abundant evidence in the social and political life of Europe in Marx's time pointed to revolution. Moreover, the failure of the social revolution to materialize in the advanced capitalist countries does not at all invalidate Marx's dialectical method. What does become invalid is the subsequent application of the dialectical method by the followers of Marx in the twentieth century. We say this because if we accept the premise of dialectics, then we accept the view that everything in social life is constantly changing, coming into existence, and passing away. But if this dialectical premise is "truth," why then is it assumed that everything in society is subject to the processes of change *except the historical role of the working class in advanced capitalist nations?* Why is this white European, North American labor movement itself exempt from dialectical change in terms of class position, ideology, consciousness, etc., and in terms of what other groups or classes this labor movement fights, supports, or compromises with in the "class struggle"? Has it not become abundantly clear that the white labor movement in the advanced capitalist countries has, indeed, abandoned the Marxian historical role assigned to it? And do we not, therefore, have the right to claim that European and American Marxists who still hew to this white working class line are practicing *mechanistic materialism* rather than *dialectical materialism?*

Classical Marxism rejects all forms of mechanistic materialism because it denies any genuine evolution in the sense of the emergence of new forms and new qualities of new things. Hence the very premise of dialectical thinking demands, in this instance, an admission that new forms of social consciousness can develop within capitalist societies which are of more political relevance than even the social consciousness of the conservative labor movement. Any other conclusion than this is manifestly anti-dialectical. Fundamental to the crisis in all the schools of Western Marxism in the advanced capitalist countries (the white nations) is the crisis that has long gripped the philosophical system of thought, the kernel around which the entire political, economic, cultural, theoretical and programmatic structure of Marxism must form. It is the crisis of dialectical materialism, which was conceived by Marx as a method which had to comprehend the reality of the world, but is no longer able to do so. The reality of world revolutionary events are running far ahead of Marxian theory.

In 1939, when the European white working classes were armed to the teeth along the borderlines of their nations ready to spread war and mayhem against themselves all over Europe and half the world, Trotsky, writing about "Marxism in the United States," could say with the most lofty detachment: "By the example and with the aid of the advanced nations the backward nations will also be carried away into the mainstream of socialism." Here is expressed in the most graphic manner the supreme illusions of the Western (or in Trotsky's case) the "Westernized" white Marxist. They cannot let go of the *idée fixe* of the white working class "saving" the world's humanity. Rooted in their preconceived notions, their undialectical ideas, is the deeply ingrained "white nation ideal." Socialism becomes, like capitalism, a white-nation conception, the great white working-class prerogative. The "white man's burden" shifts from the capitalist's missionaries to the socialist's revolutionaries, whose duty to history is to lift the "backward" peoples from their ignominious state to socialist civilization—even if the whites have to postpone this elevation abroad until they have managed to achieve it at home. But in so doing, the white Marxist's dialectical conceptions of world developments become a distorted image of the reality that is taking place before their very eyes.

The dialectical analyses that Marxists project concerning world developments are, in truth, mechanistically gross distortions of the original dialectical methods of Marx, who was essentially true to his method for his own time and circumstances. It was not the fault of Marx that the world changes, for this was already explicit in dialectics. But the distortions of today's Western Marxism lie in the fact that Marxists treat dialectical materialism only from the standpoint of how the impersonal productive forces develop, how the material forces evolve in society to go through stages from feudalism to capitalism. Or further, how capitalism penetrates the underdeveloped world and brings the latter into the capitalistic network. But Marx pointed out that "In the social production which men carry on they enter into definite relations that are indispensable and *independent* of their will." (Emphasis ours.) Which means that men are subject to the blind forces of the laws of social production unless they become socially conscious of what is happening to them. But how men become socially conscious is a problem of the theory of knowledge and reflection, which is an inseparable category in the dialectical method of social inquiry. If men did not comprehend the nature of material forces, they could not intervene in the process of these forces in order to shape events, i.e., to control blind forces. Thus men, or classes, or groups, or even nations cannot assume the task of "revolutionizing" societies unless they are strategically situated to do so and also have the necessary consciousness to shape events. In this regard, social developments can situate certain classes to shape events, give them the potential; yet such classes can remain without the consciousness or the will to make history. But there are always other classes, and it is the implied function of dialectics to correctly perceive which classes are being brought to the forefront of social consciousness by blind material forces. These classes will become the social force chosen by "historical laws" for historical roles, rather than preconceived classes that history has left behind.

Lenin dealt most thoroughly with how men or classes receive their sense perceptions of the real world; but Marxists today bypass this aspect of dialectics because they believe the social role of the "proletariat" alone settles this question for all time. White Marxists have tried to make world reality fit their dialectical preconceptions; but world developments require that dialectical conceptions embrace world reality. Such conceptions cannot come from the minds of Western Marxists whose philosophical views have become provincially rooted in the crisis-reality of the Western world and cannot transcend the conceptual limitations of that world. They talk revolution, but revolution is being made by others. World social developments are running ahead of their world social theory. William F. Warde says that the principles of historical materialism are applicable everywhere "provided they are applied with full consideration of the facts in each case." But the question Warde does not discuss is: Who is to determine this, those who are making the world revolution or those in the West whose dialectical views are anchored to the lethargy of the white working class?

The Marxian Theory of Knowledge (dialectics) implies that if the backward peoples of the world are carrying themselves into the mainstream of socialism instead of being led there with the aid of the advanced nations as Trotsky saw it, then the backward peoples must replace the white working class as the "chosen people" of the dialectical functionings of world society. Hence if "historical science" or dialectics is to be considered truly scientific, it must be developed and verified in life by the inclusion of the social experiences, the history, the ideas and political philosophies, and the points of view of the backward peoples. In short, it is the social realities of backward peoples that count today the world over. For it is their social consciousness that is determining which way history is moving. Dialectical materialism is no longer the philosophy of the proletariat (i.e., the European proletariat), as the Western Marxists would have it.

It is the fate of the Marxists to be imprisoned within their illusions and that is the source of their crisis. They cannot deal with the race question in America in terms of their dialectical method except superficially, which they must attempt to conceal by all too obvious practices of political expediency, such as the DeBerry nomination. This must, of necessity, bring them into serious conflict with the Negro movement itself, for the spiritual affinities of the Negro movement are not with the white working class of America whose status vis-à-vis American capitalism is qualitatively different from Negroes'.

White labor's heyday is behind them in the history of the
1930's. The American Negro movement is currently a semi-
colonial revolt that is more inspired by events outside America than within it. We can much better explain the Negro
movement's relationship to world developments today by
quoting Leopold Sedar Senghor, president of the African
republic of Senegal, from his pamphlet on *African Socialism:*

We are not communists . . .

The paradox of socialistic construction in communist countries
in the Soviet Union is that it increasingly resembles capitalistic
construction in the United States of America. . . . And it has less
art and freedom of thought.

But a third revolution is taking place, as a reaction against capitalistic and communistic materialism, and which will integrate
moral, if not religious values, with the political and economic
contributions of the two great revolutions. In this revolution the
colored peoples including Negro Africans, must play their part,
they must bring their contribution to the construction of the new
planetary civilization.

Of the Negro American in this "third revolution" Senghor
quotes Paul Morand as saying:

The Negroes have rendered an enormous service to America.
But for them one might have thought that men could not live
without a bank account and a bathtub.

The living facts of the world revolution today are more
persuasive than any revolutionary theory that came out of
western Europe after the death of Marx. We do not hold
Marx accountable for any deviations or distortions that either
history or men have imposed to detract from his doctrine. He
was a towering product of his times and his conclusions about
the society of men tore away the veil that hid the profound
forces that moved societies. His forecasts have been negated
by the very dialectical process he revealed; yet to say, nay
insist, that history should act just the way Marx thought it
would is to do an injustice to a great thinker and to imply
that dialectics is a philosophical fraud, as many have tried to

do (even some who called themselves Marxists). Neither history nor dialectics, which is history's inner clockworks, stands still. Neither is history prone to bestow special historical prerogatives on any special class of people forever. It is the peculiar juxtaposition of time, place, and social circumstances which decide who is going to play the role of prime movers of history. Considering this, we can well understand Marx's own assertion, "I am not a Marxist." It would have been a historical tribute to Marx's self-effacement if Leon Trotsky had admitted: "Though I played fast and loose with Marx's laws, I am no dialectician."

In America today the Socialist Workers Party must strive to conceal the theoretical bankruptcy of Western Marxism by the highly questionable political strategy of entering into political competition with a Negro political party (which is not even established) by presenting a Negro candidate for high office. Some capitalists trying to crash in and exploit the Negro economic market could not have been more crass and opportunistic. But what is revealed here that is more striking than mere crassness is the unreality that hovers around much of what American Marxists do. Basic to all this unreality is the Marxist illusion about the "working class-socialist myth" as it concerns the Russian experience. For the Trotskyites to be forced to let go of this dead issue would be to force the admission that the Trotskyite Fourth International is and always has been rather utopian. For after the seizure of power in Russia by the Bolsheviks and the creation of soviets, the problem became more Kantian than Marxian. The Marxist revolutionary idealists assumed that Marxist elites, once in power, act in accordance with the Kantian "categorical imperative" and perform their functions according to an ethical code of "right conduct." This has been and always will be a problem of revolutions.

The hard American realities and the Negro movement force the Trotskyites to push into the background all these issues that once agitated the international revolutionaries years ago, and to depart from the book and play it pragmatically by jumping on the bandwagon of the black political party idea. But this cannot work. The Freedom Now Party will not permit itself to be used to save the Marxist tradition in America from its own illusions about the nature of social reality today. Clifton DeBerry's role as a Negro Marxist of the Western mold is a contradiction that cannot be solved within the context of the political, social, and cultural philosophy which the Freedom Now Party will attempt to shape. In view of what Leopold Senghor says on the matter of Communism, an American Negro Marxist becomes a rather misplaced figure in the real scheme of things. And his position is made all the more ridiculous if he is involved politically in beating the dead horse issue of Stalinism vs. Trotskyism. What can this really matter to the "third world" in view of the fact that Russia's place and impact on the twentieth-century revolution is established and well-known? Trotskyites in the West have been reduced to the role of ferreting out Stalinist vestiges in world revolutionary currents, analyzing the "distortions" of revolutions already made, and projecting an ideal of the "socialist revolution" that has never been seen or experienced, while rehashing Trotsky's theory of "permanent revolution"—an undialectical concept because everything, including revolutions, is a process of change and development. Trotskyites are the purists of the Marxist camp—astute, analytical, and possessed with the insight to refine, from their own point of view, every aspect of historical materialism. But they cannot escape the theoretical net of the crisis of Marxism in the West. Clifton DeBerry is a mere pawn whom the Trotskyites can attempt to foist on the black political party wearing a king's crown that is much oversized.

The Negro movement possesses inner qualities of different degrees of nationalism and integrationism whose economic, political, cultural, and psychological implications are too much for Marxian theory today. To attempt to confuse these unknown qualities with the white labor mystique of the Marxian left would be to disrupt the natural development of the Freedom Now Party and confuse the real native issues of the Negro with the unreal and irrelevant view of the Marxists concerning American realities. Such intrusions will be fought with every weapon at the FNP's disposal.

The Freedom Now Party is predicated on the ideal of achieving independent black political power in the United States through economic, cultural, and administrative approaches. In this way, the Negro movement in America becomes aligned with the real nature of the world developments involving non-white peoples. In this realignment of world social forces the reality is that white capitalist nations, including all the different classes within these nations from upper bourgeoisie to lower proletariat, have become, in fact, bourgeois and relative middle-class strata vis-à-vis the non-white peoples who have become, in fact, the "world proletarians." This is the real outcome of dialectical processes in our age. If world unity of different peoples is ever to be achieved within a democratic framework, it must be sought along the paths of "social consciousness" that clearly reveal future possibilities rather than the dead ends of the past that we have encountered in radical politics.

11

The Economics of Black Nationalism

The great conflict between W. E. B. Du Bois and Marcus Garvey in the early 1920's had its roots in the earlier leadership rivalry between Du Bois and Booker T. Washington that had agitated Negro leadership circles from the turn of the century until 1915 when Washington died. The basic underlying issues that gave rise to this Washington-Du Bois-Garvey continuum were fundamentally economic, although Negro historians do not tell the story this way. The historians, both Negro and white, have so distorted and confused the issues involving Washington, Du Bois, and Garvey that it is impossible for the present generation to comprehend the real meaning of the roles these leaders played. Du Bois had deep conflicts, first with Washington and then with Garvey. But in reality these conflicts were more concerned with leadership tactics than with certain racial principles involved in such goals as "civil rights," "racial equality," "higher education," "voting rights," "gradualism," "accommodationism," "political power," "back to Africa," "separatism," "integration," "nationalism," etc., etc.

In the attempt to explain the conflicts between Du Bois and his rivals, historians have done the Negro a serious disservice by elaborating on the slogans and the ideologies of these leaders without bothering to explain the fundamental economic compulsions behind these ideologies. Neither Washing-

ton nor Du Bois nor Garvey can be understood in their proper
contexts unless one at the same time comprehends the basic
economic realities and motivations behind Negro class ideologies at any given time. For while it is true that ideologies move
men, it is economics that feeds, clothes, and shelters them.
If ideologies are not understood in terms of economics, then
these ideologies are not understood at all.

Individual leaders can project ideologies of many kinds and
color them with the hues of their own personal aspirations
which very often obscure the very fundamental issues which
are of crucial interest to the people for whom the leaders
speak. Then the historians come along and completely forget
or overlook what the basic issues were for the people in the
mass, and center their attention on the personal characteristics of the leaders. In this fashion was the fundamental economic question that first split Du Bois and Washington, and
then Du Bois and Garvey, almost completely lost in the historical accounts of these men. Thus both the historians and
the partisan followers of these leaders—Washington, Du Bois,
and Garvey—will have you believe that these three leaders
represented three clearly defined and separate schools of racial
thought concerning the Negro in America. But for all these
seeming differences—and they were very marked at certain
times—they were essentially tactical rather than substantive.
This can be shown by the fact that Du Bois wound up essentially agreeing with both Washington and Garvey on the
necessity of the "black economy" which was Washington's
original idea, and then on the "back to Africa" possibility
which was Garvey's main platform—which in turn was a
further elaboration of the black economy theme. In his autobiography *Dusk of Dawn* (1940), W. E. B. Du Bois protested
against the charge that he had any serious differences with
Washington. He stated he was "not against Washington's
ideas," but he insisted on the rights of other Negroes to express their ideas. But Du Bois admitted in his book that Washington was the undisputed leader of ten million Negroes of his

time. If so, who were these "other Negroes" and what were their views on Negro leadership? Du Bois admitted of himself, "I was not a natural leader of men." But then he argued that "the question was as to how far educated Negro opinion in the U.S. was going to have the right and opportunity to guide the Negro group."

Here were the seeds of Du Bois' "talented tenth" elite leadership conception. In other words, Du Bois' conflict with Washington was a leadership power struggle expressed mainly through a difference of theories of Negro education. Du Bois, being a Northern-born product of Fisk, Harvard, and Berlin Universities, would naturally have a much different point of view on education of the Negro than Washington, a Southern product of slave parentage. Du Bois had, thirty-seven years before *Dusk of Dawn* was published, stated much more clearly the real basis of his opposition to Washington's "undisputed leadership." In his *Souls of Black Folk* (1903), he summed up his views on Washington most thoroughly in his essay, "Of Mr. Washington and Others." If one analyzes this essay very thoroughly and also very objectively, without the partisan emotionalism common to most Negroes these days, one can arrive at a clearer comprehension of what the Negro problem is all about and also better understand what is wrong with the Negro movement today, and why this movement is hung up in a programmatic crisis.

Booker T. Washington had stated his position in 1895 with his famous (or infamous—depending on how you look at it) Atlanta Exposition speech. Du Bois quoted him:

In all things purely social we can be as separate as the five fingers, and yet one as the hand in all things essential to mutual progress.

This went down in Negro history as Washington's "Atlanta Compromise" which, according to Du Bois and others (mostly from the safer Northern states), was a "civil rights" sell-out. Washington's soft-pedalling of civil rights agitation in the South was interpreted as counselling Negro submission. And so it might seem if we were to look at the South of 1895 to 1910 and mistake that South for the South of today. Du Bois' attitude was:

Mr. Washington's counsels of submission overlooked certain elements of true manhood, and that his educational programme was unnecessarily narrow.

Notice the reference to education theory. Du Bois did, however, have to recognize that circumstances had elevated Washington to the rank of "the one recognized spokesman of his ten million fellows, and one of the most notable figures in a nation of seventy millions." Therefore, Du Bois softened his criticisms of Washington by saying: "One hesitates, therefore, to criticize a life which, beginning with so little, has done so much." Then Du Bois continues with what is the essence of his conflict with Washington's leadership:

This is an age of unusual *economic development,* and Mr. Washington's programme naturally takes an *economic cast,* becoming a gospel of Work and Money to such an extent as apparently almost completely to overshadow the higher aims of life. (Emphasis ours.)

Here the question of *economics,* the real underlying social compeller, forces its way into the picture. Du Bois, then, elaborates on this economic theme as follows:

[Mr. Washington] is striving nobly to make Negro artisans business men and property owners; but it is utterly impossible, under modern competitive methods, for workingmen and property owners to defend their rights and exist without the right of suffrage.

Washington's views on "suffrage" were expressed as follows:

Brains, property, and character for the Negro will settle the question of civil rights. The best course to pursue in regard to a civil rights bill in the South is to let it alone; let it alone and it will settle itself. Good school teachers and plenty of money to pay them will be more potent in settling the race question than many civil rights bills and investigation committees."

Du Bois countered this by voicing the sentiments of his own and "the other class of Negroes who cannot agree with Mr. Washington . . ." He said, " . . . Such men feel in conscience to ask of this nation three things: (1) the right to vote; (2) civil equality; (3) the education of youth according to ability."

This reference to "education of youth according to ability" was a reflection of the Washington-Du Bois disagreement over education theories. Washington favored "common-school and industrial training" for Negroes in the South and, according to Du Bois, "depreciated institutions of higher learning," which implied that, for most Negroes in the South, what Washington was teaching at Tuskegee was not "higher learning." Here, again, Du Bois' educational "elitism" and "talented tenth" ideas were in conflict with Washington's functional or practical educational ideas as they concerned the mass of illiterate or semi-literate Negroes who had to be fitted into an industrial society. Washington did not see what the study of French, Latin and Greek had to do with enabling the class of Negroes he was most concerned with to earn a "practical" living. This educational controversy is no longer valid today, but it is noteworthy that Carter G. Woodson, in his book *The Miseducation of the Negro* (1933), apparently favored the Washington school of thought and does not mention Du Bois anywhere in his study. Woodson observed that: "The large majority of the Negroes who have put on finishing touches of our best colleges are all but worthless in the development of their people." He speaks of the "contempt for Negroes on the part of educated Negroes" and added that:

Negro scholars taught in universities outside the South—languages, mathematics, and science—may serve well. . . . But what has been taught in economics, history, literature, religion, philosophy is propaganda and cant and a waste of time and has misdirected Negroes thus trained.

This was, without a doubt, a slap at the Du Bois "talented tenth" idea. Woodson added that classical education produced no Negro thinkers or philosophers. Woodson did not disagree with Washington's "industrial education" theory in principle, but observed that it resulted in no uplift of Negroes as artisans and mechanics because of lack of facilities and obsolete methods and techniques which did not equip Negroes to keep up with rapid changes in industrial techniques based on the division of labor. As was to be expected the inevitable economics of the race question found its way into Woodson's remarks. He observed that:

In the schools of business administration Negroes are trained exclusively in the psychology of and economics of Wall Street and are, therefore, made to despise the opportunities to run ice wagons, push banana carts . . . among their own people. Foreigners, who have not studied economics but have studied Negroes, take up this business and grow rich.

From all of this it must be seen that the Washington-Du Bois controversy over race leadership and politics was fundamentally economic, but fought out in terms of rivalry over education theories mainly because the Washington school of thought was getting the lion's share of white philanthropy for Negro education. Washington had more pull with the "big white folks" than Du Bois. But Washington's position in all this forced him to soft-pedal civil rights and politics to placate Southern opinion in order to further his own economic platform, which he considered more important than civil rights. The latter, he felt, could not be won under Southern conditions of that time. Du Bois, as we shall see later, did not really disagree with Washington over economics, but had to force Washington's hand on civil rights by posing (1) the right to vote; (2) civic equality; and (3) higher education, as a civil rights program. This Du Bois position on civil rights soon flowered into the Niagara Movement—a protest group composed of the very small number of articulate critics of Washington. This dissident group was soon absorbed by white

liberals and assorted socialists to form the NAACP. Thus it
was that the official civil rights protest movement was forever
separated from the basic economics of the Negro situation in
America as first posited by Booker T. Washington and given
organizational form in the National Negro Business League
established by him in 1900. This business league still exists in
Washington, D.C.

Time has proven that the issues first raised by Washington
and Du Bois are still very much with us. Neither the "civil
rights" of Du Bois nor the "economics" of Washington has
won a full measure of acceptance, and the "education" problem on another level is more a bone of civil contention among
the races than ever before. Moreover, even Du Bois' educational elitism was given a critical downgrading by Carter G.
Woodson, the founder of Negro History Week and the Association for the Study of Negro Life and History. But fundamental to all issues growing out of the original clash
between Washington and Du Bois is the central fact that has
still not been resolved in Negro thinking: It is impossible to
separate civil rights from the economics of the problem of
Negro existence in America. And by civil rights and economics we do not simply mean the question of jobs and discrimination in employment. The question goes much deeper.
This was brought home to Du Bois more profoundly several
years after his conflict with Washington when the Garvey
Movement came into being. For Garvey, even before he came
to America, had been a student of Booker T. Washington's
economics, which Du Bois had already said grew out of "an
age of unusual economic development."

This was an important observation on the part of Du Bois,
for it is assumed by too many people of various political per-
suasions (both Negro and white) that there is something very
strange in the idea that Negroes would want to develop a
capitalist class. Or that it is even necessary in terms of capitalist development that such a class should come into existence,
or that Negroes should strive to cultivate a capitalist (bour-

geois) ideology even though a real capitalist class well entrenched in the corporate structure of American capitalism
is never achieved. This has been a unique problem for the
American Negro. We have cultivated among us a very strong
bourgeois outlook among our articulate, educated classes. But
this bourgeois mentality is not matched by any parallel
achievements as capitalist producers, entrepreneurs, or managers. Hence, this bourgeois mentality becomes, in many
ways, a troublesome intellectual abnormality in many Negroes. These bourgeois trappings are worn like expensive but
ill-fitting clothes by people who harbor exaggerated bourgeois ideals but who lack the substance to back up these ideals.
It would not be half so bad if these bourgeois ideals grew out
of a profound knowledge of economic thought—of which the
public libraries are full. But our bourgeois-oriented Negroes
are, economics-wise, the most ill-equipped of all people. They
clutter up the Negro civil rights movement with their strident
protests and really believe that American capitalism is going
to grant them racial equality, while they remain in blithe ignorance of the inner workings of American capitalism.

These Negroes have been kept in ignorance about economic realities not only by themselves but by their white
liberal, radical, and "revolutionary" friends from left of center to left. The liberals have promised them "full integration"
without economic integration above the level of token jobs,
which makes it a lie. The white leftists have advised them to
forget about the capitalist economics of the market place today and place their hopes on "socialism" tomorrow, which is
a dishonest deception. It took Du Bois almost a lifetime to see
through the first lie of the white liberals concerning "civil
rights." Washington saw through that tale by pure common-
sense reasoning. But then Du Bois had much longer to live
than Washington, a much broader life's canvas to paint on,
and more horizons to conquer. Right after Washington died,
Garvey came on the scene. Hence, Washington's original
"black economy" theories took on broader implications than

he gave them in 1900. For now the "black economy" theory was pushed onto the international scene and had to include the continent of Africa and the American Negro's relationships to that continent.

Characteristically, W. E. B. Du Bois had already seen the implications of Africa's incipient emergence into international politics at the beginning of World War I. In 1915, the year Washington died, Du Bois published an article in the *Atlantic Monthly* entitled "The African Roots of the War." Du Bois had seen this war brewing for several years. But before Garvey arrived on the scene, it is very doubtful if Du Bois could have foreseen that African nationalism, which would be heightened by this war, would have a parallel effect on those of African descent in the Western world to the extent that was evidenced in the Garvey Movement. As one writer has said, "Until 1914, Pan-Africanism, if not forgotten, was dormant amongst Negro Americans, probably because the increase of colour problems in the United States temporarily narrowed their horizons."

Residual forms of "Pan-Africanism" had, since the end of the Civil War, lain dormant among the American Negroes. Most of them were the romantic "back to Africa" dream kind of African recall and were often hotly opposed by Negro politicians. But the opening of World War I reactivated those historical ties between Africa and the American Negro which had been tediously and carefully cultivated by various Negro seers, leaders, missionaries, educators, even soldiers of fortune, in search of the regeneration of the "African personality." Among them was Booker T. Washington himself who, though no great militant in his views, had influenced many Africans with his self-help educational and economic policies. Washington had organized the African Union Company scheme for promoting trade between American Negroes and the Gold Coast, which was destroyed by the World War I interruption of Atlantic Ocean trade routes. This again has bearing on Du Bois' observation that Washington was influenced by "an age of unusual economic development," because everything Washington pursued was "cast in an economic mold." And it was in this fashion that Washington actually laid the basic economic foundation and motivation for Negro nationalism in America even though he himself was no militant nationalist. Washington was the Negro bourgeois prophet par excellence, which is an important fact to keep in mind when discussing nationalism of any kind. For nationalism is usually bourgeois in its origins. It is only after bourgeois leaders express nationalist politico-economic platforms and ideologies that the masses of people pick up the slogans and the ideals and support such leaders.

The reason why it is difficult to understand the bourgeois motivations and origins of black nationalism in the United States is because of the uneven, distorted, stunted and fragmented development of the Negro bourgeoisie. In viewing the phenomenon of black nationalism, people are so misled by the mystiques and racial ideologies expressed by nationalism that they overlook the underlying economic motivations behind the slogans.

Thus Negro nationalism in America could not have arisen under the leadership of Marcus Garvey without an economic philosophy having been laid down by Booker T. Washington. And Marcus Garvey could not have been inspired to put Washington's philosophy into practice without the added ingredient of African nationalism, given impetus of release through the international shock of World War I, which shook European imperial capitalism to its very foundations. It was not for nothing that Du Bois was moved to describe World War I in terms of its "African roots." For this war was fought over little else but the African treasure trove of untold natural wealth and colonial labor. Once African nationalism was released in Africa it could not help but leap the ocean and send its currents through many peoples of African descent scattered throughout the Western Hemisphere. For the seeds had been planted long before. What was needed now was merely an economic framework, an economic conception, a racial philosophy, a messianic leader, a world in an uproar, and world capitalism tottering on the brink and striving to maintain itself. The time was ripe for a Garvey, and when he arrived on the scene the old conflict between Washington and Du Bois over "economics" vs. "civil rights" took a qualitative leap to another level of leadership conflict.

In America Du Bois was still committed to the civil rights stand of the NAACP, which he had created in opposition to Washington. But now Washington's economic philosophy, having been negated in practice because the Negro bourgeoisie could not prevail against the overwhelming power of American capitalist institutions and develop Washington's ideas of a black economy, was taken over by Garvey with the added ingredient of black nationalism geared to an organizational vehicle of trade, commerce, steamship lines, land, resources, businesses big and small, African nations' revival, black unity, "Back to Africa," and universal improvement of the Negro race. The only real difference between Washington's Gold Coast African Union Company for two-way trade and Garvey's dream was that Garvey's was more grandiose and dynamic. Garvey and Du Bois clashed bitterly despite the fact that both of them were "Pan-Africanists" because Du Bois' Pan-Africanism was of a different blend. Moreover, Garvey's Pan-Africanism was a dire challenge to Du Bois' strongly white-influenced civil rights movement, which was no threat at all to American capitalist institutions. Du Bois was not yet a revolutionary, but Garvey's movement was fundamentally revolutionary and a threat to American capitalism at home and European capitalism in Africa—despite the fact that it was bourgeois in motivation. Hence, Du Bois had to fight Garvey. Yet, whatever slogans and verbal criticisms were used by the two antagonists against each other, basic to all was the underlying unsolved problem of the Negro's economic fate under American capitalism. One twentieth-century revolutionary, Josef Stalin, was most apt when he said: "The market is the first school in which the bourgeoisie learns its nationalism." For many years of his life Du Bois was not much interested in the economics of the market place. In fact, he had complained that Booker T. Washington's "gospel of Work and Money" overshadowed too much the "higher aims of life."

12

The Blacks and the Idea of Revolt
(Les Noirs et l'idée de révolte)

The nearest living contact I have ever had with French culture was in North Africa during World War II. I took part in the Anglo-American landings in Oran, Algeria, in November, 1942. During those fateful days few if any of us Americans were intellectually or politically prepared for what we encountered in French North Africa. We knew next to nothing of North Africa's ethnic composition, history, or politics. Some of us were vaguely aware that North Africa and, indeed, all Africa, was under European rule; but what this implied in human relationships was remote from our experiences. We learned things very fast.

As for myself, being an American black, the Army had rudely opened up to me the grand new world outside the limits of the United States. My shipload of troops had come in from England, where my regiment had arrived the previous July. We had already been "seasoned" for overseas service. Unlike the troops who came into North Africa directly from the States, we had already run the North Atlantic convoy gauntlet. We had met the British, the Scotch, and the Irish, and also the "Free French" and the "Free Poles" and others in British pubs and dancehalls. But in Oran we met something we didn't at all expect and that was the resistance of Vichy France, which gave us a rather hot welcome. The Vichyite military forces had no respect at all for the conspicuous American flags we had stitched on our shoulders as a sign of "liberation." Needless to say, there were many American blacks in North Africa who had serious qualms about serving under that same flag, but there were very few black conscientious objectors before the fact—the bitching began after being drafted. Today, twenty-four years later, things are different. The war in Vietnam has, for the American Negro, accentuated the world's "race conflict," and we see today young Negroes resisting the draft on the premise that they object to fighting a race war for "democratic" principles that have never applied to them in America. My generation also learned something about war and race in North Africa; yet it would be difficult to explain to the current generation that World War II was a different kind of a war.

The world as we know it today is in the throes of revolution and counter-revolution as a result of World War II. But as I look back to those tensely exciting and dangerous days of the North African landings I am amazed at how innocent I was of what it all entailed; how blind and untutored we were; how little we surmised of what the aftermath of World War II would be like. The Army was the beginning of my real education about the reality of being black. Before the war, being black in America was a commonplace bore, a provincial American social hazard of no particular interest or meaning beyond the shores of the Atlantic. It was simply a national American disability—a built-in disadvantage to us all that we had to put up with, similar to a people that has to endure the constant imminence of droughts, floods, famines, or native pestilences. Race in America is her greatest "natural calamity," but it has today become internationalized into a global scandal because she is so rich in everything else, including democratic pretensions. A global war has made all this a global fact. But it is also a fact that it took this global war to initiate a personal metamorphosis that has culminated in what I am in 1966, as an American black.

This metamorphosis did not actually begin in Oran but in

England. Leaving England on October 29 to whither we knew not, I had left the compensations of a wartime romance in Liverpool. She was intensely and typically English and highly romantic. There was I acting out a wartime love affair similar to those I had seen in movies about World War I, except that my truth was stranger than film fiction. It all ended with the usual vows about "meeting again after it is all over over there," which was, of course, the sheerest nonsense inasmuch as I was certain we were all doomed. I said to myself: For an Army group we are obliged to do an awful lot of sea voyaging; how long will our luck hold out? In England life had been a tolerable mixture of hard soldiering and frenetic loving, but in Oran we heard the hard-bitten, rasping voice of a regular Army colonel admonishing us that "The party is over, this is War!" We marched into the fallen city of Oran from Mers-el-Kebir some distance west of the main city. On the way we saw our first representations of French North Africa's race problem—Arabs, or as our black American natives would say—"*Ay*-rabs." The ones in uniform scared hell out of most of us because they looked so gloomy and quietly ferocious. Again, visions of old American movies came to mind—the saga of "Beau Geste," Foreign Legion battles on the sands of the Sahara, Ronald Colman, shots of beleaguered French officers rallying their troops against Arab onslaughts while blood ran in the sands under a sweltering sun. I was certain that just beyond the high rocks on the Mediterranean coast was the Sahara, from whence a sandstorm would come any moment and blow us all back into the sea. This does not begin to describe how ignorant we were.

Later many of us were surprised to find that Oran was a fair-sized cosmopolitan city we had simply never heard about in our geography lessons. I could tell of many incidents that happened when Oran fell to the Allies, but the one that made the deepest impression on me was when I and my closest Army buddy met two Arab women who stopped us and inquired in broken French if *we were also Arab*. No, we were Americans, we said. But they insisted that we were Arab *but didn't know it because our fathers had been stolen from Africa many years ago*. This surprised us because our ingrained provincialism about America made us feel impossibly remote from these people. But it was later a severe jolt to our established perspectives when we discovered that these people were able to learn English faster than we could learn French or Arabic. Their responses were more alert to us than ours to them. Immediately Army orders came down to the effect that we ought not to associate too much with the Arabs. Then we learned that the French prejudice against the Arab was as intense as the American white prejudice against Negroes. The French were more outraged than the Americans when they saw Negroes associating with Arabs. The resultant race conflict among American blacks, American whites, French and Arabs was very enlightening and had a curious amalgam of racial and political overtones.

A soldier is, for the most part, in a separate world from the ways of the civilians, even in a country where the coercive power of his own Army prevails. I have since understood that despite being face to face with a colonialism that was new to our experience, what we saw were merely the surface manifestations. We were never able to get inside the intimate areas of native response to the colonial situation. We were outsiders who had to subsist on very tentative alliances with the French and Arabs. I have often wished I had been schooled on North Africa prior to arriving, because by the time I had begun to learn how to dig into the secrets of North African existence, we were shipped to Italy. But I had seen the condition of the Arab population and had spoken with several Algerians who revealed the existence of a mysterious underground resistance movement that never showed its face. Some of them were black marketeers who reasoned that since Negro troops handled most of the Army's supplies, friendly contacts with Negro soldiers were a political necessity. They were right.

After my fifteen months' experience in North Africa, I was a changed political animal. I went to Italy in February, 1944, and returned to the United States in May, 1945. The reason I did not get to France on the southern invasion route was that my outfit had been declared physically unfit by that time. Back in the States I immediately plunged into the politics of the radical left on the question of the Negro in American society. (This was a direct result of my contacts with Italian Partisans in Italy, most of whom were Communists.) Here began my first scholarly aquaintance with French history, politics, and literature. I filled my mind with Marxian interpretations of the French Revolution—*The Civil War in France*, *The Eighteenth Brumaire of Louis Bonaparte*, *The Class Struggles in France (1848–1850)*, etc. There was *Toward Singing Tomorrows* by Gabriel Peri, the poetry of Louis Aragon. And then I came across *Literature of the Graveyard* by Roger Garaudy, the critical assault on Jean Paul Sartre, François Mauriac, André Malraux, and Arthur Koestler. M. Garaudy was described on this pamphlet as a member of the French National Assembly. He described Sartre as a "false prophet," François Mauriac a "great writer in bondage," spoke of "The Death Mask of André Malraux," and of Arthur Koestler as "The Lie in Its Pure State."

Garaudy's pamphlet was printed in America in 1948 and, being an aspiring writer myself, I was inwardly puzzled and bothered by what he said. But I accepted it inasmuch as it was the official line of the radical left on what in literature should be assigned to the nether regions. Four years later, I ran up against Communist Party literary dictation and censorship towards Negro aesthetics. This, among other grievances on my part, precipitated my departure from the radical left. It took me about eight years to finally decide that the Communists had no program for the American blacks. The Communist influence on Negro writers was retarding and stifling. Communist social theory left no room for the critical Negro theorist to deal with Marxist inadequacies on the facts of Negro existence—which were many and glaring. I was forced to quit the left in order to reorient myself on my own reality in America, which for me is an indictment of the Communist Party for its grave mishandling of the Negro question in this country. This is not to say that I did not profit from my exposure to Marxism. In fact, my postwar Marxist experience, added to my foreign exposures, made me a better rounded fellow who, around 1953, stepped out into open society to fight my special problem alone. But I had learned how to write and to think inside the left, and it stamped me as the kind of writer I was to become—one with many pressing things to say and many ikons to smash, but with no literary outlets through which to launch an attack. So I carried with me into my ivory tower (a new experience) twelve years of accumulated impressions to mull over. Even then, the war was still fresh. My personal biographical memory-file was filled with people, places, and impressions which would always remain alive. The fact that I met Josephine Baker for the first time in North Africa in 1943, and again in New York around 1951 was like the fusing of time, place and circumstances into one continuum that defied the division of eras. During the same time a Monsieur Courtade—Pierre, I believe—the correspondent from L'Humanité, visited New York where I met him at a leftwing press conference. His dapper and continental manners made me believe that French Communists were, happily, not sectarian and drab, depersonalized priests such as were many American Communists. These austere people frowned on an article I wrote about Josephine Baker's New York performance. They admonished me that Baker was a "Gaullist" during the war, which made her suspect politically. I replied that none of them had been in North Africa when Josephine Baker left a sick bed to entertain Allied troops in the desert. My descent from favor in the radical left was steady and inevitable. I don't know what the French Communists thought of Josephine Baker, and it did not occur to me ask Monsieur Courtade of L'Humanité.

What opened my eyes to some of the issues of French Communism was my introduction to the ideas of Albert Camus. During the 1950's Camus had attained a unique stature in America, especially among the intellectuals left stranded on the shores of doubt and empty anxiety over their disaffection with the radical left. Camus' *The Rebel* became something of a new bible that offered many renegades from the true faith a soul-comforting rationalization and a one-way literary ticket back from perdition. It appears that Camus' retreat from Communism came too late for him to be consigned to the graveyard by Roger Garaudy. At any rate, Camus was the reason many American ex-Communist intellectuals could stride by Communist Party headquarters in New York with their heads held high in proud if not sad disdain. I think I must have read and reread *The Rebel* a dozen times. For a long spell it was one of the chief topics of random analysis by the eclectic intelligentsia of the coffee shops of Greenwich Village. To be able to quote Camus was a modish sign of being (or having been) politically or literarily (and intellectually) engagé. The majority of these Camusian "rebels" were, of course, white. They had much to be rebellious about, but found it extremely difficult to be "revolutionary" against the bourgeois Establishment. Theirs was a revolt in terms of aesthetics, sex, interracialism, life-styles, the cult of the *materia medica* of narcotic elixirs, the movement of "beat" * spirituality, etc., all of which were the ingredients of nonconformism, American style.

After reading Sartre's 1945 Paris lecture on the meaning of existentialism, I began to think that the American "Left Bank" movement of Greenwich Village, San Francisco, etc., was an American version of existentialism in practice without theory (Americans abhor theories and theorizing). American philosophers like Peirce, James, and Dewey—all pragmatists—once

---

* Beat—a word out of the lexicon of Negro Harlem of the late 1930's. It entered the language of the whites via jazz, where it became "Beatnik." Its Negro meaning was "drab, ugly, poor."

upon a time glorified as truly American the practical results of native pragmatism. But the American refusal to sanction theoretics has today become the idea behind the intellectual defense of social status quo. For this reason and others, American social rebels can find much to console their point of view in Camusian ideas. This is because, as Camus himself said, a rebellion (or a rebellious mood) "is only the movement that leads from individual experience into the realm of ideas." But to transform rebellious ideas into revolutionary social action is a horse of another color. To achieve this, Camus said, is to "attempt to shape action to ideas, to fit the world into a theoretic frame." I have always liked this phrase of Camus because it relates so well to the American intellectual and creative (and social) impasse. The white American intellectual is caught in the trap of this theoretic impasse that Camus describes, but he cannot admit this even when intuitively aware of the nature of his ideological cul-de-sac.

To be really engagé today the intellectual must be involved in the Negro civil rights movement on some level (for or against). There is, of course, our "dirty war" in Vietnam, which has absorbed the moral imperatives of our intelligentsia. But, apropos of Camus, no one is able to oppose American involvement in Vietnam in a revolutionary manner. Intellectual opposition is carried out on the level of studied dissent. Actually, the revolutionary potential on the American scene lies within the rebellious capabilities of the Negro. Hence, American race components become the main clue to the reasons why white intellectuals do not and cannot transcend what Camus called the rebellion of "a fruitless struggle with facts, of an obscure protest which involves neither methods nor reasons." To be sure, even the Negro struggle has barely begun to approach a revolutionary intensity. The methodology of this struggle has not even acquired a "theoretic frame." This is fundamentally because the American Negro has been conditioned to strive for the exact same status in politics and social status long ago achieved by the whites.

This means that his revolutionary disenchantment with values capitalistic will not be engendered by a surfeit of material surplus leaving him blasé, but through the realization that a larger slice of the integrationist pie is not in the capitalistic cards. It is not, therefore, surprising that many of the young Negro activists in the Students' Non-violent Coordinating Committee (SNCC) began reading Camus' *The Rebel* a few years back. Chief among these was Bob Moses, one of the leading young Negro radicals in the Mississippi freedom movement, who recently went to Africa in search of the sources of his "identity." However, for the young Negro generation, Camus is difficult fare, and it is problematical how much relevance to their own situation and *Weltanschauung* they will find in Camus. Relevance there is, but all the sources of Camus' philosophical conclusions are thoroughly and historically Western, as are all his conceptions of "freedom." For the Negro in America this Western idea of freedom has been both and at once a fervent hope and a dire delusion. It is only Camus' "metaphysical rebellion" that appears to have any connotations immediately applicable to the Negro revolt in America.

Within the purview of Camus' thought metaphysical rebellion would seem to be the Negro's point of departure in his quest for freedom. From that stance onwards it would seem that "historical rebellion" as described by Camus is a philosophical distillation that is so thoroughly Western (and so morally discredited by the Russian end-product of that historical quest) as to be nonapplicable to the Negro without some further philosophical and ethical refinements. "Metaphysical rebellion is the movement by which man protests against his condition and against the whole of creation," wrote Camus in *The Rebel*. Before that he asked:

What is a rebel? A man who says no, but whose refusal does not imply a renunciation. . . . A slave who has taken orders all his life suddenly decides that he cannot obey some new command.

However:

The slave who opposes his master is not concerned, let us note, with repudiating his master as a human being. He repudiates him as a master.

Yet:

The slave protests against the condition in which he finds himself within his state of slavery; the metaphysical rebel protests against the condition in which he finds himself as a man.

The Negro experience in America blurs the fine distinctions that existed in Camus' point of view on the essence of rebellion. In American terms the Negro revolt is highly metaphysical and even existential in many respects. But where does the Negro in America go from there? (He has no philosophers.) If it is true, as Camus claimed, that all revolutionary principles of the Western tradition, which is to say, the ebb and flow of historical rebellion, have been tried and found morally wanting and jeopardized in advance by doubtful ends, then to where must the Negro's radical momentum take him once he assumes the fateful position of metaphysical rebellion? One can still swear by the abiding principles of Christianity even when this faith has attached itself to the banners of war and imperialism. But Camus wanted no more to do with the Lenins after historical rebellion ended with Stalinism. Said he in *The Rebel*: "Revolution, in the dilemma into which it has been led by its bourgeois opponents and its nihilist supporters, is nothing but slavery. Unless it changes its principles and its path, it can have no other final result than servile rebellions, obliterated in blood or the hideous prospect of atomic suicide." On this point, Raymond Aron, of whom more later, was more precise, skeptical, and therefore less passionately moral. He called the whole prospect, "The Myth of the Revolution." * But the problem this all presages for

* Aron, *The Opium of the Intellectuals* (New York: Norton paperback, 1962).

the Negro revolt in America is clear and also most unprecedented. If the Negro revolt proceeds from metaphysical rebellion to revolutionary social action (with a theoretic frame),
the Negro must change the revolutionary "principles and its
path" in order to avoid ending up with another form of slavery. But for the Negro to do this would be not only a historical disaster but also a joke. In such an eventuality the Negro
in America would be doomed to wait the arrival of a metaphysical Abraham Lincoln in the form of another Hegel. It
simply wouldn't be worth all the historical travail—unless one
would say that any kind of slavery is better than atomic suicide ("Better red than dead"). The question is: Can the Negro in America change the principles, the path, the style, the
content, the aims, etc., of social revolution? It would have
been impossible for such a question to have occurred to me
during or immediately after World War II. I understand that
such heresies *did* occur to Albert Camus even as a director
of *Combat* during the Resistance.

I would wager that Camus' full doubts about the contemporary virtue of the materialistic scheme of historical rebellion
in the Western tradition must have arrived at the same time
that my own doubts arose from the Negro point of view. I
note that *The Rebel* was copyrighted in France in 1951 as
L'Homme Révolté. It did not appear in English until 1956
(the year of the 20th Congress Report in Moscow). My real
disaffection set in about 1951, and by 1953 I bid adieu to the
radical left. But even in the late 1940's I already sensed that
there was something profoundly wrong about the left's approach to the Negro. I could not abstract my own differences
with Marxian practices and cast them in a theoretic frame.
My own heretical tendencies could not then carry me that far
from political grace. What was wrong with America? With
us . . . we . . . them? In my newly aquired "ivory tower," I
would think back to the War, to North Africa, to Italy, to Europe. How could *I* write off the Italian Partisans, those heroes,
many of them Communists? How could one write off the

Italian Communist Party or the French? Not to speak of the Chinese! But Camus wrote off the theoretic frame of the Communist parties. What a man, thought I. But Albert Camus, a Western intellectual, could afford such presumptuous heresies. He had intellectual and social status in his own country (with or without the tenets of historical rebellion). But what the hell am I, an American black, in America *without* a philosophy of rebellion? Camus was born in Algiers, but he was a man of France in all his fibers, and to him Algeria was *also* France. When I read his novel *The Plague*, I noted that there was not a single Arab character of any important dimensions—and the story was set in Oran, which is full of Arabs. I wondered, once, what the Arab women, who told me I was really an Arab displaced by historical kidnapping, woud have said to Camus, who was certainly not a kidnapped Frenchman. Unlike my ancestors coming to America from Africa, the ancestors of Camus went to Algeria of their own free will to settle. They remained, of course, safely situated within the national prestige and glory of France. For them, when the Algerian Revolution began *in* Algeria, it was not *for* Algeria but was *against* the prestige and the glory of France. This Algerian rebellion was not cast in the same mold of the "historical rebellion" that Camus deprecated in *The Rebel*. This was a new thing in revolutionary styles, and I wondered to myself (in my ivory tower) what those two Arab women I met on the Rue Mostegenem in Oran, 1942, were doing in the late 1950's?

What I am trying to say is this: Because I am black, the rebellion in Algeria and in other parts of Africa made it impossible for me, in America, to agree with Camus on the Western version of "historical rebellion" *and leave it at that.* Anyone who does not understand why Camus was so silent in the face of French excesses in attempting to put down the Algerian rebellion has not seriously read *The Rebel*, and has not objectively followed the man's philosophical reasoning on revolution. Camus gave moral sanction to the revolt of a

slave just so long as it remained on a metaphysical plane. Anything beyond this posture engendered excesses and violence
that consumed both the slave and the slavemaster in a vortex
of mutual moral and spiritual debasement. In such a fateful
clash the slave grasps for enough power to bend his erstwhile
master to his liberated will, and thereby himself becomes an
insensate being corrupted by power. Camus said:

We now know, at the end of this long inquiry into rebellion and
nihilism, that rebellion with no other limits but historical expediency signifies unlimited slavery. To escape this fate the revolutionary mind, if it wants to remain alive, must therefore return
again to the sources of rebellion and draw its inspiration from the
only system of thought which is faithful to its origins: thought
that recognizes limits.

What troubled, immobilized, and silenced Camus was that
the rebellion in his beloved French Algeria was a catastrophe
of unlimited violence in which neither side gave any quarter
nor recognized any limits. No doubt Camus's long exposé in
May, 1939 of the terrible living conditions of the Kabyle
tribes (his Alger-Republicain period) symbolized his heart-
felt concern that the tribes receive "justice," a "fair deal,"
etc. (Didn't Camus understand that imperialism is intrinsically
and generically the direct opposite of justice?) He saw, very
clearly, that if these conditions were not ameliorated the
French would be faced with an Arab revolt that might lead
to a revolution. One of his friendly critics quoted Camus as
having once said, "I have with Algeria a love-affair which undoubtedly will never end." North Africa, this critic said, "led
Camus to an immediate enjoyment of life, to a kind of volup-
tuous, never satiated epicureanism masterfully expressed in the
four essays of *Noces*," in which he said:

I like this life . . . and would like to talk about it in freedom; it
gives me pride in my human condition. Yet I was often told:
"There is nothing to be proud about!" Indeed, I do believe there
are many reasons to be proud: the sun, the sea, my heart leaping

with youth, my strong and salty body, and this huge decor where tenderness and glory mingle in yellow and blue.*

When Camus departed from Algiers in the late thirties, his destination was a "sad, dark, and fear-stricken Europe." Naturally, a man conditioned by such idyllic concentrations of his homeland would react to the prospects of a revolution in Algeria as if it were an act of sacrilege. One does not rip the canvas of a beautiful painting with knives and splatter it with blood. Such social vandalism was to be expected in Europe, the home of "historical rebellion." When France fell to the Germans Camus joined the Resistance as if it were ordained by fate rather than national oppression. It was simply 1870 and 1914 all over again, except that Camus' theme for resistance to Nazism was (it seems) philosophically universalist rather than nationalist. Nazism was not simply Hitlerism; it was, for Camus, the logical outcome of the German philosophers of history—principally Nietzsche and Hegel whose "deification of history" furnished the ingredients of "historical rebellion" which ended apocalyptically with Germany in the role of what he called "the supreme example of Western Nihilism." But with Germany reduced to rubble and political bifurcation, Camus was faced with the prospect of seeing the phoenix of revolution reborn, not from the ashes of Central Europe, but in his colorful and sun-kissed Algeria across the blue Mediterranean. Here would appear another Resistance movement he could not join either actively or philosophically. He had done his bit by exposing the effects of French colonialism before the war. He demanded reforms as a preventive against the threat of revolution without moral limits. One of Camus's critics remarked:

If French authorities had followed the recommendations Camus made it is not impossible that the post-war outbreaks and the rebellion in Algeria might have been prevented. In any case, the

* Georges J. Joyeaux, "Camus in North Africa," Yale French Studies, #25, Spring, 1960 pp. 110–19 (Yale University Study of Camus).

trial articles and the series on Kabylia are further evidence of the continuity and integrity of his ethical stand.*

No doubt Camus really, honestly, believed this. Ethical man that he was, I, as an American Negro, cannot condemn him. I can only shake my head with grave misgivings about his grasp of the compulsions towards a kind of rebellion that was as real and persuasive as the nihilistic Western revolution, but destined to be cast in another "historical" context—the African, the "East," etc.; i.e. the underdeveloped world. Does this historical rebellion of the "East" which cannot rest content with "metaphysics" have any relation to the American Negro? A lot of people in America, both black and white, are debating this question on different levels. Many of them are denying and affirming this revolutionary kinship. Some say, disdainfully, that the American Negro has little or no real ties with the African revolution. Others cite the various expressions of "racial identification" with the East (rather than the West) as potent factors in the Negro's politics to-day, even if it is metaphysical. All through the late 1950's I could not help but remember those two Arab women in Oran in 1942.

Not long after *The Rebel* appeared in English I met an expatriate young French aristocrat in New York who had been banished from France for aiding and abetting rebellion in various parts of French Africa. Jacques du Visme claimed descent from the old aristocracy, the "ancien régime" that preceded the advent of Napoleon Bonaparte. He had been one of the young intellectual idealists who volunteered to go into Senegal after the war to investigate the revolt of Senegalese soldiers against French officers. The issue was allegedly a claim to back pay owed them for having been imprisoned by the Germans. Du Visme revealed that he hadn't believed reports of French colonial excesses in Senegal. When he saw what the facts were he virtually renounced his French citizen-

* Carl A. Viggiani, "Camus and Alger Republicain," Yale French Studies, #25, pp. 138–143.

ship and became, in his own words, an "African Nationalist," his white skin to the contrary notwithstanding. A close friend of du Visme was a French Negro, Léon—the son of a French-woman and a Senegalese father, both of whom had been killed in an automobile accident in Africa when he was a baby. Léon was raised in Paris by his mother's wealthy family as one of "their own" and given an expensive and exclusive educa-tion. However, when he grew older, "I felt out of place." After his schooling Léon visited his father's Senegal where he met Jacques du Visme. Both of them eventually came to America. I met them in Greenwich Village where the three of us sat up late into the night discussing Africa, the Ameri-can Negro, and the politics of rebellion. Léon, an expert lin-guist, worked for a medical journal and a Catholic magazine for which he translated scientific and political articles from Europe. Jacques du Visme taught French at the Berlitz School of Languages and swore he was still being shadowed by French intelligence, the "Deuxième Bureau." For a time du Visme represented Josephine Baker in New York. Talk-ing with him always caused me to relive my days in North Africa. I haven't seen Jacques for several years now. But the last time I met Léon he was very gay and inebriated. He was strolling through Washington Square Park one late evening singing to himself while waving a miniature French flag. He had just left a party celebration of Bastille Day! I smiled to myself and wondered who was more (or less) French—Léon or Jacques du Visme. Both of them had argued that the American Negro was having trouble with his identity and needed to become more Africa-conscious.

By 1960 the American Negro's consciousness was not only being quickened by the advent of new African states but by events in Latin America. During July of that year I was in-vited to visit Cuba to "study" the new revolution there. Ex-cept for a brief visit to Montreal around 1948, this Cuba trip was my first excursion outside the United States since the war. Accompanied by several other Negro writers, I ven-

tured down to this Caribbean country where Fidel Castro had
been installed into supreme power through another kind of
rebellion which, like that of Algeria, was not at all historical
in the Camusian sense. Although the Cuban Communists later
inveigled Castro into proclaiming that "I am a Marxist to the
day I die," the fact of the matter was that the Cuban revolution was not only made without the Communists but also
despite them. While traveling across Cuba by train I found it
remarkable to realize that once again I had to be picked up
and transported out of the confines of the United States in
order to be schooled in the living dialectics of rebellion and
war, rebellion and the identity of racial resistance to Western
colonialism. One-third (or thereabouts) of the population of
Cuba is made up of Negroes or "Afro-Cubans" as they are
sometimes called, or as my two old Arab ladies of Oran would
have said "kidnapped Arabs." In 1960 the Castro regime was
proud to announce that for the first time since Columbus discovered the "Pearl of the Antilles," and these "Arabs" had
been "kidnapped" and brought over the Atlantic to replace
the Indians that the Spanish had slaughtered—these "Arabs"
were now "free and equal." They had been liberated by the
Cuban Revolution. I must confess that while I glorified in this
revolution (I didn't have to fight in it), it was like the celebration indulged in by visiting dignitaries to some one else's country whose deeply intimate problems of survival an outsider
could never know. It was like the gulf that always separated
me from the French and Arabs of North Africa and their
under-the-surface realities. For example, I was mystified by
race relations in Cuba, which were quite unlike American
race relations. On the one hand Cuban Negroes in Havana
swore that there was never any race prejudice in Cuban society; on the other hand the Cuban Revolution was hailed for
abolishing once and for all time all racial discrimination. However, as a veteran student of revolution, historical, metaphysical, and otherwise, I knew that the revolutionary struggle
against Batista was neither very ethical nor bracketed within

"limits." Moreover, it did not escape me that Havana was full of Cubans (white and black) who were visibly skeptical about the new regime and did not hesitate to say so. How the Cuban Negroes would fare it was too early to predict in 1960. Yet, the effects of the Cuban Revolution, the appeal of Fidel Castro (who was not black) penetrated even into the Negro ghettos of the United States. Fidel Castro himself even visited Harlem in the Fall of 1960 when he came to speak before the United Nations. This euphoria of rebellion was very catching. I had to think deeply and philosophically about the meaning of all this (remembering Camus). In a strange, historical fashion Cuba was seemingly a manifestation of two divergent revolutionary trends. First there had been the traditional Cuban Communist Party that had been cast into moral disfavor by all the idealists because of its record of sleeping with Batista at night while proclaiming revolutionary virtue and purity by day. Thus the Castroite rebellion was (in the Camusian sense) both indigenous and a-historical. It caught the Communists off guard and in a compromised position. But then, as soon as Castro mounted the throne, they switched and embraced him.

Before this Communist switch I was ready to conclude that Castroism represented that form of rebellion (without nihilism) that Camus sought after—a rebellion that "recognizes limits," at least insofar as its own revolutionary aims are concerned. Interestingly enough, Jean-Paul Sartre thought the same thing, and as a result wrote what was for me the most celebrated book on the Cuban Revolution—*Sartre on Cuba*. In the last chapter of this book, "Ideology and Revolution," Sartre discusses the concept "The Revolution is a Praxis," i.e., a movement which forges its ideas in action. For several years now the radical wing of the Negro civil rights movement in America has been a "praxis," a movement that forged its ideas in (direct) action. As a praxis, direct action could only propel this movement a certain distance before it would encounter well-entrenched social barriers that would force it to alter and qualify its philosophy. The truth of the matter is that, unlike Cuba, the Negro movement in America *must* cast its praxis into a theoretic frame in the final analysis. This is basically because the American Negro does not exist within an underdeveloped country with a large population of tribes and impoverished peasantry. This is the challenge of the Negroes' position in America. His revolutionary wing seeks methods for which there are no real guides either in the "historical rebellion" of Camus in the Western tradition, or in the experiences of Algeria, black Africa, or Cuba. The social realities of the United States force the Negro to create a brand new revolutionary synthesis, in the event that social revolution rather than *slow reforms* (which Camus favored for Algeria) is possible. The great dilemma of the Negro rests in the fact that while a real social revolution for solving American racial problems is not a guaranteed possibility (based on accumulated historical knowledge), neither is slow social reform. I have never been able to discover what were Camus' reactions to the Cuban Revolution.

Camus probably did not know it, but he did present some ideas in *The Rebel* which are more relevant to the American Negro than to the Western European compatriots he was addressing. These ideas are found in his section on "Rebellion and Art," in which he points out:

In every rebellion is to be found the metaphysical demand for unity, the impossibility of capturing it, and the construction of a substitute universe. . . . This also defines art. The demands of rebellion are really, in part, aesthetic demands.

But inasmuch as America is not a society that produces philosophical originality (the race psychosis blocks this), such ideas as rebellion as art do not take root. White intellectuals are unoriginal, imitative, and puerile, and black intellectuals are brainwashed by the whites. In such a social and intellectual situation a Negro movement with revolutionary potential is like a ship in a black night and stormy sea with many captains who know nothing about navigation. Only a miracle will save such a ship from foundering on the rocks of chaos. If Western Europeans wonder in trepidation about the crucial events within America that will ultimately shape its destiny, they are war and race. With these facts in mind one cannot blame the European for contempt and cynicism not only for the American international highmindedness which she practices behind the shield of democracy, but one can also understand the roots of the blasé American reactions to certain alleged "revolutions of liberation." A Camus will take ethical exception while maintaining a certain principled perspective. A Sartre will do likewise. But I was struck, while in Cuba, with the reaction of Françoise Sagan to the Cuban experience. I traveled to Oriente province on the same train coach with this celebrated young writer in 1960. She thought the entire Cuban phenomenon an immense bore. I imagine she typifies many French intellectuals, if not all or even the majority, but even *they* can be understood in the context of their times.

There is another trend of thought in French intellectual circles which I cannot ignore without comment. This trend is neither "Left" nor "Right"; neither Camusian, Sartrean, nor Saganiste; neither politically a "true believer" nor "Godless" in the revolutionary sense. A person reflecting this trend is best described, from my point of view, as a "political agnostic," which has for critical purposes much intellectual value. Such a man is Raymond Aron, and many of his conclusions about revolution have relevance to the Negro in America.

While Albert Camus eschewed the avowed ends of the Western revolution because revolutionaries resorted to immoral and nihilistic means, Raymond Aron criticizes both the means and ends of historical rebellion, because for him the ends were a grand myth to begin with. Carrying his reasoning further, it was these mythical or unattainable ends which forced the nihilist turn of revolutionary events. The process of rebellion becomes revolutionary process with apocalyptic visions which are unrealizable. Blocked from its avowed ends, the revolutionary process turns and feeds on itself (the revo-

lution eats its own children), establishing a tyranny which is
Intellectuals, Raymond Aron asserts:
a perversion of its avowed aims. In his *The Opium of the*
The idea of Progress is implicit in the myth of the Left, which
feeds on the idea of continuous movement. The myth of the
Revolution has significance which is at once complementary and
opposed to this: it fosters the expectation of a break with the normal trend of human affairs . . . [but]

Are revolutions worthy of so much honour? The men who con-
ceive them are not those who carry them out. Those who begin
them rarely live to see their end, except in exile or in prison. Can
they really be the symbol of a humanity which is the master of
its own destiny if no man recognizes his handiwork in the achievement which results from the savage free-for-all struggle?

In America today there has flowered a young black breed
in the ghettos of the North who says that Negroes must be
prepared to die for their "freedom," and that they themselves
are prepared to do just that. Many of them also talk avidly
of "revolution," but aside from their volatile activistic pro-
clivities their "revolution" is a borrowed term abstracted out
of the revolutionary ideologies of the "Third" or "Bandung"
world. It is the revolutionary sentiments of identification with
movements as close as Cuba and as distant as China, but its
native methodology is one of pure and simple protest, both
non-violent and violent. In Camusian terms theirs is a movement without a "theoretic frame" but with a content which
is nationalistically racial in one degree or another. The conclusion is that all of this puts the elements of the so-called "Negro
(or Black) Revolution" in America outside the conceptual
framework of the "historical rebellion" analyzed in *The
Rebel.* For the Negro in America, for example, the Communist Revolution is assuredly a myth, but not for the same reasons offered by Raymond Aron. It is not a myth because the
ends of the Communist Revolution became nihilistically per-
verted, or because "The myth of the Revolution serves as a
refuge for utopian intellectuals . . . [an] intercessor between

the real and the ideal." The Communist Revolution is a myth for the Negro precisely because its class-struggle methodology is nonapplicable in America. Aron's own conclusions on "The Myth of the Proletariat" are better demonstrated in America than anywhere else in the world. But if the American proletariat has no evident revolutionary sentiments, the Negro movement (as a racial thing) most assuredly does, even if these sentiments are metaphysical and lacking in standard historical methodology. To be sure, this phenomenon deeply troubles the American Marxists who are hard put to make the Negro movement fit into their own Marxian "theoretic frame." Certain Marxist tendencies have attempted to see the Negro as *the real proletariat* (not white labor) because he is the most economically disfranchised. But this is an oversimplification which unrealistically blurs the peculiar class stratifications within the Negro minority. The civil rights movement, for example, is led by bourgeois Negroes. Thus, if the revolutionary wing of the Negro movement fails to create its own theoretic frame, its own peculiar methodology, it too will end up in blood and tears and its own "myth of the Revolution."

One of the great disadvantages of political and social theorizing in America is that all of our native politicians (both reform and revolutionary) must study, absorb, and attempt to imitate foreign models and foreign philosophies in pursuit of their own native utopias (including our utopia of constitutional democracy unlimited). Unlike the French who, as Raymond Aron describes, "have a weakness for the word revolution because they cherish the illusion of being associated with past glories" (the French Revolution), Americans cherish no such illusions. They do not allow themselves that nostalgic luxury. So afraid are (white) Americans of the contemporary meaning of social revolution that they have all but denied the heritage of their own American revolutionary tradition of 1776. Any American radical with the temerity to cite the Revolutionary War against Great Britain as our historical mandate for perpetual war against tyrants both foreign and domestic is suspected of being an agent for Moscow. Aron, however, does have a point when he writes:

The United States on the other hand has preserved its constitution intact for nearly two centuries; indeed it has gradually come to acquire an almost mystical prestige. And yet American society has never ceased to undergo continuous and rapid transformation. Economic expansion and the social meltingpot have been absorbed into a constitutional framework without weakening or modifying it. A federation of agrarian States has become the greatest industrial power in the world without recourse to illegality.

This conclusion is more apparent than real. It is what most American whites have led themselves to believe and want the rest of the world to believe. In the first place, America pretended to be a social melting-pot but never truly was. Its great and unprecedented economic expansion has been nothing but a late-epoch extension of the Industrial Revolution blessed by the energy of pragmatism and the unlimited ingredients of natural resources. America, however, has remained behind the constitutional façade, a "nation of nations," an aggregation of national and religious groups vying for power and economic status with the white Protestant Anglo-Saxon ruling the roost. Moreover, the melting-pot which Aron thinks he sees has never included the Negro. This fact has always been the Achilles heel (as the Communists used to say) of American constitutional capitalist democracy, only the Communists called it "American Imperialism." Of this fact, Aron says, "Colour prejudice in the United States has put a brake on the realization by the Negroes of the equality promised by the American constitution. If they have not responded to the appeal of Communism, it is to a large extent because of this promise." But it is demonstrated these days that this promise has failed in preventing Negroes from responding to the appeal of revolution (non-Communist). Historically excluded from the social melting-pot, the Negro subsociety in America becomes the spawning ground for a form of rebellion that has no historical precedent in philosophical content.

If it is true, as Aron contends, "that colonial civilizations are subject to different laws from those of civilizations which have a long history behind them and are geographically confined," then it might be possible (theoretically) to say that the Negro in America represents a unique type of colonized man never before seen anywhere else in the world. He has been effectively excluded from the laws of Western civilization, American style. He is no more (or less) an integral part of American civilization than were the Arabs in Algeria before the uprising, the salient difference being that the Negro is colonized *within* the geographical confines of the United States. Hence, the Negro intellectual class exists with one foot in and one foot out of the "Metropolitan" country even when they imagine themselves to be well ensconced within it.

In 1942 when I landed in Oran I was far from thinking such thoughts. But my conversation with those two Arab women inadvertently started a unique intellectual process which, with experiences added, has led me to these conclusions about the nature of rebellion. It is not to be thought that Negro intellectuals as a class all share these opinions, despite a more manifest identification with the revolutionary "world of color" than they have ever shown. On the contrary, the Negro intellectuals in America have their own "opium." It is not, today, the "Left"; it is "racial integration," a great myth which the ideologues of the system and the Liberal Establishment expound, but which they cannot deliver into reality. When Raymond Aron says of the French intelligentsia that none suffers as much as they do—"from the loss of universality, none clings so obstinately to its illusions, none would gain more from recognizing its country's true problems"—the same would apply to the American Negro intelligentsia, with but a small change in the wording.

This, of course, applies to the majority, which is not to say that the Negro intelligentsia is all of an ideological piece. On the contrary, there are deep conflicts developing within this class growing out of the worsening crisis within the civil rights movement, a movement which is blocked from achieving its end—complete racial integration. When Aron contends that Western intellectuals "suffer from the fragmentation of their universe," etc., this applies to the Negro only to the extent to which he strives to adopt the complete cultural value system of the white world (which he can hardly ever achieve). Thus Aron's "The End of the Ideological Age?" proposition *cannot* apply to the Negro in America, but *only to the whites*. Professor Daniel Bell of Columbia University, after reading Aron, came out with his book *End of Ideology—The Exhaustion of Political Ideas in the Fifties*. This book revealed how dependent are white American intellectuals on European initiative not only for the philosophies of rebellion and revolution, but also for philosophical rejections of rebellion and revolution. At this juncture of Western civilization, the American Negro is free from the necessity of either accepting or rejecting rebellion or revolution, which is at once his hope and the challenge of his unprecedented and precarious position.

13

Behind the Black Power Slogan

Back in the middle fifties I severed my connections with the Marxist Socialist movement because I had come to the conclusion that its theory of the struggle for socialism did not apply to the real situation of the Negro in America. Even as a fledgling black radical of the late forties I was ill at ease with the Communist approach, which I felt was not tuning in on the Negro presence. The main reason I stayed in the movement as long as I did was to learn more thoroughly *why* the Marxists could be so dogmatically wrong about Negroes.

In the process it was inevitable that I would absorb a residue of some of the dogmas I rebelled against with such outspoken candor that I became a marked man in the eyes of Communist officialdom. For example, I once believed that Marxism *did* have all the answers, that it was merely a question of *interpretation*. But despite the depth and scope of Marxian resources, I now consider it a dogmatic error to believe this implicitly. One of the dogmas I seriously questioned was that concerning the everlasting necessity of the "Negro-Labor" alliance. I said, "Since most Negroes are of the laboring class, this unity scheme sounds spurious even if white labor *were* pro-Negro, which it is not." This querulousness got me into deeper disfavor with the bureaucrats of the Left. Long before certain black militants of the sixties made black nationalism a familiar topic for the media, I was one of those

* Note: Footnotes refer to Biographical Notes at end of chapter.

people ostracized by the white Left (and the black) for being tainted with the ideology of "bourgeois nationalism," considered to be detrimental to the cause of "Negro-White" unity, etc., etc.

Today, some fifteen years later, here I am taking part in a Socialist Scholars' Conference which takes up the question of "The Political Economy of Black Power"! I find this fact absolutely amazing. Here we have a slogan, "Black Power," put forth by the most militant black nationalist trend in America since the Garvey movement of the Twenties, and the socialists (at least some of them) consider it relevant enough to invest it with a "political economy." In 1950 I never thought it would come to pass. There is no hankering after an alliance with white labor in this slogan, and no reticence about alienating other would-be white "allies." Yet some socialists are taking it up for serious study. I suppose it proves the correctness of a Harlem adage that was popular during the Forties—"*It ain't what you do, it's the way* how *you do it!*"

Now, when a socialist scholars' group in America calls a conference (even if it includes Black Power on the agenda), this conference is, obviously, to be mainly concerned with the problems of socialism in America. I would not go so far as to say that Black Power is meant to be merely incidental to such a discussion, because the long-range issue of socialism *is* relevant even if few of the new Black Power theorists are aware of it. For the white Socialists (as well as the black), however, it follows that the "method" pursuant to the socialism scheduled to be examined, from various theoretical and intellectual vantage points, will be the Marxian "scientific method" toward the achievement of American socialism. It is assumed here (but not with absolute certainty) that none of Eduard Bernstein's revisionist methodology will be officially placed on the agenda, but that some of this social-democratic ideology might intrude anonymously without being declared. In other words, a conference unanimity is anticipated on socialism as a goal whose *means* and *ends* are of equal (and dialectical) importance and relevancy in the United States.

Immediately a serious problem is posed for the socialists (white and black), for how do they propose to verify the viability of the Black Power doctrine by way of the Marxian "scientific method," and also the compatibility of this doctrine with socialist practice? As we all know by now, both modern socialism as a creed and the Marxian method are of European origin. Unlike Black Power they are not native American conceptions. Although our socialism and our Marxian method are today the cumulative results of a hundred-year-old tenure of naturalized "Americanization," the Marxian method still bears highly recognizable European trappings under its American cloak. Marxism has tried to become truly American, but it has never lost its European accent and continental prejudices. In the spirit of genuine internationalism this ought not to be deplored; it has, very often, been simply politically embarrassing.

For one thing, it is permissible for white socialist scholars in America to feel at home with Marxian socialism and its method. But when you involve the Afro-American in such deliberations, you encounter a sociological and psychological contradiction—the Negro is not a European-American but an Afro-American. If many American whites take a jaundiced view of Marxism as a "foreign doctrine," the Afro-American has other justified reasons for being just as critical. He could say it is a European (white) revolutionary doctrine meant primarily to liberate white workers, leaving non-whites to shift for themselves. No matter how vocal the Communists were, for example, on "Negro rights," in the final analysis they looked upon the white labor movement as the dominant factor and considered the Negro as merely an appendage in their strategy and tactics. Other Marxist tendencies such as the Socialist Workers Party (Trotskyite) have attempted a more flexible approach. The SWP, for example, attempts to come to terms with the realities of black nationalism, while clinging

mightily to the orthodox Marxist position on the primacy of
the white labor movement, on the supposition that labor will
ultimately rise to the revolutionary occasion. However, no
Marxists of any tendency have succeeded in "Afro-Ameri-
canizing" Marxism (if such is possible).

I realize that Marxists will demur most vehemently against
the notion that there is any contradiction involved in trying
to relate the Marxian method to radicalized Negroes functioning in the midst of a quiescent and conservatized white
labor movement. They will insist (as they must) that even
this unique situation can be squared with the Marxist method
as it stands. But this remains for the Marxists themselves to
demonstrate. In the meantime, you are not going to induce
radicalized Negroes to believe in the potentialities of white
workers today. The white Marxists may try, but in the meantime the reality leaves the black Marxist up a tree. The latter
becomes one of the most irrelevant political animals of our
times, because the radicalized black movement in America is
on the ascendancy not because of Marxism and its theory and
practice, but despite it. The Negro Marxist will object: "But
am I not in full support of all civil rights efforts? Do I not
support the aims of Wilkins, King, Young, SNCC, CORE,
etc.? I might not agree with *all* of their methods, but I support
them. Therefore, I am not irrelevant." The Negro Marxist
is relevant *only* to the extent in which he participates in these
movements as an individual. The truth is that these movements were not Marxist-inspired and do not need Marxist
support to achieve their aims. Hence the Negro Marxist qua
Marxist is superfluous to the aims, imperatives, and methods
of these movements that comprise the main thrust of black
activism today. For what, in fact, do Negro Marxists actually
bring to these movements in terms of ideology or direction?

Paradoxically, it is only the Negro Marxists who have any
firm, theoretically oriented, long-range commitment to socialism! The Wilkinses, Youngs, Kings, SNCC, CORE, the Black
Powerites, the urban guerrillas of northern uprisings, etc.—

none of these has any long-range commitment to socialism. "Ah," says the Negro Marxist, "so you see, the aims of these leading activist movements who dominate the scene *cannot* achieve all of their aims unless we achieve a socialist society. Therefore we Negro (and white) Marxists are not that irrelevant, especially in the long haul of history."

But wait a minute. "Is that really true? How can you be so certain that *some*, if not *all* of the activists' aims are unattainable except under socialism?"

"Capitalism is doomed. Look at the way the world is going. Besides, it has been demonstrated that capitalism is unable to make room for black equality in its economics, politics, and institutions," says the Negro Marxist.

"You have a point. But when you say 'look at the world,' we must look especially at the *Western world*. No socialist revolution there that was not imposed by the Russian military and political presence."

We have all heard various sides of this debate ever since the Prague coup of 1948, so let us stick closer to home in the United States. If we agree, for the sake of argument, that there is no hope for the Negro under capitalism, how can this Socialist Conference include Black Power, essentially a capitalistic slogan in economic terms, on its agenda? How can this slogan Black Power, whose intended meaning is not adequately defined as yet, a meaning which varies from group to group, from spokesman to spokesman, be given a sociological category universally agreed upon to the extent that it warrants a school of "political economy"? The whole idea is very interesting, for it implies that a more provocative designation would be "Black Power and Socialism." At any rate, it strikes me as a signal departure in Marxist theoretical investigation. Before we can ask, What is implied here?, we must ask, What do we think the Black Power theorists mean to imply by the slogan? We must note that many of the rebellious urban youth think Black Power means "Get the cops!" "Burn, baby, burn!" "Down with Whitey!" or "Let's get the loot!"

The recent Black Power Conference in Newark, New Jersey, produced so many resolutions of an economic, political and cultural nature that they cannot be quoted or analyzed here. But previous to this, the Harlem CORE organization published last winter an issue of their magazine *Rights and Reviews* called the "Black Power Issue" (Winter 1966/67). A number of spokesmen decribed Black Power as follows:

Julian Bond:

> Black Power must be seen as a natural extension of the work of the civil rights movement over the past few years. From the courtroom to the streets in favor of integrated public facilities; from the streets onto backwoods roads in quest of the right to vote; from the ballot box to the meat of politics, the organization of voters into self-interest units.

Floyd McKissick:

> The doctrine of Black Power is this new thrust which seeks to achieve economic power and to develop political movements that would make changes that are vast and significant.

Lorenzo Thomas:

> Our attempts to think out loud have often been taken up by the news and represented to the nation as our plan of action. Black Power, for instance. Forget Black Power. There is more to it than that, and our life might perhaps become the truth of the moment we seek without the need of slogans. In times past people were content to *experience* their lives, but today one is not really living unless one has a program.

Ralph Edwards:

> Any true proponent of Black Power should be *committed* to a special kind of violence—*defensive* violence. Yes, defensive violence as opposed to the aggressive violence heaped upon us.

(It is not clear whether Edwards considers defensive violence and the urban rebellions of Watts and Detroit, etc., as one and the same thing. If he does, then we have a new form of American revolutionary anarchism which demands a more critical examination.)

Yosef Ben-Jochannan:
> What is Black Power? It is that power which black peoples had in Africa before the invasion and domination of Africa by the Europeans under the guise of "taking Christianity to the heathen Africans."

(This definition of Black Power comes from the old Garveyite Back to Africa movement. At a Harlem Black Nationalist Youth Conference in May, 1965, this tendency said that any Negro who opposed "Back to Africa" with fighting for equality in the U.S. is an Uncle Tom-House Nigger. It is not clear how the Garveyite tendency views Black Power in the U.S.A.)

Roy Inniss:
> There is a compelling need to emphasize the socio-psychological aspect of Black Power. We can cry "Black Power" until doomsday . . . [but] until black people accept values meaningful to themselves, there can be no completely effective organizing for the development of black power.

(Note that both Inniss and Ben-Jochannan consider Denmark Vesey, Harriet Tubman, Nat Turner, Marcus Garvey, Elijah Muhammad, and Malcolm X as representative leaders of black people in America, but *not* Booker T. Washington and W. E. B. Du Bois.)

So much for Harlem CORE's definition of Black Power—and there are other definitions to come. However, the *Amsterdam News* of July 29, 1967 asks the question, What was accomplished at the Black Power Conference? It then says, "Despite the encomiums of success from many at the conference, a definitive meaning for the phrase Black Power eluded circumscription and remained . . . dangerously ambiguous." So let us examine certain other attitudes on Black Power.

In the New York *Post* series on Black Power (week of June 19), Bayard Rustin says of the slogan:

Three times Negroes have engaged in these politics. First with Booker T. Washington at the turn of the century, after the failure of Reconstruction. His slogans were "Self-Help" and "Drop Down Your Buckets Where You Are." Then with Marcus Garvey in the 1920's, during the racist regression just after World War I. Garvey had two slogans: "Build the Negro Economy" and "Back to Africa." Now aren't they inconsistent? Slogan politics are always inconsistent.

Another critic, Tom Kahn, along with Rustin believes that "Black Power is conservative, is a retreat." An NAACP official, Henry Lee Moon, thinks Black Power is a "naive expression, at worst diabolical, in the sense that at worst it's designed to create chaos." He added, "Actually people with power never speak of power." Roy Wilkins agrees generally with Moon.

John R. Lewis, a former chairman of SNCC, does not see any hope in the future of Black Power. However, a present member of the leading echelons of SNCC, Ivanhoe Donaldson, when asked by Rustin what kind of *program* SNCC offers for Black Power, answered, "I'm not sure we have to justify ourselves with a program in this country. We have a program because we have a base." This reply brings us face to face with one of the most challenging problems of the Black Power slogan. We have a situation wherein Stokely Carmichael, who has been the most vocal exponent of Black Power within SNCC, is described as a spokesman whose strong points are not structure and plan (i.e. program); his gift is speech. The same was true of Malcolm X, who could inspire but who did not plan, structure, or plot an organized course. Martin Luther King believes that the slogan of Black Power is "really a cry of disappointment, it is a cry of hurt, it is a cry of despair."

What really lies behind all of these varied and conflicting reactions to the slogan of Black Power? Strange to conclude, there happens to be a certain validity in nearly all these reactions. For any slogan that has not been adequately defined, there will be reasons for doubt as well as for strong support. Bayard Rustin has put his finger on something very crucial about the Black Power slogan. *Black Power is nothing but the economic and political philosophy of Booker T. Washington given a 1960's militant shot in the arm and brought up to date.* The curious fact about it is that the very last people to admit that Black Power is militant Booker T-ism are the Black Power theorists themselves. A Roy Inniss and a Ben-Jochannan, for example, will characterize Booker T. Washington as a historical conservative (if not an Uncle Tom) and refuse to recognize him as a part of their black nationalist tradition. Both of them will, of course, uphold Marcus Garvey with much nationalist fervor—completely overlooking the fact that Garvey was a disciple of Booker T. Washington. When Garvey came to the United States in 1916, he came to see Booker T. Washington, who had died in 1915. Both Garvey and his wife Amy-Jacques Garvey thought: "Since the death of Booker T. Washington, there was no one with a positive and practical uplift programme for the masses—North or South." [1] But the NAACP "radicals" of the time, especially the Du Bois tendency, were staunchly opposed to Washington's program. Later on all the Marxist Communist and Socialist tendencies combined to relegate poor old conservative Booker T. Washington to historical purgatory for having failed to conduct himself like a respectable militant or radical in Negro affairs. Dr. Herbert Aptheker, the chief Communist Party historian on the Negro, for example, also became the chief castigator of Washington. The prejudice of the political left against Washington accounts in part for Bayard Rustin's denigration of Black Power in 1967, the only difference being that Rustin is perceptive enough to see that Black Power is, clearly, Booker T-ism. Few Marxist Socialists and other radicals will see the truth of this when they honor Black Power with a political economy. Even Bayard Rustin did not point out that W. E. B. Du Bois put forth a program for economic and political Black Power in his autobiography *Dusk of Dawn* (1940) when he clearly enunciated his abandonment of the NAACP philosophy. Du Bois did not call his plan "Black

Power"; he called it a plan for the Negro "economic cooperative commonwealth." The radical left, especially Aptheker, will also overlook this fact in their estimate of Du Bois' career. A Bayard Rustin did not see that Du Bois, along with Washington and Garvey (with whom Du Bois fought bitterly) also had a "self-help" phase of "Drop Down Your Buckets Where You Are." This phase has (and will) always recur in Negro life from era to era. In fact, this nationalist (self-help, self-identification, black unity) phase appeared simultaneously with the civil rights-radical protest tradition of which Frederick Douglass was the first outstanding historical prophet. The spokesman for the black nationalist phase of Douglass's day was Martin R. Delany, who was, for a time, Douglass's co-editor of the abolitionist newspaper *The North Star*. Thus the civil rights protest phase of Negro leadership began simultaneously with its opposition, the black nationalist phase, within the Abolitionist movement.

The ambiguity, the lingering vagueness over the exact definition of Black Power is rooted, first of all, in an exceedingly faulty and unscientific interpretation of Negro historical trends in the United States. This faulty interpretation of black social trends in America negates any attempt to deal *theoretically* with the Black Power concept in any definitive way. In other words, the subjectively faulty way in which Negro history has been interpreted by all conservative, liberal, and left schools has cut the ground from under any possibility of setting up a theoretical structure around both the nationalist-separatist-black power trends and the civil rights protest-integrationist trends. The result is *the black American as part of an ethnic group has no definitive social theory relative to* his *status, presence, or impact on American society*. It is for this reason that when a Black Power phase repeats itself in the Sixties, it comes at such a crucial moment in the history of American race relations that a Black Power movement cannot escape being taken over and commandeered by a *revolutionary anarchist tendency*. Coming at a moment of racial crisis in America, there has been no school of *social theory* prepared in advance for Black Power that could channel the concept along the lines of positive, radical, and constructive social change. In this regard, the most derelict and irresponsible school of thought has been the Marxist tendency in America. The abject forty-five-year-old failure of the American Marxist movement to comprehend the meaning of the Negro presence in America amounts to an historical disaster of the first magnitude.

Consider the case of the leading Marxist historian (on blacks and whites alike), the perennial Dr. Herbert Aptheker of the Communist Party. This historian published his first pamphlet on Negroes about thirty years ago and still has not grasped the basic fundamentals of Negro social development to this day. I quote Aptheker's comments in *Studies on the Left* to illustrate this problem:

I do not find an "enormous influence" exerted by Booker T. Washington upon black nationalism. And Genovese's acceptance of Mr. Washington's own public rationalizations for his program of acquiescence is extraordinary. Thus, Washington justified his insistence that Negroes avoid political activity on the grounds that they were not experienced in such activity; but this was not why he put forth the program of acquiescence. He put forth that program because of the insistence of Baldwin of the Southern Railroad, and Carnegie and Rockefeller who subsidized the Tuskegee machine. And they insisted on that program for obvious reasons.

The differences between Du Bois and Washington were basic and not simply tactical, and no single quotation from a 1903 essay will change that. Du Bois rejected subordination; Washington accepted it. Du Bois rejected colonialism; Washington assumed its continuance. Du Bois was intensely critical of capitalism, long before World War I; Washington worshipped it . . .

. . . Further, integration is necessary to this nation exactly because the Negro is integral to it . . .

. . . The realities of black nationalism are exaggerated by Genovese; the power and force of Negro-white efforts are minimized by him.[2]

One could quote more, but this is enough to demonstrate that Herbert Aptheker is one of the most un-Marxist Marxists quotable these days when it comes to heaping radical mystification on the Negro movement. In native American terms, Aptheker's Marxism is European "book" Marxism; hence his approach to the Negro is totally lacking in imagination, depth, or perception. For one to see no "enormous influence" of Washington on black nationalists is like seeing no enormous influence of Hegel or the Greeks—Democritus or Heraclitus—on Karl Marx's dialectical materialism. For Aptheker to quibble in 1966 about Washington's avoidance of political activity throws absolutely no light at all on the nature of Washington's Tuskegee machine in 1905. This machine got a Negro, Charles Anderson, appointed to the post of Collector of Internal Revenue in 1905, which was no mean achievement in the New York City of those days. Aptheker does not distinguish between what Washington said (tactically) and what he *did* practically, both North and South. In 1900 he established the National Negro Business League, which still exists in Washington, D.C. Long before Du Bois' Niagara Movement (which sold itself out inside the NAACP) Washington was organizing Southern Negro farmers, sharecroppers, and small businessmen through yearly Tuskegee conferences. During the same period, it was Washington's protegés in the North, Philip A. Payton and others, who organized the Afro-American Realty Company, which waged a most militant economic struggle against entrenched white real estate interests in order to win living space in the previously all-white Harlem of 1900. The winning of Harlem and better housing for Negroes between 1903 and World War One was a direct outgrowth of Washington's National Negro Business League, of which both Payton and Anderson were members.

Booker T. Washington built a school in Alabama, a permanent, lasting, and functional institution in the deep South.

Aptheker is rather naive about Southern life-realities in 1900 if he thinks that one built institutions in Dixie without "acquiescing" to something sacred within the status quo. Apparently Aptheker does not have much respect for such all-black institutions where they are socially necessary and tactical compromises are required to create them. What Aptheker says reveals that not only does he not understand the social imperatives behind these institutions, he also does not understand the nature and imperatives of black nationalism as a trend (and this is not to imply that he *must* be sympathetic to black nationalism). The point is that as a *historian* he should understand certain facts that he doesn't. Marcus Garvey had so much admiration for what Washington had done with Tuskegee that he wanted to get his advice on how such a school could be developed in Jamaica, B.W.I. When Garvey established his U.N.I.A. headquarters in New York, Emmett J. Scott, who was Washington's personal secretary at Tuskegee, became a close working colleague of Garvey's. Now since black nationalists admire the memory of Garvey, it stands to reason historically and ideologically that Washington's influence on black nationalism was rather enormous. But Aptheker professes not to understand this phenomenon; and this is because Aptheker refuses to understand what black nationalism is all about. A historian *must* understand *all* social phenomenon out of history or stop pretending to be a historian. Negro historians are not much better. Many of the young black nationalists of today are misinformed on the real meaning of Booker T. Washington's role because of the obfuscation that permeates Negro historiography and that has prevented the development of a black social theory on historical and class trends in Negro history.

Again, consider Aptheker's attitude towards Washington's views on capitalism: "Du Bois was intensely critical of capitalism, long before World War I; Washington worshipped it . . ." Here is revealed the roots of Aptheker's vulgar Marxian prejudices. What he is saying is that Du Bois was historically virtuous because he was always anti-capitalist, and that Washington was historically unworthy as a leader because he was pro-capitalist! Such an attitude is not at all Marxian, but *anti-Marxian*. It is also a form of liberalistic Marxian Victorianism and leftwing sectarianism which has always been known to believe that everyone has a right to have capitalistic ambitions in America (and does) except a Negro. To put it another way, it is a traditional form of American Communist ideology which has said, or implied, that *capitalistic development of a Negro bourgeois class is neither desirable, necessary, nor historically relevant*. This is what a Herbert Aptheker believes retroactively to the age of Booker T. Washington, and it is also what an Aptheker believes today. But an Aptheker is historically and theoretically wrong. His limited views on black nationalism and his distortions of black capitalism are all of a piece. It goes without saying that an Aptheker cannot accept the intent of the Black Power slogan today, not only because it *is* neo-Booker T-ism, *but also demonstrably pro-capitalist*. The fact that some fifty industrial corporations are reported to have helped finance the Black Power Conference in Newark is not unrelated to the historical fact that Booker T. Washington, the pro-capitalist, had his Tuskegee machine subsidized by the Baldwins, Carnegies, and Rockefellers of his day.

The fact that the Black Power movement is, in part, pro-capitalist *should not*, but *will* pose problems for those socialists who desire to construct a political economy for the slogan. The Black Power ideology is *not* socialistic in its economic and political orientation; it is, however, nationalistic. Another problem is that the Black Power ideology is *not* at all revolutionary in terms of its economic and political ambitions; it is, in fact, a *social reformist* ideology. It is not meant to be a criticism of the Black Power movement to call it "reformist"; there is nothing wrong or detrimental about social reforms. But we must not fail to call reformism what it in fact is. The Black Power theorists who believe their slogan is in fact a revolutionary slogan are mistaken about the social essence of the slogan. What *does* have a revolutionary implication about Black Power is the "defensive violence" upheld and practiced by its ultra-extremist-nationalist-urban guerrilla wing, which is a *revolutionary anarchist tendency*. Thus we have a unique American form of black revolutionary anarchism with a social reform economic and political "program." For the Marxists it is Marx versus Bakunin on another level (with Eduard Bernstein in the shadows).

The term Black Power was first enunciated by Adam Clayton Powell, a member of the radical wing of the black bourgeoisie, at the Howard University commencement exercises of 1966. The slogan was later picked up and popularized by Stokely Carmichael, a member of the lower middle-class student's front. Thus the "radical" or "revolutionary" verbiage surrounding the Black Power slogan obscures the fact that this movement is bourgeois-oriented in its class and economic and political ambitions. Note the fact that the first Black Power conference was organized and engineered by a moderate middle-class Negro spokesman with alleged financial support from big business. Note also that this conference was well attended by black nationalist-oriented representatives of the black working class, and the black professional, intellectual, and student segments. That working-class blacks attended this conference and staunchly supported economic and political aims which are bourgeois, pro-capitalistic, reformist, and cooperative, as well as private enterprise-oriented, should not surprise socialists who understand black nationalist historical antecedents. But Marxists do not grasp these imperatives. Even a Frank Kofsky, who was a member of the radical left tendency that supported Malcolm X, does not understand black nationalist historical imperatives in the United States. Kofsky wrote in *Studies on the Left:*

It makes about as much sense to construct a lineage tying Malcolm X to Washington as it does to confuse the ideas of Marx and Engels with those of the "feudal socialists." . . . Where

Washington was the quintessence of a social conservative, Malcolm was a revolutionary and, in his last days, an international-socialist one at that . . .

Later on Kofsky said:

But the fires of resistance never completely died out [from the black radical movement]. And when a public figure who appealed to these remaining sparks did develop—a Marcus Garvey or a Malcolm X—the response he obtained from the masses was dramatically in contrast to that given the white-appointed "official" Negro leaders.[3]

By rewriting Negro history to suit present-day political lines, Kofsky lands himself in Aptheker's corner where the angle of historical vision permits one to see only what one *wants* to see. Kofsky simply cannot grasp the fact a Malcolm X *cannot* accept a Marcus Garvey's stance out of history unless he also accepts a Booker T. Washington, who was Garvey's ideological mentor. How do white radicals in America dare to assume the privilege of speaking and writing so authoritatively on the Negro while refusing to take into account and to explain who the Negro heroes were and *why?* Booker T. Washington was a *hero* to hundreds of thousands of Negroes in the United States, and one *cannot* wipe this fact out of history—regardless of what W. E. B. Du Bois or anyone else said against him. The deeply ingrained paternalism of the white radical prompts him to attempt to pick the Negro's heroes out of history for him. He does this for the purpose of justifying an expedient political line which is usually predicated on political opportunism rather than on scientific social understanding. For Kofsky's edification, let me quote Marcus Garvey's wife again on her husband's attitudes towards Washington:

[Garvey] heard of the help Booker T. Washington got for his work in the Southern States, so he wrote him, and Washington encouraged him to come up. Garvey felt that if he could get funds, he would return and open a Trade School like Tuskegee.

This would give practical help to the masses who then had no such opportunity for training; at the same time he could inculcate in them Race-love, and strengthen his African programme in the entire island.[4]

Elsewhere:

While in Alabama we went to Tuskegee Normal and Industrial Institute. Primarily to pay homage to the late Booker T. Washington, at his monument erected to his memory in front of the chapel.[5]

Since Frank Kofsky upholds Garvey (as a black radical resister), which the other Marxist Herbert Aptheker does not (Garveyism was reactionary race-chauvinism), I should also inform Kofsky that Garvey's African program was preceded by Booker T. Washington's African program by several years. Washington organized a successful conference on Africa at Tuskegee in 1912. Following this, Washington organized the Africa Union Company, for the purpose of promoting trade between American Negroes and the Gold Coast. This business scheme was destroyed by the World War I interruption of Atlantic Ocean commerce in 1914. Thus not only did Garvey learn his black nationalist economics from Booker T. Washington, he also based his "Back to Africa" movement on Washington's earlier groundwork of 1912–1914.

On these questions, Kofsky and Aptheker take positions which at once merge and diverge. Both of them reject Booker T. Washington out of hand historically. Aptheker worships Du Bois, but the Trotskyites were always critical of him and his "talented tenth-NAACP" philosophy. The Trotskyites, however, accept Marcus Garvey as a good man defeated by fate, but refuse to accept Garvey's personal idol, Booker T. Washington. Aptheker, of course, must reject both Washington and Garvey because Du Bois was down on both of them, but agrees with Kofsky that he simply can't see any "lineage" between Malcolm X and Washington. Aptheker, however, has no love for Malcolm X with or without Washington's direct lineage, and he disagrees with Kofsky for exaggerating the importance of black nationalism. Frank Kofsky makes this muddled mess on black nationalism even more of a muddle by calling Washington the "quintessence of a social conservative," and calling Malcolm X a "revolutionary and, in his last days, an international-socialist one at that." But Kofsky (as well as the Trotskyites) is so bent on claiming that the Socialist Workers Party actually won over Malcolm X that he overlooks the fact that Malcolm had hardly emerged out of the Nation of Islam, led by Elijah Muhammad, an organization also called a politically conservative movement. Kofsky misunderstands the essence of black nationalism so thoroughly that he misses the point that nationalism has both its *conservative* and *radical* tendencies; *but it is still nationalism!*

What is wrong with these so-called radicals? Can't they think at all? It seems that the American system has not only brainwashed a great number of Negroes so that they can't think straight, it has also brainwashed a great number of radicals who pretend to be great experts on brainwashed Negroes but who are themselves brainwashed to the extent that they can't even use their own highly touted method of analysis consistently. While I do not, for example, agree with much of what historian C. Vann Woodward had to say apropos of Genovese's remarks (it is my opinion that Genovese was more consistently correct than Aptheker and Kofsky on black nationalism), I can well understand why Vann Woodward would remain in support of Aptheker (aside from the fact that Communists always misled white liberals). Both Kofsky and Genovese should have been lined up solidly *against* the old-guard Aptheker's Communist conservatism and the old-guard Woodward's dated liberalism. However, none other than Frank Kofsky, a young-turk radical, messes up the game and swings so far to the left on black nationalism that he commits the "infantile disorder" of what Lenin called "Leftwing Communism."

Kofsky, in assessing Malcolm X, does not see that his former Nation of Islam was nothing but a form of Booker T. Washington's economic self-help, black unity, bourgeois hard work, law-abiding, vocational training, stay-out-of-the-civil-rights-struggle agitation, separate-from-the white-man, etc., etc., morality. The only difference was that Elijah Muhammad added the potent factor of the Muslim religion to a race, economic, and social philosophy of which the first prophet was none other than Booker T. Washington. Elijah also added an element of "hate Whitey" ideology which Washington, of course, would never have accepted. The reason that a Washington would have considered a Malcolm X a madman was that Washington practiced moderate accommodationist separatism while Malcolm and Elijah preached militant separatism. *But it is still the same separatism whose quality only changes from one era to another.* The Marxists and other radicals cannot see that when Booker T. Washington said to the Southern whites—"In all things purely social we can be as *separate* as the five fingers, yet one as the hand in all things essential to mutual progress"—that Washington was saying in 1895 what Elijah Muhammad was to say under changed conditions sixty-five years later. They were both prophets of a kind of nationalist-separatism, one moderate, one assertive. When Malcolm X was in the Nation of Islam he, too, believed in this separatism, but it was a militant separatism that Malcolm X preached at the behest of Elijah Muhammad. Washington preached a form of separatism which laid the ideological groundwork for both Garvey and Muhammad. But can anybody be serious if he thinks that Booker T. Washington could have preached Muhammad's kind of militant separatism *in 1895 in the deep Alabama South?* Anyone who thinks so must be a consummate fool and romantic (after the fact)! Why can't white Marxists put aside their provincial and infantile prejudices, use their analytical method (which is the best in the world) and THINK. Jesus Christ preached peace and good will to all men, but when the Christian believers go out and wage war it does not stop them from being Christians in belief. Washington's nationalism and Malcolm's nationalism are related; it is merely a question of *how* they are used, and *why* and *when*.

The Marxists call Booker T. Washington an accommodationist and a conservative because he shied away from the militant civil rights struggles. But the Marxists fail to see (although they are looking straight at it) that this was precisely the reason Malcolm X broke with Elijah Muhammad. Malcolm claimed that the Nation of Islam had grown conservative, that Elijah refused to become embroiled in the "broad struggles." Malcolm X then joined the broad struggle and became another kind of a black nationalist. Did this mean that Elijah Muhammad ceased to be his own brand of black nationalist? Of course not! He simply remained a conservative separatist nationalist. Why can't the Marxists understand this? It is really very simple.

Why can't a Herbert Aptheker understand that when W. E. B. Du Bois, a younger generation radical, broke with the conservatism of Booker T. Washington on civil rights questions, he did what Malcolm X was forced to do in breaking with Elijah Muhammad. It was merely a case of the young breaking with the old. Herbert Aptheker applauds this action (historically), but does not truly understand it. Aptheker is so engrossed in drooling sentimentally over his enduring love for W. E. B. Du Bois he loses all his historical objectivity (if he ever possessed that quality). I can assure you that when some of the sons and daughters of certain of Aptheker's Communist Party leadership cronies broke with their parents' beloved Communist Party because it had grown superannuated and conservative, Herbert Aptheker did not applaud so loudly. History has the ironic faculty of repeating itself, much to the consternation of all dogmatic die-hards—whether they are Marxists, black nationalists, conservatives, liberals or revisionists.

The young-guard radicals, too, have their troubles with social perception. Trotsky, for example, taught them many things, but apparently not how to think originally. Frank Kofsky is drooling over the exploits of Malcolm X much as Herbert Aptheker moons over W. E. B. Du Bois. But with all that Marx, Lenin, and Trotsky wrote, poor Kofsky simply cannot understand Malcolm's "lineage" to Booker T. Washington through Marcus Garvey to Elijah Muhammad. Why? Because neither Marx nor Lenin nor Trotsky were able to see black nationalism develop in America and thereby instruct a Frank Kofsky how he should view this native American social phenomenon "scientifically" or according to a real Marxist analysis. The trouble with our current breed of American radicals (on the Negro) is that they use their method of analysis *not* to understand the Negro but to make some outstanding black leadership symbol fit the political line of their own preconceptions. The radicals have had the convenient advantage in recent years of capitalizing on the derelictions of the Communists on the Negro. Hence they were able to overcome the indigenous American Marxist prejudice against black nationalism. As a result they were able to form a tentative kind of alliance with Malcolm X's tendency. This has led Frank Kofsky to go completely overboard in his claim that Malcolm X was not only a revolutionary nationalist but an "international-socialist one at that." Come, come, Frank Kofsky, Malcolm X did not have time to become all of that. Do not confuse black nationalist militancy with "revolutionary" capabilities under American capitalism! A revolutionary has to have a revolutionary social program, which Malcolm X did not possess. And don't repeat again that naive SWP belief that Malcolm was about to announce his program "just before he died." It is not in the nature of the inner development of the black nationalist movement that this would have been possible. Malcolm X was neither genius nor miracle worker. Had he lived, it is very doubtful that he would have developed any further than what the Black Power movement has pronounced to date. Malcolm X was headed toward what became the Black Power position—which is *not* a revolutionary position. It is a reformist position which has given vent to the revolutionary anarchism which had existed before by way of Watts, etc. Before he died, Malcolm's statements on politics, economics, and self-defense were no different from what were put forth as resolutions at the Black Power conference. Moreover, none of Malcolm's views on economics, politics, and self-defense was original with him. Malcolm X remained a militant black nationalist until the moment he died. He was evolving into something undefinable because present circumstances make definitions highly conjectural and tentative.

To return to the problem of the political economy of Black Power, you will note that the vagueness and indefiniteness among blacks on the meaning of Black Power matches the vagueness, conflict and indefiniteness among white Marxists over the meaning of black nationalism (both conservative and "revolutionary"). This puts the socialists (black and white) in an ideological dilemma and a theoretical bind. It creates an almost insurmountable gulf between black and white radical forces. The causes here are profound—racial, historical, and theoretical. They can be overcome *only* by the right kind of critical analysis of the social phenomena involved by both sides, black and white. How is this to be done? It can only be accomplished if both sides drop their subjectivity and put aside all their preconceived notions about this and that and go back to first principles. Negroes must go back and reinterpret their own black history in America, and the Marxists (white and black) must go back and re-examine their Marxist methods of analysis. Even here, it must be said that a proper analysis of our current situation *must* bring forth completely new conceptions, because the American black and white social phenomenon is a uniquely new world thing. It is not European, thus there are not many theoretical precedents for dealing with it. Therefore, the Marxists have to go back to *their* books in order to review what *they* have failed to master in *their* own theoretical tradition, in order to be better able to meet the new theoretical and creative demands imposed on them by this unique American reality.

With apologies to Herbert Aptheker, we must attempt to get to the roots of this problem by starting with the historical conflict over "program" between W. E. B. Du Bois and Booker T. Washington. The problem with the Marxists is that they have never comprehended the deeper meaning of this controversy. Moreover, the Marxist socialist conferees have been looking for the "roots of black nationalism" in the wrong place. The era of slavery is too far back. Slavery explains some things, but not all or enough. In dealing with black nationalism today, we are dealing with what is essentially a *twentieth-century movement* which has its origins, main compulsions, and ideologies in the twentieth century.

It is strange that the Marxist socialists who participated in the scholars' conference of 1966 should not understand this fact. The legacy of slavery certainly did establish ideological patterns that carried over into the twentieth century, but they could not be crucial influences in the rise of black nationalism in this century. Such a conclusion would have to leave out the results and effects of the Reconstruction period, which was an attempt on the part of the radical and progressive forces to win the democratic inclusion of the Negro in American society. However, the roots of black nationalism in America must be found both in the *failures of black Reconstruction and the rise of the American imperialistic age*, which is to say the age in which American foreign policy became openly imperialistic, coupled with renewed national oppression inside the country.

I do not believe that the slave revolts constitute the real leadership ideology of pre-Civil War black nationalism. This prewar and postwar black nationalism involves itself more politically and socially with the emigration-back to Africa movement or separate state idea led by such men as Martin R. Delany and his associates who, in 1859, organized the Niger Valley Exploring Party which went to Africa in search of possible sites for the repatriation of black freedmen to Africa. They also sought out possible emigration sites in Latin America and Canada. It should be recalled here that Frederick Douglass, the first prototype of the Abolitionist-civil rights-protest leadership was thoroughly opposed to this black nationalist trend, personified in Delany, which sought a solution to the emancipation problem through emigration. Douglass considered any Negro interest in Africa as a troublesome, impractical, and worthless diversion of energies needed to win full equality for Negroes in America. And it appears that the advent of Reconstruction so absorbed all the Negro leadership, even the emigrationists, that emigration efforts diminished radically. Even Delany submitted to giving full time to health and welfare work among the freedmen. Delany was a graduate physician. His leadership role was considerable, but he was overshadowed by the personality of Frederick Douglass before and after the Civil War, into the Reconstruction period.

Frederick Douglass, who died in 1895, was replaced by another leader, Booker T. Washington, who came into prominence the same year through his famous Atlanta Exposition "separate fingers" declaration of "mutual race progress." Then came the young W. E. B. Du Bois in 1903 to challenge Washington's accommodationist doctrines. He challenged Washington on his Negro educational philosophy of industrial training and also on civil rights and racial equality. It is worth noting that Frederick Douglass fully supported Washington's industrial training program for the "masses." However, Du Bois differed with Washington on other grounds besides civil rights and higher education, and for our purposes of dissecting the roots of black nationalism and the meaning of Black Power today, these other grounds are much more crucial for our deeper understanding of what the Washington-Du Bois controversy was all about. Note very carefully what Du Bois said about Washington's philosophy:

Mr. Washington represents in Negro thought the old attitude of adjustment and submission; but adjustment at such a peculiar time as to make his programme unique. *This is an age of unusual economic development, and Mr. Washington's programme naturally takes an economic cast, becoming a gospel of Work and Money to such an extent as apparently almost completely to overshadow the higher aims of life.* (Italics added)

Note the high idealism inherent in Du Bois's outlook. Further:

He is striving nobly to make Negro artisans business men and property owners; but it is utterly impossible, under modern competitive methods, for workingmen and property-owners to defend their rights and exist without the means of suffrage.

He insists on thrift and self-respect, but at the same time counsels a silent submission to civic inferiority such as is bound to sap the manhood of any race in the long run.

He advocates common-school and industrial training, and depreciates institutions of higher learning . . .

To counter what he called Washington's "accommodationism," Du Bois said he was "in conscience bound to ask of this nation three things: 1. The right to vote; 2. Civic equality; 3. The education of youth according to ability." [6] The substance of Washington's reply to Du Bois and other critics of his program was this:

Brains, property, and character for the Negro will settle the question of civil rights. The best course to pursue in regards to a civil rights bill in the South is to let it alone; let it alone and it will settle itself. Good school teachers and plenty of money to pay them will be more potent in settling the race question than many civil rights bills and investigating committees.

The real implications of this dialogue between Du Bois and Washington will become clearer if we keep in mind that while Du Bois was criticizing the shortcomings of Booker T's program, Washington's protégés of the Afro-American Realty Company were engaged on the Harlem real estate front carrying out an aggressive and militant struggle of *black economic nationalism* for economic control of a quality area for the housing of hundreds (later thousands) of Negroes. In 1907, when the last edition of *The Souls of Black Folk* was printed, Washington also published his important book, *The Negro In Business*, in which he described the development of twenty-five Negro businesses from banking to building. These included businesses in the following fields: agriculture, catering, hotels, mortuaries, manufacturing, publishing, and real estate. Washington wrote that in the year 1900, when he founded the National Negro Business League, "Of the 76,026 persons of Negro blood in this country who are engaged in the professions and in the trades requiring skill, 21,161 are teachers and professors. Only 9,838 are in businesses requiring capital." By 1907 this situation in Negro business had improved. In 1900, for example, Washington's business league had helped found the New Rochelle Cooperative Business League with a capital stock of $25,000. Later on, Washington founded "Negro Health Week." In 1892, Washington established regular Tuskegee conferences with farmers and sharecroppers in Alabama in which he educated them "on the evils of the mortgage system . . . buying on credit." He printed and circulated small tracts and circulars explaining to black farmers the essentials of improved farming methods. Washington performed all of these practical, educational, and progressive functions, but the Du Bois radicals did not like his general program and philosophy. Were they justified? Let us see.

Did Booker T. Washington really counsel "submission," as Du Bois contended? In view of the Southern situation in the 1890's, a period of intense post-Reconstruction political and racial oppression, was Washington's program abject submission or a tactical compromise with reality? Remember, Du Bois was not a Southerner and built no institutions in Alabama. How can one seriously maintain that Washington's economic, educational, and organizational activities were a form of submission? It is true that Washington was no civil rights militant, but the tenor of his approach on civil rights can be gauged from his message to the Louisiana State Democratic Organization in 1898 on the institution of the "grandfather clause" device that disfranchised Negroes all over the South. Washington said: "No one clothed with state authority will be tempted to perjure and degrade himself by putting one interpretation upon it for the white man and another for the black man." This was pure moderation, to be sure; but he *did* speak out on political affairs in this manner throughout his career. It would have been unrealistic to expect an educator whose Tuskegee Institute depended upon the support and goodwill of white politicians and financiers to act like a civil rights radical or "take to the hills."

The point here is that Washington's record clearly shows that he was *not* against the things Du Bois stood for in civil rights, any more than Du Bois was against Washington's program of making Negro artisans businessmen and property owners, or his philosophy of Work and Money. With both of them it was a question of *what is more important and what do you emphasize* as the basis of your program to advance the Negro in America. On this point they were in fundamental disagreement. But this conflict between Washington and Du Bois was symptomatic of an even more fundamental and deeper *class cleavage* than the historians (especially Aptheker) have taken into account. The Washington-Du Bois controversy was *a reflection of the split within the new, emerging, Afro-American black bourgeoisie* of our twentieth-century America. It is obvious that Booker T. Washington was the spokesman and prophet of the bourgeois nationalist wing of the black bourgeoisie which, under those 1900 conditions, was moderate or conservative in civil rights politics generally, *but* progressive, militant, and resourceful in black economics and functional education, and tactful in their methods of "power structure" politics. On the other hand, W. E. B. Du Bois was the leading spokesman for the radical civil rights protest wing of the black bourgeoisie, whose most effective spokesmen *had to be one of the militant and radical bourgeois intellectuals and professionals.* These antagonists and protagonists were all of the same *class development;* they simply represented different *tendencies* in that same class emergence. This is what the Marxists have always failed to consider, thereby violating one of the basic tenets of their own Marxian method of social analysis. It is what confounds an avowed Marxist such as Frank Kofsky who does not understand a Booker T. Washington because he does not grasp the historical roots of bourgeois nationalism within the black movement.

In 1913, Joseph Stalin, then a ranking Marxist-Leninist analyst of the "national and colonial question" wrote:

The chief problem for the young bourgeoisie is the problem of the market. Its aim is to sell its goods and to emerge victorious from competition with the bourgeoisie of another nationality. Hence its desire to secure its "own," its "home" market. *The market is the first school in which the bourgeoisie learns its nationalism.* [Italics added] [7]

Thus the rising black bourgeoisie in America of 1900 had its bourgeois nationalist spokesman in Booker T. Washington; but the bourgeois radical integrationist spokesman, Du Bois, criticized Washington's economic policies of work, money, business, profit and property, as detrimental to the cause of civil rights and, therefore, inappropriate as a program. The problem was that neither Washington nor Du Bois actually understood themselves as "bourgeois nationalist" or "bourgeois integrationist" or their movement as a bourgeois movement. Each of them was simply responding intuitively to the same situation according to his respective background, training, and convictions. Note that when Du Bois evaluates Washington's interest in work, money, property, and economic development against the "higher aims of life," he was depreciating black capitalist development just as if it were neither desirable nor historically necessary. But Marxists know (or should know) that at certain stages capitalistic development is both necessary and desirable. Historians such as Aptheker go back into slavery to find manifestations of Negro nationality in the "nation within a nation" idea of such nationalist leaders as Martin R. Delany. However, in 1913 Joseph Stalin wrote: "A nation is not merely a historical category but a historical category belonging to a definite epoch, the epoch of rising capitalism." [8]

For the Afro-American, "the epoch of rising capitalism" was *not* the epoch of white bourgeois capitalism, whose need for expansion and political dominance smashed the slave system in the South, but the epoch of black bourgeois capitalistic emergence beginning around 1900 when Washington established the National Negro Business League. Thus Booker T. Washington was expressing *the real, fundamental class aspirations of the epoch.* He was the bourgeois leader-educator who was learning his bourgeois nationalism in the politics of the market place (Stalin), but who played the capitalistic game according to the rules that prevailed (as all smart capitalists do). Thus irrespective of what a Du Bois might have thought about the role of a Washington (or vice versa), they were both representative of different wings of the same bourgeois movement. Stalin, again, explained how such movements as the black bourgeois emergence of 1900 come into being under the intensely oppressive racist conditions of America at that time:

The bourgeoisie of the oppressed nation, repressed on every hand, is naturally stirred into movement. It appeals to its "native folk" and begins to cry out about Fatherland, claiming that its own cause is the cause of the nation as a whole. It recruits itself an army from among its "countrymen" in the interests of Fatherland. Nor do the "folk" always remain unresponsive to its appeals, they rally around its banner; the repression from above affects them also and provokes their discontent.

Thus the national movement begins.[9]

In the case of the black bourgeois emergence of 1900, it is a historical fact that Booker T. Washington had more of the "folk" rallying to his banners than did W. E. B. Du Bois to his. Yet it proves very little in terms of who was "wrong" or who was "right," since it does not help us understand the real nature of the bourgeois movement by taking sides. How to approach a social phenomenon such as this 1900 movement is best explained by Marx:

Just as our opinion of an individual is not based on what he thinks of himself, so can we not judge of such a period of trans-formation by its own consciousness; on the contrary this con-sciousness must be explained rather from the contradictions of material life, from the existing conflict between the social forces of production and the relations of production. No social order ever disappears before all the productive forces for which there is room in it have been developed. . . . Therefore, mankind always sets itself only such tasks as it can solve; since, looking at the matter more closely, we will always find that the task itself arises only when the material conditions necessary for its solution al-ready exist or are at least in the process of formation.[10]

Hence, insofar as the black bourgeois emergence of 1900 is concerned, we can judge neither Du Bois nor Washington on what they thought about themselves. But Aptheker judges Du Bois on just that basis, revealing that this Marxist has learned very little from Marx, Lenin, or Stalin on how to ex-plain the black bourgeois "period of transformation" of 1900. Can Aptheker swear that in America in 1900 there existed no more room for the capitalistic expansion of the white bour-geoisie *or the black?* Can Aptheker swear that the white pro-letariat was prepared to overthrow American capitalism in 1900? Can Aptheker seriously maintain that the expansion of American capitalism from 1900 to 1929 was unnecessary, his-torically unjustified, or sociologically inappropriate? Of course he cannot. Then why would this Marxist, Aptheker, assume that there *could not, should not* arise a pro-capitalistic wing of the American black bourgeoisie with a spokesman named

Booker T. Washington? If the Marxist Aptheker believes in what the Marxist Stalin wrote about how national movements begin under the leadership of the bourgeois classes (he has to believe this, which has nothing at all to do with the question of post-Lenin Stalinism), then how would the Negro national movement begin in America unless under the leadership of a black bourgeoisie—and when? The problem of Aptheker, the Marxist, is that he has liberalistic subjective hangovers about the status of the "Negro People." He cannot deal objectively with the black bourgeoisie as a class phenomenon in real life from a Marxist point of view. He cannot bring himself to call W. E. B. Du Bois what he really was—*a bourgeois radical intellectual* whose "talented tenth" bourgeois elitism was nothing but a philosophy representing *his* tactic in an inner-class struggle for leadership. As a tactic, however, Du Bois's elitism was no more to be deplored or upheld than Washington's bourgeois economic nationalism. Both tactics had positive features. But Aptheker has another subjective problem which has little to do with Marxism; like many Americans, Aptheker cannot take black capitalist aspirations seriously. White capitalists are a class catastrophe we hard-pressed, earnest Marxists have to put up with in the course of honorable struggle for socialism. But black capitalists? My God! (Negroes in America are predominantly workers, the Marxists protest, *they are poor people*. Other corollaries to this attitude are: (1) don't let Negroes get hold of money, *that means power*; (2) keep all Negroes poor and, therefore, tractable; (3) rich Negroes are an abomination; (4) money spoils Negroes because they don't know how to handle it; (5) all Negroes—rich and poor—should reject capitalistic ambitions in favor of socialist brotherhood; etc., etc.) All of these Marxian and non-Marxian racial attitudes we American Negroes understand quite well. All the folklore of American race prejudice is familiar to us. But it is disastrously appalling when Marxists fall into this mythic pattern of thought. It is quite true that the majority of Negroes are workers, but E. Franklin Frazier pointed out what is also very true about Negroes when he wrote: "From its inception the education of the Negro was shaped by bourgeois ideals." [11] Thus the education of the black bourgeoisie veered from the making of men to the making of money-makers. Towards this end, Booker T. Washington was the prophet.

Herbert Aptheker's perennial, plodding, unimaginative blindness on Negro history has led him into the inescapable swamps of theoretical obscurantism. What he calls the "Developing Negro Liberation Movement, 1901–1910," was, in fact, the emergence of two clashing and conflicting tendencies of the black bourgeoisie. It was this class that furnished the leaders, sopkesmen, and ideologists for this so-called "Liberation Movement." It is one thing for either non-Marxist blacks or whites, past or present, to describe these historical events under such an oversimplified heading as "Negro Liberation Movement"; but for a Marxist such a description is un-Marxian and unscientific. It blurs the manifest dynamics of class motivations and inner-class contentions within this "Negro Liberation Movement." It obscures the real origins of the bourgeois nationalist tendency within this liberation movement. It fails to make clear what the conflicting tendencies within this movement were really at odds about. What was really at stake? It makes it easy for partisan prejudices of whatever political orientation to take sides with a particular tendency within this liberation movement and declare that God, Virtue, Justice, and Verity are on the side of "my favorite Negro leader." Thus, for Herbert Aptheker, W. E. B. Du Bois was forever on the side of the liberation angels and Booker T. Washington was forever to be consigned to the nether regions of those who "submitted." Yet Washington had a mass following among Negroes that Du Bois never had in his life. In fact, the new Negro radical generation of black socialism in 1920 did not view Du Bois as very radical. A. Philip Randolph's *Messenger* group said of him:

Du Bois's conception of politics is strictly opportunist. Within the last six years he has been democrat, Socialist, and Republican. . . .
He opposes unionism instead of opposing a prejudiced union. He must make way for the new radicalism of the New Negroes.[12]

Twenty years previously W. E. B. Du Bois was saying much the same about Booker T. Washington. It only serves to show that what is radical or conservative is relative to time, place, and circumstance. Herbert Aptheker has good and ample reasons for so highly lauding and apotheosizing W. E. B. Du Bois, especially in view of the venerable scholar's incomparable achievements during his long life. The point is that a Herbert Aptheker, when he discusses this so-called "Negro Liberation Movement" in which he gives Du Bois a key leadership role, must take into account what Du Bois, himself, finally said about this movement's achievements. He said, in 1940, that this liberation movement was a failure. In summing up his work with the NAACP which he helped to found, he said:

There are, however, manifest difficulties about such a program. First of all, it is not a program that envisages any direct action of Negroes themselves for the uplift of their socially depressed masses.[13]

There is no way in which the American Negro can force this nation to treat him as an equal.[14]

There faces the American Negro therefore an intricate and subtle problem combining into one object two difficult sets of facts: His present racial segregation which will persist for several decades; and his attempt by carefully planned and intelligent action to fit himself into the new economic organization which the world faces.[15]

In discussing himself and Booker T. Washington and the conflict of programs that had occurred between them, Du Bois admitted:

I was not against Washington's ideas.[16]

[Our] two theories of Negro progress were not absolutely contradictory.[17]

[Washington] did not advocate a deliberate planned segregation.[18]

I did not wish to attack Booker T. Washington . . . [etc.] [19]

But he explained:

There came a controversy between myself and Booker T. Washington which became more personal and bitter than I ever dreamed.[20]

Then:

He [Washington] never adequately grasped the growing bond of politics and industry.[21]

Let us note, here, that twenty-five years after Booker T. Washington died, Du Bois is forced to confess that what Herbert Aptheker called (in 1951) the "Negro Liberation Movement" was not really the answer for liberation at all, for it was "not a program that envisages any direct action of Negroes themselves." If this was true in 1940, how much more true must it have been in 1900 in Washington's Alabama. Yet W. E. B. Du Bois and the radicals blamed Washington for not believing in the efficacy of *their* program for racial equality in 1900. Although W. E. B. Du Bois had to admit, indirectly, that Booker T. Washington had not been *all wrong* about civil rights agitation in 1900, Du Bois still refused to give Washington his due credit. He declared, in 1940: "We must lay on the soul of this man a heavy responsibility for the consummation of Negro disfranchisement . . ." [22] which is to imply either that Washington did not care to see Negroes have the vote, or that because he compromised on civil rights agitation he aided and abetted the complete disfranchisement of Negroes in the South. Here Du Bois could not bring himself to admit that the Southern Bourbons were hell-bent on emasculating the Negro politically and would have achieved it despite anything Washington or anyone else cared to do about it. Then, after admitting that his own thirty-year effort in the NAACP was a failure, Du Bois then outlined the premises of his own "new" program for the Negro, the "economic cooperative commonwealth" (a version of Black Power), overlooking the fact that Washington not only preached the necessity of co-operative economic efforts for twenty-five years, but had helped to establish cooperatives in New Rochelle and else-where as far back as 1905. Great as he was, W. E. B. Du Bois was always late in catching up to the realities of grass-roots sentiments and necessities.

To repeat, all of the foregoing points up the fact that the Marxists' basic analytical error was to term Negro develop-ments from 1900 the "Negro Liberation Movement," when in fact it was an ideological division within the main tendencies of the emerging black bourgeoisie over which course to take for true Negro progress. Should it be basically bourgeois, self-help, group economics, plus functional, practical educa-tion with a de-emphasis of civil rights agitation? Or should it be an emphasis on civil rights-protest agitation, social equal-ity, and higher "humanities" education, etc., etc? This is how the conflict in tendencies was posed; this is how the conflict has been fought out, on one level or another, ever since the Washington-Du Bois controversy emerged. What the Marx-ian socialists who now seek a "political economy" for Black Power don't appear to understand is that the present slogan of Black Power is nothing more than a shifting back to the basic position taken by Booker T. Washington in 1900 with the addition, of course, of certain contemporary refinements. When the CORE and SNCC "direct action" protest-civil righters make a turnabout and say:

give up "integration" efforts . . .
de-emphasize civil rights protests . . .
stop agitation for more worthless civil rights bills . . .
let us go back into the black communities and build *our*

own economic, educational, and political institutions . . . let us build *Black Power!* Then we'll be *equal!*

What real difference is there between these slogans of today and those of Booker T. Washington in 1900 when he said:

brains, money, property, education . . .

plenty of good schools and good teachers . . .

tone down worthless civil rights protests . . .

let us build our group economic power . . .

let us have good farms, good businesses, thriving cooperatives . . .

let us establish these things for ourselves and all civil rights will be added as a matter of course, for we will then be truly equal.

There is, *basically*, no difference at all. When W. E. B. Du Bois said, in 1903, that Washington's program was faulty because it was "utterly impossible, under modern competitive methods, for workingman and property-owners to defend their rights and exist without the right of suffrage," it was precisely what the *opponents* of Black Power within the civil rights movement say today: *Black Power is going it alone, but that is impossible under "modern competitive (and other) methods" of the white world. You must continue to fight for more "rights of suffrage" (plus more integration).*

There are certain new features in the Black Power recurrence of Booker T-ism of our times. For one thing there is the added militant-nationalist-separatist wing in this Black Power movement. There is also the revolutionary anarchist ideology, which is far removed from the generic moderate economic nationalism of Booker T. Washington. However—and note well—*it was not these militant-separatist-revolutionary anarchist elements who organized, convened, and spearheaded the Black Power Conference.* This was done by a moderate Black Power supporter, a member of a black middle-class community establishment who, in his book on Black Power, harks back to none other than the original ideas of Booker T. Washington.* But a Marxist, such as Frank Kofsky, will still find all of this beyond his comprehension. In order to explain why, we must go deeper.

The Marxist socialists cannot deal properly with these questions because for nearly fifty years the American Marxists have been fundamentally off-base in their over-all analysis of the Negro presence in America. What certain Marxists dubbed the "Negro Liberation Movement" was a gross theoretical and analytical oversimplification of what was happening. I can well understand *why* this has happened, yet I find it strange that it *should* have happened. Consider the fact that V. I. Lenin, as far back as 1905, dealt very adequately (in Russian terms) with every issue that was to crop out in the development of what the American Marxists called the Negro Liberation Movement. A parallel situation, developing in Russia, involving the Russian bourgeoisie, was not called by Lenin any such thing as the "Russian Liberation Movement." This movement Lenin called the "Democratic Revolution" and his pamphlet on the subject was called "Two Tactics of Social-Democracy in the Democratic Revolution." Reading this pamphlet over again, I get the impression that if anyone in 1905 had dared express such an infantile conception as "Russian Liberation Movement," he would have been laughed out of the Social-Democratic (Marxist) Party in Russia.

Very obviously, the American Marxists have been thrown off balance in dealing with the Negro because of the fact that Negroes constitute a large non-white ethnic minority within a predominantly white nation with a large white working class. Desiring to see the Negro group merely as an appendage to the main body of white workers, the Marxists have been unable, theoretically and practically, *to set the Negro off and see him in terms of his own national minority group existence and identity, inclusive of his class, caste, and ideological stratifications.* If the Marxists (especially the black ones) had been

* See Dr. Nathan Wright's *Black Power and Urban Unrest* (New York: Hawthorn).

able to do this, then the Negro national minority could have been seen as developing a new movement beginning in 1900 which was essentially a "Democratic Revolution"—or better, a bourgeois-led movement aimed at completing the uncompleted *American* Democratic Revolution in terms of including Negroes (especially bourgeois Negroes) in the American democratic equation. In Russian terms, Lenin described this development more exactly. He called it the *Russian bourgeois-democratic revolution*. And the problem was how the Russian Marxist party, the Social-Democratic movement, would relate to this bourgeois-democratic revolution. Further, there was the problem of how to relate the aims and aspirations of the Russian workers and peasants to the aspirations of the Russian bourgeoisie and their bourgeois-democratic revolution. Toward this end, the Russian Marxists were faced with "Two Tactics." There is a distinct parallel here, for in the emergent Negro bourgeois-democratic revolution of 1900 there were also *two tactics* implicit in this movement—one Washington's, the other Du Bois'. They personified the fateful split within the Negro bourgeois movement—the bourgeois nationalists versus the bourgeois integrationists. On one level or another, on one issue or another, at different times and in different circumstances, these two tendencies have been at war with each other ever since 1900. First it was the conflict between Washington and Du Bois; then between Du Bois and Garvey; later between Garvey nationalism and black Communism or black socialism as during the Randolph *Messenger* magazine period; then the continuing conflict between the remnants of Garveyism and the continuing NAACP tradition; then the new, young-wave civil righters' break with the NAACP tradition, as Du Bois had already done in 1940. Very often the conflict between nationalist and integrationist tendencies is evident within *one individual* as in the case of Du Bois himself. When ths occurred, the integrationist tendency in Du Bois won out over the nationalist tendency. He said that his new plan could "easily be mistaken

for a program of complete *racial segregation and even nationalism* among Negroes . . . this is a misapprehension." (Italics
added.) [23]

Then a uniquely new force came on the scene—the Muslim
Nation of Islam. This movement used the unifying force of
religion to weld unknown thousands of Negroes into a viable
nationalist entity. In this instance, religion took the place of a
cohesive political creed which neither Marxism, socialism,
Communism, nor black nationalism alone could do. But under
the ideology of Islam we find the same economic and educational philosophy of Booker T. Washington in more updated
trappings. On a lesser scale, religion achieved what "Back to
Africa"-West Indian nationalism failed to maintain on a larger
scale in the 1920's. Because Garveyism sought no solution for
the race problem *within* the United States, and because of its
West Indian, pro-British Empire biases operating *outside* its
native Caribbean locale, Garveyism, as a force, could not out-
live its leader and became outdated. Any kind of black nationalist movement today cannot be viable unless it seeks some
kind of solution within the continental limits of the United
States. Otherwise it degenerates into political withdrawal and
escapist romanticism. This is why, among other factors, the
new, young 1960's wave of radical civil righters and radical
nationalists have come to split the entire civil rights movement
with the slogan of Black Power. But in 1968, this Black Power
movement cannot fully escape *any* of its sixty-eight-year-old
heritage—either nationalist or integrationist—nor can the
Black Power movement use *all* of its heritage in *pure forms*.
It cannot use old-fashioned Booker T-ism in pure form, but
repeats its basic slogans in a modern, updated manner. It must
use *something* from the Du Bois tradition, even though it
might attempt to disown Du Bois without understanding all
that he stood for in different phases of his long career. The
Black Power movement might claim to honor the tradition of
Marcus Garvey but it can't use the "Back to Africa" slogan
anymore because Africa is out of reach (hence the symbolism

of the African dress). The Black Power movement might claim to disown the integrationist heritage of the "Negro Liberation Movement" beginning with 1900, but this is only tactical and verbal. It does this (as did Washington) merely to de-emphasize its contemporary importance as a principled goal in life. In 1968, the Black Power movement is able to be cavalier about the few, limited gains in integration that the integrationist forces have achieved against the odds. These gains have proven insufficient for total black necessities, even though in 1900 such social gains were unheard-of and would have been considered "radical" achievements.

The only way for the Marxist socialists to analyze this sixty-eight-year-old Negro movement correctly is to see it as Lenin saw similar movements of his time, i.e., as a bourgeois-democratic revolution. These bourgeois-democratic revolutions were taking place among the colored races in practically all of the colonial and semi-colonial countries. If the Marxists in America had seen from the very beginning that the position of the Negro in America was nothing less than a Western form of *domestic colonialism,** then things programmatic would have been simpler for all concerned. It would have been seen, for example, that men like Washington, Du Bois, Garvey, Randolph, and others were of the same stripe and caliber of men like Sun Yat Sen, Gandhi, Nehru, Chiang Kai-shek, and all other "bourgeois nationalist" and "bourgeois democratic" leaders of movements that sprang up in the colonial and semi-colonial areas immediately before World War I and shortly thereafter. The great difference was that some of these bourgeois-democratic revolutions, such as the Russian, were more successful than others due to a number of unique circumstances—geographical, political, military, etc. Others were very long, drawn-out affairs. In fact, among the very longest has been the Afro-American bourgeois-democratic revolution.

* "Domestic colonialism" first used by the author in his article "Revolutionary Nationalism and the Afro-American," *Studies on the Left*, 1961, Vol. II, No. 3.

Our black bourgeois-democratic revolution started in 1900 and is still incomplete due to our unique and peculiar American circumstances and the institutional structure of race relations. Our Negro bourgeois-democratic revolution has continued for sixty-eight years through ups and downs, shifts and permutations, victories and defeats, changes of leadership, a proliferation of tendencies, refinements of programs, changes of slogans, the rise and fall and clash of integrationist and nationalist tendencies, the infusion of Communist and socialist ideologies, down to this latest development, Black Power, in which the integrationist and nationalist tendencies are in conflict on a brand new level of involvement. But the Marxist socialists cannot lose sight of the historical fact that it is still the same bourgeois-democratic revolution still being defeated, delayed and aborted. The key fact in our current developments is that the bourgeois-democratic leadership (integrationist) is fast losing its control of and prior claim to exclusive leadership of the movement after all these years. The Black Power Conference demonstrated that the middle-class establishment has not been totally dethroned as the supplier of leadership cadres (they might never be). The bourgeois-democratic revolution is now greatly infused with the fresh spirit of black working-class and petit-bourgeois student and intellectual elements. Yet the cry for "Black Unity" that emerged from the Black Power Conference reveals that the implications of class aspirations under the slogan of Black Power are not very well understood. In fact, the grass-roots radical-nationalist elements are forced to accept the moderate bourgeois leadership because *they lack any feasible goals which are sufficiently independent of the aims and aspirations of the moderates.* It is for these reasons that Black Power is now basically a reformist movement; its middle-class leadership can only aspire to reformist economic and political programs. Black Power is not revolutionary, but a movement of *rebellion* in practice and ideology and *reformist in program.*

It is enlightening for me, a nonconformist radical indepen-

dent student of revolutionary movements, to read what Lenin
had to say about the reformist goals of the bourgeois-democratic revolution:

It is to the advantage of the bourgeoisie if the necessary bourgeois-democratic changes take place more slowly, more gradually, more cautiously, with less determination, by means of
reforms and not by means of revolution . . . if these reforms
develop as little as possible the revolutionary initiative, the initiative and the energy of the common people. . . .

On the other hand, it is more advantageous for the working class
if the necessary bourgeois-democratic changes take place in the
form of revolution and not reform; for the latter is the road of
delay, procrastination, of painfully slow decomposition of the
putrid parts of the national organism.[24]

These remarks should be of interest to practicing Marxist
socialists in their quest for a "political economy of Black
Power." Lenin explains here why it is un-Marxist for Marxists
in America to expect Negro integrationists such as Wilkins,
Young, and King to act like "revolutionaries" in the civil
rights movement. Yet this is precisely what the Marxists do,
and it is because they are unscientific and muddled about the
bourgeois-democratic revolution in America *from the black
point of view.* The Marxists do not analyze how this democratic revolution has been delayed, checked, and aborted by
American capitalism. For a long, long time the Marxists were
confused over "racial integration" and "nationalism." For
example, they swallowed whole the NAACP idea that integration was legitimate in principle as a goal for *all Negroes* simply
because it appeared to be synonymous with "racial democracy," "social equality," "equal rights," "civil rights," etc.
(As a synonym for civil rights, the word "integration" did
not enter the NAACP lexicon until 1940 in connection with
the demand for the "integration of the armed forces.") For
example, as late as 1957, the Socialist Workers Party complained in its draft resolution on "The Class Struggle Road to
Negro Equality" that: "The fundamental flaw in NAACP

policy—complete reliance on the capitalist government to secure civil rights [read integration]—has repeatedly upset its organizational control over the insurgent Negro masses." [25]

The question is, What did the Trotskyites expect the NAACP to do? Storm the barricades with urban guerrillas? In the *New York Post* of August 1, 1967, a news item stated that Floyd McKissick, Wilfred Ussery, and Roy Inniss demanded that the U.S. Department of Labor "develop a crash program for jobless Negroes and a living allowance until jobs are found." They also demanded that anti-poverty funds be increased by ten billion dollars. These are all Black Power advocates, but they are also showing a whole lot of "reliance on the capitalist government" to secure Black Power reforms. I am not criticizing these reformist aims, I am only pointing out the methodological confusion of the Marxists in dealing with black social trends. For behind the Marxists' criticism of the NAACP integrationists' reliance on the capitalist government is the implication that a real revolutionary program for the Negro masses should not exhibit any such reliance on the capitalist government. And the only alternative program the Marxists have to offer the Negro masses as opposed to that of the NAACP *is the struggle for socialism.* This is easier said than done since the reality is that Negro masses do maintain a lingering reliance on the capitalist government for redress of all grievances.

The Marxists' confusion over the meaning of the NAACP's integrationist aims was revealed in another way in the SWP's 1957 draft resolution. In attacking the Communist Party's former "black belt" self-determination idea, the Trotskyites said:

This slogan ran counter to the integrationist aims of the colored people and further alienated them from socialist ideas. . . . Theoretically, the profound growth of racial solidarity . . . among the Negro people might under certain conditions give rise to separatist demands. . . . Yet even under these circumstances socialists would continue to advocate integration rather than separation as the best solution of the race question.[26]

The NAACP itself would not disagree with any of these conclusions on racial integration coming from the Trotskyites. Hence, what is the real substance of the SWP's criticisms of the way in which the NAACP pursues integrationist aims (with which the Trotskyites are in full accord)? The answer is that the NAACP wants *capitalist integration*, and the Trotskyites want *socialist integration!* And here is where the Marxists are in serious trouble over grasping the essentials of the Negro bourgeois-democratic revolution in force since 1900. The Marxists have no program that can lead the Negro workers to socialism, and also do not fully understand the real relationship of the capitalist-oriented Negro bourgeois-democratic revolution to capitalistic America. Here again we must fall back on Lenin, since he is the only one (to my knowledge) who has given clear, scientific answers to the problem:

In countries like . . . [colonial and semi-colonial] the working class suffers not so much from capitalism as from the lack of capitalist development. The working class is therefore interested in the widest, freest and speediest development of capitalism. The removal of all the remnants of the old order which are hampering the wide, free, and speedy development of capitalism is of *absolute advantage* to the working class.

The bourgeois revolution is precisely such a revolution. . . . Therefore, the *bourgeois* revolution is in the *highest degree* advantageous to the proletariat. . . . The more complete, determined and consistent the bourgeois revolution is, the more secure will the proletarian struggle against the bourgeoisie and for socialism become. Such a conclusion may appear new, or strange, or even paradoxical only to those who are ignorant of the rudiments of scientific socialism.[27]

In 1968, this will no doubt sound paradoxical to Marxist socialists in America, who will immediately object: "But Lenin was talking about the situation in Russia in 1905. What he said then has not the remotest bearing on the American situation today." Well, so he *was* addressing himself to the Russian situation in 1905; but he was also talking about the "rudiments of scientific socialism" which all Marxists maintain do not change but merely require updating. Can this postulate concerning the relationship of the bourgeois-democratic revolution to capitalist development be updated in America? Let us dispense with all of our pet sentiments about the "necessity of socialism" and look at some facts. What working class of what group in America suffers most from the lack of capitalist development? It is the Negro national minority group. The Socialist Workers Party's 1957 draft resolution stated: "There are virtually no capitalists among the Negro people and only a thin layer of middle class elements." I think the Trotskyites rather underestimated the middle-class stratum,[28] especially its ideological hold on the masses. But they added:

Revolutionary socialists are confronted with complex educational tasks in connection with the civil rights struggle. It is necessary to have a thorough understanding of the historical, theoretical and practical aspects of the fight for Negro equality in its independent character as a movement for democratic reforms under capitalism, a movement which under capitalist decay has a profoundly revolutionary character.[29]

But realizing that the Negro group is "overwhelmingly working class in composition," the SWP sees the Negro workers taking the class struggle road for both "democratic reforms under capitalism" and also a "Negro-Labor alliance" toward a "socialist solution" by taking the "leadership out of the hands of the middle-class elements." A very big order! But, apropos of Lenin's thesis, *would Negro workers be more interested in democratic reforms under capitalism or more capitalistic development within the Negro group itself, irrespective of class?* If one rules out capitalistic development within the Negro group in 1968, then one must rule out the "political economy of Black Power," because the Black Power Conference resulted in many resolutions for the building of black capitalist institutions which were supported by black working-class elements. This bears out Lenin's 1905 thesis that the working class (black in this instance) is interested in the widest development of capitalistic free-enterprise ventures for the black minority because this minority suffers from a lack of capitalist development. This brings us back again to 1900 when the Negro bourgeois-democratic revolution began.

Aptheker is correct: Du Bois was intensely critical of capitalism; Washington worshiped capitalism. *But who was right?* Taken alone, each was right. Taken together, they were both *wrong* for not understanding their own bourgeois movement well enough to get together. But Herbert Aptheker is totally wrong about *both* Washington and Du Bois because he has never admitted the real nature of the movement that obsessed them. Because Aptheker's Marxism is so diluted, he over-simplifies and politically bowdlerizes the Negro bourgeois-democratic revolution by the misnomer Negro Liberation Movement. He further compounds the original error by mis-applying the role of the individual in history by over-glorify-ing the individual (Du Bois) and by not clarifying the nature of *the basic social trends that make the individual*. He then compounds the second error by naively interpreting Du Bois' anti-capitalism as a political virtue in representing the aspirations of a minority whose gravest social disabilities are the result of a lack of capitalist development. This is typical of Marxists, and makes it clearer today why Marxists have made so little headway within the black community.

What *should* Marxists do today about the lack of capitalist development within the Negro community? They will say, "But it is much too late in the American dream for Negroes to think of capitalist development. The issue today is socialism. It is preposterous for any Negro to aspire to capitalist entre-preneuring in 1968." When we speak of Negro social disabil-ities under capitalism, however, we refer to the fact that he does not own anything—*even what is ownable in his own community*. Thus to fight for black liberation *is to fight for his right to own.* The Negro is politically compromised today because he owns nothing. He can exert little political power because he owns nothing. He has little voice in the affairs of state because he owns nothing. The fundamental reason why the Negro bourgeois-democratic revolution has been aborted is because American capitalism has prevented the development of a black class of capitalist owners of institutions and economic tools. To take one crucial example, Negro radicals today are severely hampered in their tasks of educating the black masses on political issues because Negroes do not own any of the necessary means of propaganda and communication. The Negro owns no printing presses, he has no stake in the networks of the means of communication. Inside his own communities he does not own the houses he lives in, the property he lives on, nor the wholesale and retail sources from which he buys his commodities. He does not own the edifices in which he enjoys culture and entertainment or in which he socializes. In capitalist society, an individual or group that does not own anything is powerless. In capitalist society, a group that has not experienced the many sides of capitalistic development, that has not learned the techniques of business ownership, or the intricacies of profit and loss, or the responsibilities of managing even small or medium enterprises, has not been prepared in the social disciplines required to transcend the functional limitations of the capitalistic order. Thus, to paraphrase Lenin, it is not that the Negro suffers so much from capitalism in America, but from a *lack of capitalistic development.* This is why the Black Power Conference heard so many pro-capitalistic resolutions, such as the old "buy black" slogan of Harlem's 1930's nationalist movements. Not a single one of the economic resolutions of this conference was new; they were all voiced ten, twenty, thirty, forty years ago. The followers of Washington raised them, the followers of Garvey raised them, even Du Bois raised them in his nationalistic moments. They are new slogans only for the new, young Black Power sloganeers in 1968. The significance then, of Black Power today, is not that the slogan voices aspirations which are new, *but aspirations which should have been realized decades ago.* They were not achieved because the Negro bourgeois-democratic revolution has been incomplete, frustrated, and aborted for sixty-eight years. It has, for a long time, been what Lenin prophesied it would be in Russia if Russian Marxism defaulted, "an abortion, a half-baked, mongrel revolution" mired down in constitutionalism.

If the American Marxists have not grasped the bourgeois nationalist tendencies within the Negro bourgeois-democratic revolution, they have also misinterpreted the real economic implications behind the ideology of the integrationist wing. The Marxists fail to see that bourgeois integrationism becomes a tactic which aims for *economic integration* as a substitute for the inabilities (and lack of interest) of the black bourgeoisie to achieve economic and political domination over the black community (which, historically, should be its natural function in an ideally democratic multi-group society). The "social equality" rationale used by the integrationists, plus the demand for "equal opportunities" in business, industry, the professions, etc., often uses the democratic substance of "racial democracy" as a cloak for social opportunism. For this rationale allows the integrationist to disavow any special responsibility toward developing the economic or political autonomy of the black community. While it is necessary, in our society, to uphold the right to economic integration for Negro individuals, it is also necessary to see the opportunism growing out of, or implicit in, some of its practices. For example, when the bourgeois integrationists oppose the economics of Black Power, the real motivation is their unwillingness to assume responsibility for building group institutions.

Thus, in the final analysis (and contradictory as it might appear), Marxist socialists must support all pro-capitalistic aspirations of Negroes in terms of economic institutions. This applies especially to black Marxist socialists, who must come to terms with this paradox in a *theoretical* way before they can deal with reality in a practical way. There is no need here to go into details concerning the various economic proposals made at the Black Power Conference. By now they are generally well known to anyone familiar with the conference proceedings. However, simply agreeing with these economic resolutions theoretically and politically is one thing; carrying them out is another question. For here is where the Black Power theoreticians will encounter serious if not insuperable difficulties. As said before, none of these economic objectives is new or original, and the Black Power leaders have accepted the challenge of beginning to establish economic institutions in 1968 which, if they existed now, would have taken thirty to forty years to build. Remember that Booker T. Washington's National Negro Business League, which still exists, was founded in 1900. That, too, is an economic institution which it is doubtful if many of the Black Power economic planners are aware of. Would that the political and economic slogans of Black Power been raised immediately after World War II!

It takes capital to make capital; it takes capital to establish economic institutions, whether private or cooperative. From whence will the financing of these projects come? To repeat, it is not necessary here to go into all the middle-class aims implicit in many of these economic platforms. Class factors can be dealt with in another way. But the Black Power theorists encounter another problem in dealing with economic cooperative enterprises when one considers the very real pro-capitalistic, private-gain, free-enterprise individualism which Negroes in general have imbibed from the world in which they live. This individualistic ideology will present serious obstacles in any attempts to organize black people into any kind of economic organization for their own benefit. It will demand a long siege of political and economic organization. But it is only through such a long process of economic and political education that the black masses can be taught anything at all about the real nature of the capitalistic system. If one takes the leftist Marxist position and insists that it is more "revolutionary" to demand "Socialism Now!" let it be said that the only way to teach the black masses about the necessity of socialism is to demonstrate in practice which of the Black Power economic goals cannot be achieved under capitalism, even though desirable, *and why they cannot be achieved*. In other words, educate for the essentials of socialism by educating in the essentials of capitalism. There is no other way. It is not feasible to follow Herbert Aptheker's mechanistic, anti-dialectical thesis: "Through integration one transforms. The effort is not simply to integrate into the nation; the demand is to transform a racist nation into an egalitarian one. Hence, to battle for integration is to battle for basic transformation." The NAACP could hardly disagree. They would not care what the transformation leads to just so long as it is "integrated," they would not care that the road to hell is paved with good (integrationist) intentions, just so long as hell is interracial. Aptheker's intentions are laudable but his logic is anti-dialectical because *it is the Negro himself who must be transformed before his self-projection can transform a racist society into something else*. If, after several decades of integrationism, Aptheker still cannot see that it is not transforming a racist society, then his blindness is both perverse and incurable. In our context, it is pure super-leftism for a Marxist to project the idea of "socialist integration" or integration through socialism. The statement made by Lenin in 1905, "We cannot jump out of the bourgeois democratic boundaries of the Russian Revolution" applies to the Marxists vis-à-vis the Black Power movement, which is but a belated recapitulation of the issues of the aborted, retarded, emasculated, and delayed Negro bourgeois-democratic revolution that began in 1900. While admitting that the "bourgeois-democratic revolution" does not go beyond the limits of the bourgeois, i.e., the capitalist social and economic system, Lenin argued that it was wrong for Marxists to conclude that "the bourgeois revolution is a revolution which can only be of advantage to the bourgeoisie." Since the bourgeois aims are legitimate in such a revolution, the proletarian aims can also become legitimized in such a movement, depending on how the Marxists and the proletariat functions *within* such a movement. In other words, how do various sorts of Marxist and non-Marxist radicals deal with the bourgeois and working-class aspects of Black Power within the context of the bourgeois-integrationist civil rights movement as a whole?

For those Marxists who will say that Lenin's thesis on the nature of "bourgeois democratic revolutions" for 1905 no longer applies, that would raise the question: What conclusions from Marxism-Leninism *do* apply today? I maintain that Lenin's thesis does apply, and has always applied since the founding of the Marxist-Leninist movement in America. I also maintain that this important Leninist thesis was never actually applied by the American Marxists. I find no evidence that it was ever understood or applied during the 1920's when it should have been. Again in the 1930's, the Marxists failed to grasp the essence of their Leninist thesis, caught up as they were in the black and white labor crusade and the New Deal seduction. Of course, the Marxists changed their approach to the Negro bourgeoisie during the National Negro Congress enthusiasm beginning in 1936. But the Marxist left's bourgeois alliance was with the bourgeois integrationists, *not* the bourgeois nationalists. The new Negro left leadership that emerged out of the "united front" collaboration with the radical black bourgeoisie was a *bourgeois integrationist leadership*. It brought to the fore leaders such as Benjamin J. Davis and Paul Robeson, who became the spokesmen for a new, black, essentially middle-class, leadership elite that flourished in the late 1930's, 1940's, and into the 1950's. This Negro left leadership elite was fundamentally integrationist in outlook. From 1951 to 1955, its Harlem community voice was Robeson's ill-fated journalistic venture, *Freedom* newspaper. They all represented, of course, the pro-Communist Party tendency in American Marxism. It should be noted, too, that Lenin's "two tactics" thesis was not reprinted in English until 1935 as a

pamphlet, a fact which might have some significance in relation to the new Negro left of the 1930's.

At any rate, the failure of American Negro Marxists to
come up with a suitable original theory on the implications
of the unfinished character of the Negro bourgeois revolution, and the built-in conflict between its nationalist and integrationist wings, has meant that the "Negro Liberation Movement" has lost anywhere from twenty-two to forty years of
accumulated political maturation. We can excuse the Marxist
default of the 1920's and the 1930's. But we cannot excuse the
Marxists for the wasted years between 1945 and 1968. I personally know that the critical questions raised against the
Marxist line on Negroes by the post-World War II generation of new black radicals anticipated in many ways the Black
Power demands of today. I was one of those critics, and I can
vividly recall today the words of a Harlem white Communist
leader, objecting as follows: "You are for consolidating the
Harlem ghetto as if it were a 'nation.' That is wrong. The
Party is for breaking up the ghetto and integrating the Negro
people all over New York City." And that was what every
Negro Communist leader stood for. It has proven to have
been a grievous theoretical, tactical, and organizational error
on the part of all Marxist socialists. It has brought down on
our collective heads the heavy weight of decades of social
action defaults which have left the black ghettos in a well-
nigh irreparable condition of political and economic disinte-
gration. Not only have the self-determining economic and
political foundations of the black communities been undermined by the integrationist-leftwing philosophy, but another
extremely important front—*the cultural front*—has never even
seen the promising dawn of a new day of radical programming because of the failures in black economics and politics.
The white Marxist socialists are probably not aware of a very
obvious fact, but, as a black radical, I can say that it was on the
cultural fronts of this nation that American Marxism was presented with its only social area for theoretical and program-

matic originality in a social philosophy that is generically European in radical style.

There is very little in the economic and political areas of Negro life that is conducive to originality. Economic and political innovations in black community life can only be variations of themes already tested and tried elsewhere in the world. These innovations are necessary, but they have already been adopted, in one form or another, in Russia, Sweden, Yugoslavia, Cuba, Mexico, China, etc. It is on the cultural front that there exists the possibilities for creative revolutionary activity and original radicalism. But the cultural side of the American radical potential has lain fallow, basically because the black economic and political potential has never been fully analyzed, guided, or developed. In line with certain new conclusions on the "polycentric power centers of Western societies" * arrived at by British Socialists, this is an area that radicals should study anew.

To deal adequately with this cultural front question calls for a far more exhaustive analysis than has ever been given to the American Negro's socio-cultural status and impact on American society. America is an undemocratic culture because it is underdeveloped culturally. The American Negro is culturally underdeveloped because America is undemocratic culturally. American society cannot become fully developed culturally, i.e., it cannot reach its fullest cultural potential, until it ceases being culturally undemocratic. But in order for America to reach its fullest cultural potential it must cease discriminating against the Negro and suppressing his cultural development by practicing cultural imperialism against him. The greatest crime that American society has perpetrated against the Negro is not simply its "discrimination." This is what the racial integrationists preach. The greatest crime is that the Negro has been robbed of his cultural

* See: *Towards Socialism*, Perry Anderson, Robin Blackburn, eds., Cornell University Press, 1966, pp. 42-44.

identity in America. He has been told that racial equality means he *must* meet the white standards of cultural philosophy, but then is told that he *can't* because he is black. On the other hand, he has been induced by the Great American Ideal (and his integrationist leadership) to deny the validity of a cultural world-outlook and methodology all his own. Thus the Negro is a product of two prevailing cultural negatives, and as a result he possesses no cultural philosophy with which to fight his own cultural negation.

It is not yet understood that without a cultural philosophy (or methodology) suitable for *radical politics* within the *interracial* context of American realities, it is impossible to organize the Negro masses around the political or economic platforms of Black Power. This is why all of the political and economic resolutions growing out of the Black Power Conference can be expected to remain mostly paper resolutions. The realities of American racially imbued politics makes it extremely difficult today to organize the black masses around purely reformist economic and political goals. And because it is so late, now, it is doubtful that the Black Power activists can muster up enough organizing zeal for such a task. Just as long as federal and state power is able to dangle capitalistic-welfare state palliatives, anti-poverty funds, relief, etc., etc., and as long as the two main political parties collaborate in the trading of ghetto conditions for party patronage, the mass thinking will remain tied to this paternalistic "dependency" ideology. Only a viable program for radical social change can break this dependency, and it was not a radical social change program that came out of the Black Power Conference, but a reform program. *And it had to be a reform program because there was no cultural methodology included*, merely cultural embellishments concerning the aesthetic function of black artists. A truly radical black program for social change in America must include the elements of *economics, politics, and culture* in a proper programmatic combination. These represent the basic elements in black radical social theory, though how to put them together is not understood.*

In the same way that the Nation of Islam used religion to bind Negroes together into a social and economic movement (without politics), the secular black radical movement must use the cultural ingredient in black reality to bind Negroes into a mass movement *with economics and politics.* This has to be done through a cultural program that makes demands for cultural equality on American society. Without cultural equality there can be no economic and political equality. Richly endowed as the nation is in the materialistic basis for a democratic culture, there is no cultural democracy in America, and limited cultural freedom. There is cultural freedom for only one group—the white Anglo-Saxon Protestant group, which has the freedom to deny cultural equality to other ethnic groupings in America. The white Anglo-Saxon Protestant group also sets the cultural standards for all other groups. At the same time that the Anglo-Saxon Protestant group exerts its cultural domination in the aesthetics, content, and forms of cultural expression, and its ideology dominates the philosophy of its cultural institutions, this group's level of creative originality sinks lower and lower. Thus the deepening racial crisis in America exerts a profound stress on established value-systems involved in group *cultural identity.*

From within the black movement arises a renewed thrust toward cultural identity as expressed through the art forms. For the Negro, social revolution is impossible without a *cultural revolution.* More than that, a cultural revolution in America cannot come as an after-product of a political and economic revolution; this is a foreign historical scheme of social progress. In America, the cultural revolution (which has also been aborted) must be recognized as a way of opening up the path to radical social change by removing certain roadblocks within the system which are barriers against pol-

* This is why the Freedom Now Party movement of 1964 failed in New York City.

itical and economic transformations. *This requires a special analysis of the political and economic role of mass media and communication systems within the American industrial complex.* It is apparent that any hoped-for democratization of the American economic system must be preceded by a thorough democratization (change of ownership) of the mass media and communications systems. This is the *economic* and *political* side of the problem. The *cultural* results will mark the first stages towards a complete democratization of American culture in terms of groups. As the most culturally deprived and retarded ethnic group, the Negro must be educated to raise the level of his mass politics to the point of demanding cultural revolution. There is, however, much more analysis and research involved in this question.

The emergence of the Black Power slogan serves to highlight the long recognized fact that revolutionary black nationalism and revolutionary socialism remain unreconciled in terms of theory and practice. However, revolutionary black nationalism so far manifests itself within the context of the Black Power movement, which has a contradictory duality. Its social program is manifestly a social reform program, but its social activism reveals itself as violent revolutionary anarchism, whose destructive ends are patently at variance with its avowed social reformist goals. Now inasmuch as Black Power's revolutionary anarchist tendencies range themselves against the police, the federal and state power (armed forces) and not against "class rule" (i.e. directly), Black Power serves to bring into play the forces of the federal government with its stated promises of capitalist-welfare state melioristic and reform measures to "cure" the causes of revolutionary anarchism. In other words, the state is forced to act, however half-heartedly and ineffectively. But inasmuch as Black Power demands social reform measures, the question arises: To what extent can revolutionary anarchism force the federal and state power to meet black reformist demands? To what extent does American capitalism have the ability to reform ghetto conditions? When radicals declare that the money used for the Vietnam war, the military establishment, space exploration, "foreign aid," etc., are sufficient to cure the social ills of our society, they are admitting that American capitalist society can be reformed without recourse to radical social change. Is this true? This ill-concealed hope lies behind the verbal demands of many Black Powerites. If there is any "revolutionary" sentiment in the Black Power ideology at all, it is a vision of a "revolution" carried out *with state aid*, since the revolutionary activist wing espouses no social program relating to structural social changes pursued by grassroots movements. Up to a point of diminishing capabilities, one cannot underestimate American capitalism's ability to assuage certain social ills by gradual reforms. The state can set up WPA type work programs, labor camps, conservation corps, "resettlement" projects, etc., etc. The welfare state apparatus can absorb and drain radical potential. In other words, while the Marxist socialists talk about the ultimate inability of capitalism to reform itself, it remains only talk. Hence, Eduard Bernstein's revisionist methodology becomes factually implicit, *not* in theory, but in the *real social practice* dominating the stage. And to make capitalistic reformism even more persuasive as dominant practice, the Black Powerites demand it programmatically. What kind of social change methodology, then, can transcend this state of affairs?

Then there is the question of the revolutionary anarchism of the "urban guerrillas" Black Power wing. As said before, this revolutionary chaos explodes out of ghetto desperation with an angry cry of armed defiance which says, in effect, to the powers-that-be: "We're going to make you do something by burning down the place!" When the smoke clears, the state steps in and surveys the rubble, investigates the causes, makes a plea for law and order, and talks about possible reforms pending the next uprising. It is not certain how long this can go on before we reach the stage of racial Armageddon. But in between each rebellious uprising and the disposal of the loot, the rebels and populace wait for the state power to grant them a bigger share of the capitalist-welfare state pie. There is no "socialist perspective" either among the urban rebels or the Black Power theorists. In 1898, Eduard Bernstein wrote:

The present generation will see the realization of a great deal of Socialism, if not in the patented form then at least in substance. The steady enlargement of the circle of social duties and of the corresponding rights of the individual to society and *vice versa;* the extension of the right of supervision over the economy exercised by society organized either as nation or as state; the development of democratic self-government in community, county, and province; and the enlargement of the tasks of these bodies—all these signify for me growth into Socialism or, if you wish, piecemeal realization of Socialism. The transfer of economic enterprises from private to public management will, of course, accompany this development, *but it will proceed only gradually.* (Italics added here.) [30]

Bernstein prophesied the rise of bourgeois-capitalistic welfare state gradual reforms (into socialism), and excluded violence as "unethical." In 1950, the Marxist tendency, as represented by the Socialist Workers Party (Trotskyite), stated:

Since 1932, the majority of the American people have shown by their votes that they believe the government is obligated to ensure their welfare and security. But the big question remains: Can any "welfare state" assure full employment, decent living standards, life time security and peace *under the capitalist system?*

We of the Socialist Workers Party say, "No!" We charge that Truman's "welfare state" is a fraud to fool the people into "buying" a decayed capitalism. We say that Truman's capitalist "welfare state" can lead only to unemployment, degraded living standards, dictatorship and possible annihilation in H-Bomb war. We say that the only way you can achieve real welfare and security is by abolishing capitalism and building socialism.[31]

Thus the sixty-eight-year-old argument between Bernstein's revisionist "Marxism" and Marx's orthodox Marxism-

Leninism continues in America, although the younger generation of revolutionaries (black and white) is hardly acquainted with Eduard Bernstein. The older generation of Marxists remembers Bernstein as the first "revisionist," but still gives "tactical" support to democratic capitalist reforms. They believe, of course, that anything less than the complete revolutionary overthrow of capitalism is a bourgeois-revisionist illusion. The "economics and politics" Black Powerites are closer to Eduard Bernstein than any of them could possibly know because they are, in effect, upholding capitalistic reforms in favor not of the white working class, but for all black people. This is because the Black Powerites are dealing with realities in the United States, a Western capitalistic country similar to the German society to which Eduard Bernstein's revisionist ideas applied. America is *not* Cuba, China, Vietnam (Asia), Africa or Latin America.

Although the Trotskyites did not mention Bernsteinism in connection with the welfare state ideology, the revisionist ideas of this German socialist have cropped up in America under various other names. It is also a curious fact that Bernstein's book, *Evolutionary Socialism,* appeared in 1909, the period Herbert Aptheker cites as the beginnings of the "Negro Liberation Movement." * The Marxists may claim that the "welfare state is a fraud to fool the people," but it is impossible to deny that Negroes have experienced what "piecemeal socialism" has been handed down (social security, medicaid, medicare, etc.). It also cannot be denied that Negroes are overwhelmingly in favor of *more* welfare state innovations (even if they are frauds). What does all this mean for the future of "revolutionary" prognostications?

It is a serious mistake for the black revolutionary exponents of "urban guerrilla" warfare to take their cues from Asian or Latin American experts on guerrilla warfare when the geographical and communication realities of the United States

* Certain "Bernstein" Socialists helped W. E. B. Du Bois found the NAACP in 1909.

indicate the existence of little or no conditions for the establishment of the all-important "guerrilla base" and the security maintenance thereof. The outlook here is that urban uprisings (even if coordinated) will be shortlived cataclysms of destruction which will waste themselves through both armed suppression and the lack of the necessary resources for sustained warfare. Revolts even with arms are not necessarily *social revolutions*. We are living in America, the most technologically advanced and coordinated of all Western societies. If the American Negro is a victim of domestic colonialism (which he is), it does not follow that his war against oppression can be conducted solely along the lines of resistance established in *pure* colonial or semi-colonial countries. It means, rather, that the exigencies of struggle grow out of *both* Western social conditions and a unique kind of colonialism not experienced in Cuba, China, Asia, Africa, or Latin America generally. This reality is even demonstrated in the peculiarities of the American Negro's revolt—the revolutionary anarchism of urban uprisings always ends up by demanding more state aid from the capitalistic-welfare state governmental apparatus (or Bernstein's revisionist piecemeal "socialism").

There is a very unique and complex set of contradictory factors involved in all of this. Marxist socialists can neither disavow the necessity of revolutionary violence, nor can they disavow their support for what are called "democratic capitalist reforms." As one of Eduard Bernstein's friendly critics recently remarked:

"The inevitability of gradualism" should not have been taken as an axiom that stood above dispute. Bernstein and his followers were doubtless right when they decried rigid revolutionism as foolish. But whether or not parliamentarism can work depends on the social structure and political institutions of a country. The change from capitalism to Socialism involves a drastic transfer of power from one social group to another. Whether that transfer can be accomplished without violence is a tremendously complex problem that allows no dogmatic answer. . . . There is nothing inherently wrong with a Revisionist theory of social change. But to establish it without correctly analyzing the society to which it is supposed to apply can only lead to disaster.[32]

In view of the fact that orthodox revolutionary Marxists do not disavow short-term support for "democratic capitalist reforms," i.e., "parliamentarism," might not these latter conclusions on gradualism suggest that a completly new theoretical synthesis is required for the United States? For how are we going to deal with a black movement that is being called revolutionary, which also projects a pro-capitalistic social reform program involving welfare-state aid, which also calls for urban guerrilla warfare, which also has a pronounced black middle-class orientation, and which functions in a society whose organized labor movement has "sold out"? In addition to these contradictory characteristics, we also aim to invest the economics of Black Power with the theoretical framework of a political economy. I believe not only that a new theoretical synthesis is demanded, it is also implicit in the American social makeup and has always been present. It is the *Negro presence* that represents the basic social ingredients of the native American theoretical synthesis; it is only that the revolutionary Marxists have never understood or acknowledged it. *They have always attempted to apply a European theoretical schema to the United States,* which has been a monumental mistake. America is not Europe. Its social, ethnic, cultural, political, economic, and other ingredients did not coalesce in the European fashion. Therefore it is apparent by now that to thoroughly democratize American society it is necessary to depart from the dialectical conclusions that European societies revealed to the orthodox Marxist social theorists.*

American Marxists find it next to impossible to break with this established European Marxist revolutionary schema. One chief reason for this difficulty is the inability of Negro radicals

---

* This also demands a reinterpretation of Marx's original dialectical findings.

themselves to break with it. Whenever someone conjures up "social revolution," the Negro radical of experience immediately thinks of the old European socialist formula. For example, Bayard Rustin, who rejects Black Power because he sees it as another phase of neo-Booker T-ism with militant nationalist embellishments, also argues with the "black revolutionaries" over the meaning of social revolution. He wrote: "Whatever separatist impulses exist among American Negroes cannot find appropriate models in the colonial world." [33]

He is right. He explains that "American Negroes do not constitute a popular majority struggling against a relatively small white colonial ruling group." (But it is a unique form of domestic colonialism nevertheless.) Rustin adds, however:

If independence revolutions are no model, what of social revolutions? [As if to imply that independence revolutions are not also social revolutions!—H.C.] This is a more interesting subject because the phrase "social revolution" has been widely used by the civil rights and liberal movements generally. But in this sense—and the sense in which I have been using it for 30 years—the phrase designates fundamental changes in social and economic class relations resulting from mass political action. Such action would be democratic. That is, it would aim to create a new majority coalition capable of exercising political power in the interest of new social policies. *By definition the coalition has to be interracial.*

As a minority, Negroes by themselves cannot bring about such a social revolution. They can participate in it as a powerful and stimulating force. [Italics added.] [34]

Like all Negro leftwing radicals, Bayard Rustin's problem is that in thirty years he has learned nothing new. He has done nothing creative in radical theory in American terms and he boasts about it. His historical and social perceptions allow him to see no more than what the real essence of Black Power amounts to historically. Beyond that, Rustin reveals that he has never gotten over the very real intellectual subordination that white radical versions of social revolution imposed on

Negro radicals of the 1930's. They were taught that Negroes could neither think nor act on a revolutionary plane without white participation. They were induced to believe that there was no viable revolutionary social theory but a white-created theory and practice. Hence the Negro was historically fixed in a position wherein he might participate in a social revolutionary movement as "a powerful and stimulating force," *but he could never hope to lead such a movement in America.* No matter what revolutionary fortunes accrue to a radical "new majority coalition," the Negro participants would always be doomed to bow and scrape before the will of the white liberal, radical, intellectual, and labor (we hope) dominant majority. The established radical schema has fostered an axiom which says: *The Negro can never, should never, will never, create a definitive theory on social revolution wherein he is placed in hegemonic leadership as the guiding source of inspiration, ideas, strategy, tactics, and direction even if the coalition is interracial.* In America it does not follow that the Negro (or anyone else) can stimulate any movement and then step back to participate merely as followers. To do this would be to invite being sold out by one's "allies." What Bayard Rustin is advocating is a policy of radical accommodationism to an established radical creed. Since his social imagination cannot conceptually transcend this 1930's doctrine of radical interracial coalitions, he is forced to fall back on a program that only amounts to a massive capitalistic-welfare-state reform measure:

This is just the challenge posed by A. Philip Randolph's $185-billion "Freedom Budget"—a carefully designed, economically feasible program for the obliteration of poverty in 10 years. Unless the nation is prepared to move along these lines—to rearrange its priorities, to set a timetable for achieving them and to allocate its resources accordingly—it will not be taking its own commitments seriously. [35]

Not a bad plan at all! Everybody should support such a program. But no matter how you cook it and serve it up it is still gradualistic Bernsteinism which, as the critic said, should not stand "above dispute" as an antidote or an alternative to social revolution. Rustin scoffs at the pretensions of black revolutionaries who believe they can go it alone. He believes that the only possible revolutionary formula *must* be interracial, yet he cannot proffer the black revolutionaries any palpable hope for the eventuality of this interracial coalition. Instead Rustin holds up a modern version of Bernstein's gradualistic reforms, $185 billion worth, which he thinks the black revolutionaries should accept as "above dispute." This is *not* leadership!

This leaves an old radical like Rustin dangling hopelessly, both in theoretical and practical terms. For he has neither *his* social revolution nor *his* gradualistic federal funds on anybody's agenda. More than that, Rustin's essential integrationism negates in advance any real consideration of how this $185 billion would be spent in ghettos. How would such funds be allocated in terms of class, cultural, educational, welfare, institutional, and other terms, i.e., *in structural terms?* Idealistically, Bayard Rustin is not "racialist"; his program of gradual reforms is for all Americans. But the Black Powerites are concerned only with black people's social advancement. Tactically and stategically this is sound, since the Black Powerites cannot think any other way without falling into the integrationist camp. Although their social visions are poorly etched out in details, and their conceptualizations vague and ambiguous, the Black Powerites correctly see that integrationism holds no cures at all for ghetto ills. Thus they emphasize, however indefinitely, the building of black economic and political institutions. They have devised no program, or better, method, as yet, for organizing people into the core of these institutions. Neither do they understand yet how or where the *main thrust* must be made for Black Power (this has to do with the "theory of cities," as yet undeveloped). They also are in a dilemma over the reality of their black bourgeoisie, without whom they cannot build their power institutions effectively. The Black Powerites have no class theory on how to deal with the black bourgeoisie and the black intelligentsia. Here again is where the missing theory of the cultural revolution becomes of paramount importance. Without such a theory the Black Powerites cannot deal positively with even the progressive elements of the black bourgeoisie. The main reason the black bourgeoisie cannot give economic and political leadership for Black Power, either in practice or in terms of ideas, is because the black bourgeoisie cannot give *cultural leadership in the areas demanded*. (I have expanded on the historical roots of this cultural defection in class terms elsewhere.) The integrationist philosophy must of necessity deny the validity of any ethnic cultural critique or method whether in art, literature, theater, historiography, aesthetics, form, content, criticism, or cultural communications media. Hence, without a cultural philosophy or method predicated on self-identity, the parallel political and economic philosophy has to be integrationist throughout. A Bayard Rustin's integrationism makes him shy away from Black Power imperatives because, he says, he mistrusts "slogans." But this is not the main reason. He wrote: "Slogan politics are always inconsistent." But it is doubtful if Bayard Rustin disagreed with that very naive slogan advanced by the NAACP during the euphoria of the Supreme Court decision of 1954: "Free by '63."

It is true that the mere slogan "Black Power" can lead to an ideological dead-end trap if the Black Powerites fail to mobilize people in pursuit of the institutional substance of what is implied. They are in danger of being thwarted in any positive and practical organizational efforts by their own built-in revolutionary anarchist-activist wing. Beyond calling for "guerrilla warfare," this element possesses no theoretical knowledge and very little interest in political, economic or cultural organization (methodology). Brought to the leadership forefront by the press and the summer uprisings—which are more spontaneous than contrived—this young leadership style functions not on the force of organizational ideas but on the fuel and momentum of a crisis situation in race relations that has gotten beyond the control of both conservative and "revolutionary" leadership. What is required now, difficult as the task may be, is the kind of constructive organizational planning that only a new school of radical theory and practice can achieve.

Bibliographical Notes to Chapter 13

1. Amy-Jacques Garvey, *Garvey and Garveyism*, published by the author, 1963, p. 26.
2. *Studies on the Left*, Vol. 6, No. 6, 1966, pp. 33, 34.
3. Ibid., pp. 48, 49.
4. *Garvey and Garveyism*, cited, p. 13.
5. Ibid., p. 124.
6. W. E. B. Du Bois, *The Souls of Black Folk*, Chicago, 1907, pp. 52–53.
7. Joseph Stalin, *National and Colonial Question*, New York, 1913, pp. 14–15.
8. Ibid., p. 8.
9. Ibid., p. 15.
10. Karl Marx, "A Contribution to the Critique of Political Economy," *Selected Works*, Vol. 1, pp. 356–57.
11. E. Franklin Frazier, *Black Bourgeoisie*, Glencoe, Illinois, 1957, p. 60.
12. *The Messenger*, March, 1919, p. 22 (A. Philip Randolph, Chandler Owen, editors).
13. W. E. B. Du Bois, *Dusk of Dawn*, New York, 1940, p. 193.
14. Ibid., p. 194.
15. Ibid., p. 197.
16. Ibid., p. 196.
17. Ibid., p. 196.
18. Ibid., p. 196.
19. Ibid., p. 225.
20. Ibid., p. 69.
21. Ibid., p. 243.
22. Ibid., p. 243.
23. Ibid., p. 197.
24. V. I. Lenin, "Two Tactics of Social Democracy in the Democratic Revolution," New York, 1905, pp. 39–40.
25. "The Class Struggle Road to Negro Equality," SWP Discussion Bulletin, New York, April, 1957, p. 11.

26. Ibid., p. 26.
27. Lenin, op. cit., p. 39.
28. SWP Discussion Bulletin, op. cit., p. 22.
29. Ibid., p. 30.
30. Peter Gay, *The Dilemma of Democratic Socialism*, New York, 1962, p. 221.
31. Art Preis, *"Welfare State"* or *Socialism*, New York, 1950, p. 4.
32. Peter Gay, cited, pp. 235–237.
33. Bayard Rustin, "A Way Out of the Ghetto," *The New York Times*, August 13, 1967, Section 6, p. 54.
34. Ibid.
35. Ibid., p. 65.

INDEX

Abolitionist movement, 202, 216
Abyssinia, 31
Accommodationism, doctrine of, 86, 156, 211–12, 216–17
Activist movement, 127, 176, 188, 197, 246, 248–49, 257
Actors and acting profession, 34, 42–43, 46, 55, 58, 65, 122–23
Adowa, battle of, 31
Advertising media, 109
Aesthetic functions, 172, 174, 186, 246, 257
Africa, 68, 73, 76, 86, 94, 120, 176, 183, 215–16, 251; black, 121, 186; colonialism in, 252; conference on, 209; and Europe, 168, 199; and France, 182; history of, 31, 52; nationalism of, 70, 165; North, 167, 169, 172–73, 178, 180–81, 184; peoples of, 50, 164, 168; South, 69; subjugation of, 105
African descent, 21–22, 49–50, 52, 71, 164–65
Africans at home and abroad, 48, 62
African Socialism (Senghor), 152
African states, 32, 79, 118, 183
African Union Company, organized, 164, 209
Afro-Americanism, 15, 23, 50, 71–72, 107, 118, 196, 221, 232; cultural patterns of, 20–22, 31, 48–49, 52–55, 58–59, 61, 65, 74, 114, 116, 119, 195, 219
Afro-American Realty Company, organized, 204, 217
Afro-Cubans, 184
Agriculture, 142–43, 190, 218
Aid, federal and state, 249, 253, 256
Alabama, 204, 209, 211, 218, 226
Algeria, 60, 109, 168–71, 179–81, 184, 186, 191
Alhambra Theater, 11
Allied Armies, 17–19, 33. *See also* World War II
Americanization, 13, 81, 105–6, 195
American Society of African Culture, 21–24, 118–19
Amos 'n Andy production, 120
Amsterdam News, 199
Anarchism, 198, 212, 207, 214, 228, 248–49, 252, 257
Anderson, Charles, Collector of Internal Revenue, 204

Anderson, Ivy, 11
Anderson, Perry, 245
Anglo-American cultural relations, 22, 49, 52, 54–55, 63–64
Anti-poverty funds, 235, 246, 255
Apollo Theater, 11, 34
Aptheker, Herbert, philosophy of, 83–84, 86, 88, 201–6, 208–10, 213, 215, 219, 221–26, 238, 242, 251
Arabian tribes, 60, 170–71, 179–80, 182, 184, 191
Aragon, Louis, poetry of, 172
Architect, profession of, 122
Aron, Raymond, 177, 187, 190–91
Artist, profession of, 36, 49, 57–58, 64, 66, 114, 123–24, 135–37, 246
Artistic creativity, Negro, 22, 26, 34, 48–49, 52–53, 55, 66–67, 117, 122, 134–35, 161, 217, 219, 247, 257
Ashanti, early culture of, 31
Asia, 86, 94, 251–52
Assimilation, 87, 93, 95, 105
Association for the Study of Negro Life and History (ASNLH), 86, 162
Atlanta Exposition, compromise speech at, 158, 216
Atlanta University, 60
Atlantic Monthly, 164
Atlantic Ocean commerce, 164, 168, 209
Authors and novelists, 21, 51–52, 55, 58–59, 67, 118, 133. *See also* Writers

Back to Africa movement, 71, 77, 85–86, 156, 164, 166, 199–200, 209, 215, 231
Backward peoples of the world, 149, 151
Baker, Josephine, 14, 17–19, 38, 40, 134, 173, 183
Bakunin versus Marx, philosophies of, 207
Baldwin, James, 14, 23, 53, 72, 120, 203, 206
Balenciaga, 37
"Bandung" world, 188
Banks and banking, 106, 218
Bantu tribe, 59
Barton, Ralph, 46
Basic consumer products, 70, 112
Basie, Count, 11
Batista, Fulgencio, 184–85

261

Harold Cruse (1916–2005) was a social critic, essayist, and teacher of African American studies at the University of Michigan. His other books include *The Crisis of the Negro Intellectual* and *Plural but Equal: A Critical Study of Blacks and Minorities and America's Plural Society.*

Cedric Johnson is associate professor of political science at Hobart and William Smith Colleges. He is author of *Revolutionaries to Race Leaders: Black Power and the Making of African American Politics* (Minnesota, 2007).